HOME HEALTH CARE for THE AGED

HOME HEALTH CARE for THE AGED

How to Help Older People Stay in Their Own Homes and Out of Institutions

PHILIP W. BRICKNER, M.D., F.A.C.P.

Director, Department of Community Medicine
St. Vincent's Hospital and Medical Center
New York, New York

APPLETON-CENTURY-CROFTS / New York

78 79 80 81 82 / 10 9 8 7 6 5 4 3 2 1

Prentice-Hall International, Inc., London
Prentice-Hall of Australia, Pty. Ltd., Sydney
Prentice-Hall of India Private Limited, New Delhi
Prentice-Hall of Japan, Inc., Tokyo
Prentice-Hall of Southeast Asia (Pte.) Ltd., Singapore
Whitehall Books Ltd., Wellington, New Zealand

Brickner, Philip W   , 1928–
    Home health care for the aged.

    Includes bibliographies and index.
    1. Home care services. 2. Aged—Home care.
3. St. Vincent's Hospital and Medical Center of
New York. I. Title. [DNLM: 1. Aged. 2. Home care
services. WY115 B849h]
RA645.3.B74   362.6′3   78-8993
ISBN 0-8385-3809-6

Text design: James Wall
Cover design: Kristin Herzog

PRINTED IN THE UNITED STATES OF AMERICA

To
Alice Brickner, My Partner

And To
Richard M. Brickner, M.D., Ruth Brickner, M.D.
William J. Grace, M.D., and
Dickinson W. Richards, Jr., M.D.

They taught that concern
for patients as people, and
medical care of the highest
quality, are inseparable.

Contents

Acknowledgments

The Chelsea–Village Program was created and has flourished through the encouragement and support of the Sisters of Charity of Saint Vincent de Paul; and the administrators of St. Vincent's Hospital, New York City, Sister Evelyn M. Schneider, President. These are progressive people, willing to put forth extra effort and make sacrifices in order to help old, sick, poor patients.

To my associates and co-founders of the Program, Sister Teresita Duque, R.N., James Janeski, M.S.W., and Arthur Kaufman, M.D., I offer gratitude for their wisdom, hard work and common sense.

The following sources of financial support for the Chelsea–Village Program have been of major assistance to us; in fact, we could not have survived without them: Agnes Saalfield, the Bernhard Foundation, the Guttfreund Foundation, and the Scherman Foundation, through Joint Foundation Support; Alfred Jurzykowski Foundation; American Brands; Bankers Trust Company; Charles Culpeper Foundation; Charles A. Frueauff Foundation; Charles E. Merrill Trust; Foam Plastics Corporation; Frank E. Clark Trust, through Manufacturers Hanover Trust Company; Henderson Brothers, Incorporated; Margaret Milliken Hatch Trust, through the Irving Trust Company; New York City Department of Health Ambulatory Care Unit Grant; New York Community Trust; New York Foundation; United Hospital Fund of New York; and the Vinmont Foundation.

Particular credit is due to the following individuals who have given advice and assistance to the Chelsea–Village Program when help was needed: Fred Brancato, Marjorie Cantor, James Capalino, Rita Conyers, Joseph Corcoran, John Dolan, Mary Ellen Doyle, Joseph English, John Ferguson, Peter Ghiorse, Edward Haggerty, Hazel Halloran, Mary Hart, Patricia Hewitt, Robert Higgins, Mina Knezevich, Edward Koch, Susanne Kohut, Mary Mayer, John Moore, Dorothy Murray, Stephanie Newman, Teresa Nicholas, Carl Nolte, Ralph O'Connell, Herbert Price, Nancy Rankin, Meg Reed, Peter Rosenthal, Albert Samis, Linda Keen Scharer, Al Schwarz, Sister Mary T. Boyle, Sister Marian Catherine

Muldoon, Sister Mary Robert Nagle, Sister Margaret Sweeney, Philip Toia, and Lise Weisberger.

Jed Brickner, who created the computer program; John Boehringer of Boehringer Associates, who developed the financial analysis cited in Chapters 14 and 15; and the Community Committee for Clinic and Emergency Room Patients of Saint Vincent's Hospital, under the Chairpersonships of Patrick Ward, Cheva A. Thompson, Ernest Cahn, and John Short deserve special acknowledgment and gratitude.

To all our associates in the Chelsea–Village Program—the professional and nonprofessional staff members who have worked with us since 1973—thank you: Andrew Ayson, Alex Bruton, Ray Bucko, Robert Campion, Joseph DeFillippi, Joan Donnellan, Daniel DuCoffe, William P. Duggan, Richard Epstein, Thomas Flannery, Michael Garvey, Tom Gradler, Elizabeth Healy, Joseph Healy, Sister Margaret Rose Ibe, John Intravia, Ellen Isaacs, Jeffrey Jahre, Ellen Katsorhis, F. Russell Kellogg, Priscilla Kistler, Louis Larca, Richard LaRocca, Anthony Lechich, Raymond Lippert, Mildred Lopez, Samuel Madeira, Michael Makowski, Katherine Marino, Margaret Mason, Susan Maturlo, Edward Navarro, John Novello, Lila McConnell, Hugh McDonald, James McEnrue, Carol McGarvey, Ellen McGuire, Michael Melcher, Mary Ann Mosher, Anthony Mure, Jeffrey Naiditch, Zorquina Naranjo, Jeffrey Nichols, Barbara Olvany, Ellen Quirke, Gloria Rich, Marilyn Rogers, Nancy Roistacher, Barbara Ruether, Ponce Sandlin, Michael Sarg, Bruno Schettini, Marc Sherman, Irma Stahl, Jeffrey Stall, Laura Starita, J. Reed Sterrett, Christine Vitarella, Ira Wagner, Duane Webb, Steven Werlin, and Richard Westfal.

Introduction

This book discusses methods of finding and assisting old, home-bound people through the development and implementation of home health care programs for the aged. These programs bring professional health services into the dwelling places of people who cannot themselves reach a source of care and help them remain independent, in their own homes, and out of institutions.

The first chapter describes the number and characteristics of the home-bound aged, how and why they have become disabled and isolated, and their relationship to our larger society.

The remainder of the book is concerned entirely with how to develop and carry out a home health care program for the aged. Section One defines goals for the program; discusses methods of organization; and analyzes a working project, the Chelsea–Village Program of St. Vincent's Hospital, in operation since 1973 on the Lower West Side of Manhattan. Case reports and material from conferences of this program are used illustratively throughout the book.

Section Two discusses the functions of the nurse, physician, and social worker; their combination into teams; how to make health teams work; and the importance of the medical chart in organization and in patient care.

Section Three provides information about life support services and how to obtain them. Food and nutrition, housing, transportation, homemaking services, and relief from social isolation are included.

Section Four considers the financial aspects of home health care: how much it costs, a comparison with institutions, and how to find a program.

The appendices contain basic data pertinent to the general subject of the home-bound aged.

There is a reference section at the end of each chapter, to permit confirmation of sources and the obtaining of material for wider discussion and analysis.

We recognize that old people in rural areas face difficulties as severe as those in cities. Our work emphasizes the latter because by numbers this is where the problems are greatest and where we are most experienced.

HOME
HEALTH CARE
for THE AGED

SECTION ONE
Goals, Guidelines, and Model

CHAPTER 1

THE HOMEBOUND AGED

Aged, homebound people are among the medically unreached. Often impoverished, living in single rooms, welfare hotels, or old walk-up buildings, they are out of contact with the medical care system. They are often too disabled, frightened, or bewildered to reach out, nor does assistance usually go to them. Occasionally a neighbor may find a failing person and call an ambulance, but help is often found too late.[1-8]

This group of people suffers from a complex of problems which no one health worker can handle successfully. Physical and emotional disorders, poor housing, financial difficulties, and social isolation are commonly intermixed.

They can be helped only through the development of comprehensive programs that provide services in the home. Doctors, nurses, and social workers, as teams, must pool their skills in order to create a viable plan of care for patients whose medical-social needs are this complex;[9-19] and these teams must be based in hospitals, with the full support of a consultative staff that is willing to go to the home if needed.[20-30]

Success depends, as well, upon a close integration of the program with community people and agencies. Home health care for the aged is a combined hospital-community responsibility. Program planning, case finding, and organization of the network of care require participation by both sectors.[9, 31-34]

A successful home health care program achieves two major purposes. It helps older people remain in their own homes, where they often desperately wish to stay; and it meets the needs of society at large, because home health services are substantially less expensive than nursing home care.[17, 25-27, 35-46]

3

The common alternative to this kind of program for the homebound aged is the enforced transfer of a disabled but functioning older person to a chronic care institution or hospital bed, or an unattended death at home.

IDENTIFYING THE HOMEBOUND AGED

How Many People

Estimates of the numbers of homebound, aged people are hard to make. These individuals are hidden and unable to call attention to themselves. They have often outlived or been abandoned by friends and family, ignored by neighbors. Nobody knows them.

The most reliable data available come from the United States Bureau of the Census and the National Health Survey.[47] These sources show that about 5 percent of the population in this country aged 65 and over (or a total of slightly more than one million people) are homebound or bedbound. Other estimates run even higher, up to 8 percent.[48] These numbers will increase as the aged population grows larger[47,49] in the next 30 years.

Personal Characteristics

AGE, SEX Homebound aged women outnumber men by a ratio of three to two[50] or greater (Table 1-1).

This is, of course, simply a consequence of the fact that women live longer than men, as made clear in the life expectancy table[51] (Table 1-2). The disparity in life expectancy has increased steadily from the turn of the century, when it was two years, until today, when it is almost eight.[52]

In 1900, 1 in every 25 Americans was 65 years or over. In the 1970s

TABLE 1-1
Age and Sex Composition of the
Civilian Noninstitutionalized Population, March 1975

AGE	BOTH SEXES	MALE	FEMALE	RATIO: FEMALE/MALE
65–69	7,844,000	3,463,000	4,381,000	1.27
70–74	5,580,000	2,362,000	3,218,000	1.36
75 and over	7,703,000	2,897,000	4,806,000	1.69
65 and over	21,127,000	8,722,000	12,405,000	1.42

Statistics from U.S. Department of Commerce, Bureau of the Census: *Current Population Reports.* 1975, Series P-23, No. 57.

4

TABLE 1-2
Expectation of Life by Age, Race, and Sex, 1973

| AGE | TOTAL | WHITE | | NONWHITE | |
		Male	Female	Male	Female
Birth	71.3	68.4	76.1	61.9	70.1
65	15.3	13.2	17.3	13.1	16.2
70	12.2	10.4	13.7	10.7	13.2
75	9.5	8.1	10.4	9.2	11.3
80	7.3	6.3	7.9	7.9	9.4
85	5.4	4.7	5.7	6.3	7.3

Statistics from U.S. Department of Commerce, Bureau of the Census: *Statistical Abstracts of the United States,* 96th ed. 1975.

the proportion is 1 in 10. Projections of the number of older people in the United States by the year 2000 depend on many variables (birth, death, and immigration rates, for instance). A reasonable assumption[53] grants an increase in the number by 40 percent, to 30.6 million people over age 65, up to 1 in every 8 individuals. More than 18 million will be women. The number of the homebound aged will be nearly 2 million people.

MONEY, RACE, GEOGRAPHY, ISOLATION   Poverty and severe disability go hand in hand. The lower the income, the more likely one is to suffer from both acute and chronic illness.[49] Elderly people with incomes less than $3,000 per year, for instance, are twice as likely to be homebound, or to have limited mobility, as those with earnings greater than $15,000[54] (Table 1-3).

A larger share of the white population is 65 or over than that of nonwhites (10.8 percent to 7.2 percent),[51] a consequence of the relatively poor life expectancy of nonwhites in this country (Table 1-2). And yet, a nonwhite older person is more likely to be homebound than is his or her white counterpart by a three to two ratio.[54]

The proportion of homebound people among those 65 or older varies markedly around the country[54] (Table 1-4). Causes for these differences include internal and external migration patterns, availability of institutions, attitudes toward these institutions, and variations in the pattern of family structure and feeling toward older people.

As people age, the likelihood of isolation increases. A spouse dies, friends also; children move away, are unable to care for the parent, or are uninterested.

Furthermore, people who are homebound and alone, according to our

TABLE 1-3

Percent of Population 65 and Over with Limitations due to
Chronic Conditions According to Family Income, 1972

FAMILY INCOME	WITH ACTIVITY LIMITATION	WITH MOBILITY LIMITATION	HOUSEBOUND
All incomes	43.2	17.6	5.2
Less than $3,000	52.0	23.6	7.4
$3,000-$4,999	45.1	15.8	4.1
$5,000-$6,999	39.1	15.4	4.2
$7,000-$9,999	37.7	13.7	4.2
$10,000-$14,999	34.3	14.9	4.3
$15,000 or more	34.5	14.9	3.7

Statistics from U.S. Department of HEW, Health Resources Administration: *Vital and Health Statistics,* 1972, Series 10, No. 96.

TABLE 1-4

Homeboundedness among Those over Age 65

South	6.4 percent
Northeast	5.9 percent
West	4.0 percent
North Central	3.7 percent

Statistics from U.S. Department of HEW, Health Resources Administration: *Vital and Health Statistics,* 1972, Series 10, No. 96.

data, are likely to have been loners all their lives. There is a higher frequency of spinsterhood and bachelorhood among this group than in their age group counterparts, according to United States Census figures[51] (Table 1-5).

FREQUENCY AND DEGREE OF DISABILITY   In the United States about 80 percent of people in the 65- to 74-year age bracket have chronic medical disorders of some kind. This rises to 87 percent for those 75 and over.[55] While some of these disabilities are relatively trivial, about 45 percent of older people have sufficient disability to be limited in activity, and, in addition to the homebound, about one in eight older people have difficulty getting around. The majority of these require the help of another person to be mobile.[54]

Nationwide, the major health problems producing loss of mobility among older people are, in decreasing order of frequency, arthritis, or-

TABLE 1-5
Single Status of Chelsea-Village Program Patients
by Sex and Age,
Compared to Total United States Population

| | PERCENT NEVER MARRIED | |
SEX AND AGE	Chelsea–Village	US Population[†]
Female		
65–74	35 (N = 74)	6.6
75+	23 (N = 183)	6.0
Male		
65–74	18 (N = 47	4.3
75+	26 (N = 91)	5.0

*Chelsea–Village Program Statistics as of January 1977. Includes present
and former patients by age of entry into program.
[†]Statistics from US Department of Commerce, Bureau of the Census:
Statistical Abstracts of the United States, 96th ed. 1975.

thopedic disorders of the legs and hips, heart disease, and stroke.[54] Lung
disease and psychological problems are common as well.

Programs designed to help older people must recognize the meaning of
these facts. The following points deserve emphasis:

1. Chronicity of disease in the elderly requires that we often must work
   for amelioration of symptoms rather than for cure. Emphysema, for
   example, is a disorder in which the patient can best be helped by
   limiting physical demands which result in shortness of breath. A modest amount of assistance with cleaning and shopping, combined with
   medical control of respiratory infections and selection of proper medications, can create marked improvement in the circumstances of daily
   living.
2. Disorders of intellectual function, often lumped under the confusing
   term "senility," have multiple causes. Physical disease, such as congestive heart failure or hidden thyrotoxicosis, excessive or inadequate
   medication, or transfer to a strange environment, can produce dis-
   orientation. Often the process is correctable.[56-60]
3. The medical component is essential to any plan designed to maintain
   the independence of disabled older people. Health issues are both the
   most common and controllable of the major factors influencing life for
   older people. Financial, housing, nutritional, and social problems follow closely and are interrelated.

HOMEBOUND AGED PEOPLE:
SMALL IN NUMBER—CRUCIAL IN IMPORTANCE

The homebound aged form a modest proportion of our total population, but this group is of unusual significance.

These people are at a pivotal moment in their own lives. An older person, living alone, may for a while be able to sustain an independent life, to exist in safety, obtain food, to keep clean. But any small change in the state of health sufficient to restrict activity can create a major change in the quality and condition of life of the older person. A downhill spiral develops, caused by poor nourishment, confusion and panic, deterioration of living quarters, physical and intellectual failure. Often the person is unable to reach out for help—knows no one, cannot get assistance on the telephone, is ignored. The ultimate consequence is either deterioration to the degree that incarceration becomes inevitable, or death.

For every hour and every moment thousands of men leave life on this earth, and their souls appear before God. And how many of them depart in solitude, unknown, sad, dejected, that no one mourns for them or even knows whether they have lived or not.

—Fyodor Dostoyevsky, *The Brothers Karamazov*[61]

An independent life can be sustained for many of these people if comprehensive medical and social service is provided in the home at the right moment.

Homebound older people also present a critical opportunity to the society around them. This group feeds into our acute and chronic care institutions. Nursing home and hospital beds are expensive. Home health services often prevent or delay transfer from the home. Substantial financial benefit can accrue to the country at large, at all levels of government, through the development and support of these services.[62]

WHAT DO WE MEAN BY "OLD?"

The definition of the word *old*, as applied to people, is a source of confusion. For instance, do we measure age chronologically, simply by the number of years a man or woman has lived? While this measure is a useful rough guideline, our own life experiences have taught us that one aged individual may be "old" and feeble, while another is "young" and vigorous at the same age.

In fact, there is great variation in the aging process. At one extreme are people highly productive at an advanced age, such as Grandma Moses, Picasso, Casals, Churchill, Disraeli, Adenauer. At the other extreme is the odd disease progeria, or accelerated aging, in which preadolescents die of arteriosclerosis.[63, 64] Are these children old?

Aging is a variable process, and to recognize this helps us to realize that the elderly are not a monolithic homogeneous group. More properly, they are a heterogeneous part of the population, with diverse needs and capacities.

This makes questionable the wisdom of selecting a given year, 65 for instance, as the official entrance to old age. Government and business have forced an artificial and arbitrary end point to the productive lives of millions by demanding retirement from work at this age. Eligibility for Social Security at 62 or 65 and the start of Medicare benefits emphasize the point.

A biological definition of "old" has more meaning and value than either the chronological or the official. The physical characteristics of advanced age are common knowledge: loss of hair and teeth, feebleness, poor recent memory, failure of hearing and vision. Aging of the skin is probably the most visible sign. Aged skin is thin; loss of elasticity occurs, so the skin becomes baggy and wrinkled. Senile keratoses may be present. Hair is formed in the skin, and graying and loss of body hair are part of aging skin. Teeth are lost as gums shrink and bony tooth sockets become osteoporotic.

Impaired ability to see may, of course, occur at any age, but glaucoma and cataracts are usually problems of the old. Visual ability to accommodate (to switch easily from close to distant vision) decreases normally in middle life due to hardening of the lens of the eye. Ability to hear high-pitched tones normally decreases with the passage of time, because of changes in blood supply to the inner ear and in the acoustic nerve endings themselves.

The bony skeleton alters in this group, usually because the structure of the bones themselves has gradually weakened. As the human body becomes less active, the normal stimulation of physical activity required to keep bones firm disappears. Collapse or narrowing of spinal bones accounts for the stooped appearance of some aged people and the loss of height as well. Bones of older people are less elastic, more rigid, brittle, and a simple fall can produce a fractured hip.

The endocrine glands (for example, the pituitary, thyroid, ovary, testicle, and adrenal) control major bodily functions. As the human body ages the flow of hormones from these glands changes and we see such phenomena as menopause, decrease in breast tissue, and smaller testicles.

Some of the organs and cells of the body have a tendency to perform less efficiently as they age. This is so in the absence of any particular disease. Typically at advanced ages the stomach cells no longer produce

9

acid for digestion, the voluntary muscles become flexible, and the bowel functions poorly.

Any attempt to understand the needs of an older person requires that we make a biological assessment. This forces us to consider the individual and prohibits us from accepting stereotypes.

ATTITUDES TOWARD AGING

In the Western World, and in the United States in particular, our attitude toward aging and being old is negative. The evidence for this view is so widespread and so commonly understood that there is no need to review it in detail. Summarily, this is a youth-oriented country. For instance, most advertising themes are designed to sell products through the use of beautiful, young male and female actors and actresses. We do not see many elderly people chewing gum and smoking cigarettes in advertisements. The huge success of cosmetic and wig manufacturers makes the same point: the desirability of appearing young. Further evidence lies in our use of language. Characteristic is the television host who introduces an older person as being "70 years young." Older people tend to be looked upon as cute and as different from the majority.

This is a significant point. There is a hazard to the idea of seeing older people as separate from the general bulk of the population, because once we think of older people as different, it is inevitable that we think of them as less than equal. Once they are less than equal in our minds, they become dehumanized, and it becomes easy to ignore or incarcerate older people as though they were animals or inert objects. Our efforts should be directed instead toward a long-range and cohesive view of the human species at all ages, without arbitrary separation based on chronology.

The tendency in our society to consider older people as useless or irrelevant may stem from demographic changes in this century.

The primary changes have been the following: (1) an increase in the proportion of the population that is aged, (2) the population shift from rural to urban areas of the country, (3) the breakup of the extended family and the formation of the nuclear family, (4) ethnic population movements within urban areas, and the isolation of individuals left behind.

INCREASE IN THE ELDERLY POPULATION The number of elderly people in the United States has markedly increased, both absolutely and in proportion to the total population, as noted above. Reasons for this change in the relative numbers of older people include the high fertility rate in the late nineteenth century to the mid-twentieth century and the general decrease in the birthrate subsequently. A decline in the death rate has also contributed to the rise of the elderly population. The products of the so-called baby boom, which followed World War II, will join the over-65 population after 2010, causing it to expand dramatically.[52, 65]

POPULATION SHIFTS   It is a classic phenomenon of the industrialized world, including this country, that people are attracted to urban areas and centers of manufacturing. Obviously a concomitant decrease in the rural population results. From the beginning of the Industrial Revolution in the early eighteenth century, commentators have made note of this point. The United States, which in the year 1910 had a rural population of 50,164,000, constituting 54.5 percent of the people, in 1970 had a corresponding rural population of 53,887,000, which was 26.5 percent of the total.[51] The consequence of these facts upon the lives of older people is significant, because in crowded cities the elderly tend to be surplus people.

THE EXTENDED FAMILY AND THE NUCLEAR FAMILY   The classic picture of the extended family is one in which several generations live together. The home is large enough for children, parents and grandparents. Each member of the family has important duties to perform and important relationships with other members of the family. In the extended family the elders are looked to for advice based on life experience, care and teaching of children, as well as day-to-day work. Space in the home is adequate, and all family members are valued. The characteristic extended family is rural, living on a farm.

However, as people moved into the cities to find work in an increasingly industrialized society, space and usefulness for the older members of the family became harder to find. The rush of immigrants to this country, and into the larger cities, encouraged the same developments. Multigenerational families from Europe and elsewhere, who immigrated to the United States in the late nineteenth and early twentieth centuries, faced the same circumstances: small space to live in, no work or role for older people. The inevitable consequence has been a feeling among younger people that the older generation is in the way, ineffective, useless, a drag on the family fortunes; people to be tolerated, at best, and to be put away someplace if at all possible. The response of older people themselves has been, generally, to feel guilty and useless, to participate in their own disenfranchisement as family members, and to accept increasing isolation.

ETHNIC SHIFTS WITHIN URBAN AREAS   Waves of immigrants have entered our cities over the last hundred years. As these groups of people become assimilated, they have characteristically moved out of central city areas, to be replaced by new immigrants. This process continues to the present. As each wave passes, a few of the original group remain behind. As these remnants of the earlier population wave grow aged, they become increasingly isolated.[66, 67] While the numbers of people left behind to become surrounded by new immigrants are relatively few in number, they represent a substantial proportion of people who are among the isolated, aged, and helpless.

Those individuals who reach an advanced age and who outlive family and friends find themselves strangers in their own communities. Differences of social attitude and of language appear. They are alone.

CHELSEA–VILLAGE PROGRAM CASE REPORT

Mrs. O. came to the United States from Northern Ireland at the age of 19, married, and has lived in the same neighborhood ever since, in the same apartment for the last 46 years. Her husband died of cancer, as did her grown children later, within four years of one another. Friends have either died or moved away. She is homebound by arthritis of the hip and chronic cardiac failure. Her neighborhood is now predominantly Puerto Rican. The residents of Mrs. O's building do not speak English, nor she Spanish. Formerly a social woman, Mrs. O. became depressed and withdrawn. She was admitted to the hospital with malnutrition at the age of 80, saying that she was unable to eat and wished to die.

The combination of medical problems and social isolation is hazardous for the aged. They cannot go out for help, and medical services rarely go to them. These people are truly "stranded by time on the bleak shore of a forgotten or friendless old age" (Lord Shaftesbury).[68]

"Old Is Bad"

Fear of becoming old, or appearing old, is realistic in our culture. Older people commonly are poor, ignored, and abandoned. But this pattern of society is not inevitable. In the Orient, for instance, attitudes toward the elderly show reverence. The life experiences and wisdom of elders are valued, respected, and sought after. A place of importance within the family and in the larger society is reserved for the elderly, even though physical ability and beauty have faded.[69-70]

In the traditional Eskimo culture, older members of the family partici-

12

pate fully in daily activities until the physical frailties of age become too much of a personal burden. Then the aged person walks off into the snow and dies.[71]

This ability to accept the natural events of life contrasts interestingly with the unseemly and often desperate scramble to avoid the appearance of age and the inevitability of death which we see commonly in our own society.

Unfortunately, the so-called Golden Years of ease and relaxation usually do not exist for older people in this society. W. Somerset Maugham, the English writer, made the point precisely. Maugham had a severe stammer and generally avoided public speaking. The Garrick Club gave him a ceremonial dinner on the occasion of his eightieth birthday, however, and he felt the need to make a few remarks in acknowledgement. Maugham was introduced, began his address with the customary salutations, then said, "There are many virtues in growing old." Here he paused. At first his listeners thought he had stopped for effect. As the pause lengthened, it seemed that he was overcome by his stammer. Finally people became concerned that he was ill and unable to speak. Maugham stretched the suspense to the maximum and, at last, said "I'm just trying to think what they are!"[72]

Range of Reactions to Aging

The process of aging is a phenomenon that we all face from the moment of conception. Reactions to the events of a lifetime are highly individual, but there are similarities of problems and responses in each age group which allow us some generalizations.[73]

If adolescence is a time of struggle to establish independence and of learning to handle growing strength and power, it is equally true that advanced age is a time of learning to live with loss: loss of spouse, friends, family, loss of physical strength, agility, loss of independence. There is a range of response to the difficulties of advanced age. At one end of the spectrum is the person who will not give in, the survivor. Vigor and perseverance are prominent characteristics, as illustrated in this Chelsea–Village Program case report:

E.H. is an 82-year-old woman living by herself in a single room building, homebound by cardiac disease and dyspnea, referred to us by a settlement house worker.

The patient, an immigrant from Russia in the 1890s, has been a political activist for all of her adult life. In her later years she became involved in the affairs of a local senior citizen's center and founded a newspaper for older people. Her paper stresses political news of interest to the aged and is mimeographed for local distribution by the settlement house.

Since becoming homebound, the patient has not withdrawn. She continues to write her paper, obtaining information from television and from a steady stream of visitors. She maintains a correspondence with politicians near and far.

Although she has no family, through divorce and the death of her only child, she is not alone. She is ebullient and forward looking, widely recognized as an important and attractive local personality.

At the other end of the spectrum is the person who cannot bear loss. It is not uncommon to see people fail after the death of a beloved spouse, as though death were preferable to a life alone and remaining alive the ultimate disloyalty.[74] We all know stories of married couples who died within weeks of one another. Others may react to a spouse's death with shock, depression, withdrawal, delusions, confusion, or agitation.

Mrs. H. and her husband were an apartment-dwelling couple in their mid-70s. They had no children. Although Mrs. H. had been active in community groups, after her husband's death she withdrew completely, cutting off social contacts and confining herself to her apartment. She was uninterested in eating, dressing, or keeping herself or the apartment clean. She became increasingly disoriented and was eventually found and brought to the hospital by the police after she had wandered out to the street at night, in her bathrobe. She said she was "looking for someone."

We recognize the wide range of responses to the difficulties of advancing age. In order to help our patients fulfill their own basic needs and wishes, we must set aside preconceived values, avoid judgment, not be turned aside by the bizarre. Gallant, depressed, or peculiar, these people are entitled to help. We ourselves have not yet been faced with the discomforts of age and the threat of approaching death. How will we react?

CHRONIC CARE INSTITUTIONS:
WHY AND WHY NOT

Nursing homes as we know them in the United States today derive from a history of charitable care for helpless people. The poorhouse and the large public hospital are the progenitors.[41, 48, 75]

There are about 24,000 homes for the aged and dependent in this country today, housing 900,000 people, about 5 percent of the population aged 65 and over.[76, 77] These institutions range in size from under 10 to over 2,000 beds[78] (Tables 1-6 and 1-7).

Unquestionably, a proportion of nursing home residents requires this form of placement because they are severely disabled and 24-hour attention is needed. Some families incarcerate older relatives unnecessarily because of their confusion and embarrassing behavior. Still others may enter homes because there is no other means of having their basic social and medical needs met.[17, 79-89] Without question many such patients would rather be in their own homes and out of the institutional atmosphere.

The transfer of older people from home to institution has the potential to produce harm. Removal from familiar scenes, no matter how crowded and dirty, to a strange atmosphere can create depression, confusion, and

TABLE 1-6

Number and Percent of Nursing Homes and Residents by
Certification Status of Home: United States, 1973-1974

CERTIFICATION STATUS	NO. OF HOMES	PERCENT	NO. OF RESIDENTS	PERCENT
Not certified	3,613	23.0	139,335	13.0
Medicare only	338	2.2	23,459	2.2
Skilled nursing care (certified under Medicaid)	2,273	14.5	162,793	15.2
Intermediate care facilities (certified under Medicaid)	4,425	28.2	236,421	22.0
Medicare and skilled nursing care	2,665	17.0	249,144	23.2
Medicare and intermediate care facilities	–	–	3,617	0.3
Skilled nursing homes and intermediate care facilities	1,250	7.9	129,579	12
Medicare, skilled nursing care, and intermediate care facilities	1,127	7.2	130,128	12.1
Total	15,691	100.0	1,074,476	100.0

Statistics from US Department of HEW, Health Resources Administration: Unpublished data from 1973-1974 National Nursing Home Survey, March 1975.

TABLE 1-7

Number of Nursing Home Residents by Age and Certification Status
and Ownership of Home, United States, 1973-1974

	TOTAL	AGE 65 AND OVER
All Types of Homes	1,074,476	960,257
Both Medicare and Medicaid	406,348	368,479
Medicaid only		
Skilled nursing home	292,372	263,699
Intermediate care facility	236,421	206,794
Not certified	139,335	121,285
Government-operated homes	112,774	97,811
Both Medicare and Medicaid	36,858	31,664
Medicaid only		
Skilled nursing home	35,796	31,496
Intermediate care facility	22,297	20,330
Not certified	17,823	14,321
Proprietary Homes	755,487	665,486
Both Medicare and Medicaid	313,519	283,380
Medicaid only		
Skilled nursing home	193,731	171,954
Intermediate care facility	170,120	144,844
Not certified	78,117	65,308
Nonprofit Homes	206,208	196,951
Both Medicare and Medicaid	55,968	53,431
Medicaid Only		
Skilled nursing home	62,843	60,247
Intermediate care facility	44,003	41,619
Not certified	43,394	41,654

Statistics from US Departemnt of HEW, Health Resources Administration: Unpublished data
from 1973-1974 National Nursing Home Survey, March 1975.

loss of contact with reality. The consequences may be feelings of deper-
sonalization and worthlessness, a sense of isolation and separation from
society, loss of human contact, and an increased likelihood of dying.[90-96]

Older people perceive institutionalization as the prelude to death and
sense intuitively the hazard of this move.

Early in the 20th century a nursing home was maintained by New York City on
Welfare Island, a spot of land in the East River. A physician at Bellevue Hospital, then as now an acute care hospital, had arranged transfer of a gentle, timid,
confused aged lady to Welfare Island. She no longer needed hospital care. The
physician approached his elderly lady patient and told her that she was going to

16

Welfare Island. She looked up at him, anxious and frightened, and said, "But Doctor, I don't want to go to *Farewell* Island."[97]

Why, then, are people placed in institutions when they could be maintained at home? We have noted the psychological and cultural forces which create the mood: the sense that the old are ugly and useless; that they are annoying and frightening because they remind us of our own mortality; that because they are old, they are different, and should be put away.

However, the overriding reason is financial. Medicare (Title XVIII) and Medicaid (Title XIX) support the costs of nursing home care. When this legislation was originally put into effect in 1966, provision for home health services was sharply limited. These rules do not permit support at home for chronically disabled, older people. As a result, there is a steady force pushing people into institutions, because only in institutions will the money flow for care. Local welfare departments, social workers in hospitals seeking placement for their patients, families trying to find a safe way to care for an older relative, and older people themselves are stymied by the fact that money is given only for institutional services, not for home health care.

The care of aged, isolated, homebound people is a national health issue. Only through legislative change will the forces pushing toward institutionalization of the aged be reversed in favor of maintenance at home. These changes will serve the public interest because home health care is cheaper than nursing home care, and the urgent wishes of older people themselves will be met.

Professional health workers and government, along with community agencies and individuals, must make a conscious decision in favor of these people. Otherwise the needs of the homebound aged will be ignored amidst widespread demand for assistance by groups with louder voices.

REFERENCES

1. Brickner PW: Finding the unreached patient (editorial). JAMA 225:1645, 1973
2. Brickner PW, Duque T, Kaufman A, Sarg M, Jahre J, Maturlo S, Janeski JF: The homebound aged—a medically unreached group. Ann Intern Med 82:1, 1975
3. Cantor M, Mayer M: Health and the inner city elderly. Gerontologist 16:17, 1976
4. Cantor M: Life space and the social support system of the inner city elderly. Gerontologist 15:23, 1975
5. Carp F, Kataoka E: Health care problems of the elderly of San Francisco's Chinatown. Gerontologist 16:30, 1976
6. Clark M: Patterns of aging among the elderly poor of the inner city. Gerontologist 11:58, 1971

7. Hammerman J: Health services: their success and failure in reaching older adults. Am J Public Health 64:253, 1974

8. Cohen M, Rusalem H: Homebound rehabilitation: preparing the way. J Rehabil 41:31, 1975

9. Ryder CF, Stitt PG, Elkin WF: Home health services—past, present, future. Am J Public Health 59:1720, 1969

10. Cohen E: Integration of health and social services in federally funded programs. Bull NY Acad Med 49:1038, 1973

11. Hobman D: Practical care of geriatric patients. A. An old person's view of the health services. R Soc Health J 1:21, 1975

12. Lynch JJ: The Broken Heart. New York, Basic Books, 1977

13. Harris R: Breaking the barriers to better health care delivery for the aged: medical aspects. Gerontologist 15:52, 1975

14. Brody SJ: Comprehensive health care for the elderly: an analysis. Gerontologist 13:412, 1973

15. Quinn JL: Triage: coordinated home care for the elderly. Nurs Outlook 23:7570, 1975

16. Beverly EV: Unique organization helps seniors declare, win, and keep their independence. Geriatrics 30:114, 1975

17. Bell WG: Community care for the elderly: an alternative to institutionalization. Gerontologist 13:349, 1973

18. Raskind MA, Alvarez C, Pietrzyk M, Westerlund K, Herlin S: Helping the elderly psychiatric patient in crisis. Geriatrics 31:51, 1976

19. Leonard LE, Kelly AM: The development of a community-based program for evaluating the impaired elderly. Gerontologist 15:114, 1975

20. Libow LS: A public hospital-based geriatric "community care system." Gerontologist 14:289, 1974

21. Goldman F, Fraenkel M: Patients on home care: their characteristics and experience. J Chronic Dis 11:77, 1970

22. Lenzer A: Home care: the patient's point of view. Hospitals 40:64, 1966

23. Richter L, Gonnerman A: Home health services and hospitals. Hospitals 48:113, 1974

24. Griffith JR: A home-care program for a small community. Hospitals 36:58, 1972

25. Trager B: Home care: providing the right to stay home. Hospitals 49:93, 1975

26. Silver GA, Cherkasky M, Weiner H: The home care program in a general hospital. In Linn L (ed): Frontiers in General Hospital Psychiatry. New York, International Universities Press, 1961

27. Yeager R: Hospital treats patients at home. Mod Health Care 4:29, 1975

28. Kelman HR, Muller J: The role of the hospital in the care of the ambulatory chronically ill and disabled patient after discharge. Am J Public Health 57:107, 1967

29. Houghton L, Martin AE: Home versus hospital: a hospital-based home care program. Health Social Work 1:88, 1976

30. Mims RB, Thomas LL, Conroy MV: Physician house calls: a complement to hospital-based medical care. J Am Geriatr Soc 25:28, 1977

31. Herz KG: Community resources and services to help independent living. Gerontologist 11:57, 1971

32. Wilson EH, Wilson BO: Integration of hospital and local authority services in the discharge of patients from a geriatric ward. Lancet 2:864, 1971

33. Rawlinson HL: Planning home care services. Hospitals 49:66, 1975

34. Kovner AR, Katz G, Kahang SB, Sheps CG: Relating a neighborhood health center to a general hospital: a case history. Med Care 7:118, 1969

35. Morris R: The development of parallel services for the elderly and disabled. Gerontologist 14:14, 1974

36. Lepping H, Kjeer S: A Study of the Noninstitutional Care of the Elderly. Minnesota, University of Minnesota School of Public Health, 1974

37. Chapin SE: Home care advocated for the aged and chronically ill. Geriatrics 23:40, 1968

38. Lang SL, Ritchie MT: "Home" for aged. NY State J Med 73:1698, 1973

39. Wilson D: Love and common humanity could save health care dollars. Can Med Assoc J 112:1238, 1976

40. Royle GA: Practical care of the geriatric patients. C. Community care of the elderly—can we get it right? R Soc Health J 95:28, 1975

41. Sherwood S (ed): Long-term Care: A Handbook for Researchers, Planners, and Providers. New York, Spectrum, 1975

42. Markson E, Kwol A, Cumming J, et al: Alternatives to hospitalization for psychiatrically ill geriatric patients. Am J Psychiatry 127:1055, 1971

43. Rossman, I: Alternatives to institutional care. Bull NY Acad Med 49:1084, 1973

44. Soloman N: Keeping the elderly in the community and out of institutions. Geriatrics 28:46, 1973

45. Kutner B: The calculus of services for the aged. Can Med Assoc J 98:775, 1968

46. Laverty R: Nonresident aid—community versus institutional care for older people. J Gerontol 5:370, 1950

47. US Department of Commerce, Bureau of the Census: Current Population Reports: Social and Economic Characteristics of the Metropolitan and Nonmetropolitan Population, 1974 and 1970. Washington DC, US Government Printing Office, 1975, Series P/23, No 55

48. Shanas E, Townsend P, Wedderburn D, et al: Old People in Three Industrial Societies. New York, Atherton Press, 1968

49. Cantor M, Mayer M: The Health Crisis of Older New Yorkers. New York City Office for the Aging, 1972

50. US Department of Commerce, Bureau of the Census: Current Population Reports: Social and Economic Characteristics of Older Population, 1974. Washington DC, US Government Printing Office, 1975, Series P/23, No 57

51. US Department of Commerce, Bureau of the Census: Statistical Abstracts of the United States, 96th ed. Washington DC, US Government Printing Office, 1975

52. US Department of Commerce, Bureau of the Census: Current Population Reports: Demographic Aspects of Aging and the Older Population in the United States. Washington DC, US Government Printing Office, 1976, Series P/23, No 59

53. US Department of Commerce, Bureau of the Census: Current Population Reports: Projections of Population of United States, 1975-2050. Washington DC, US Government Printing Office, 1975, Series P/25, No 601

54. US Department of Health, Education, and Welfare, Health Resources Administration: Vital and Health Statistics: Limitation of Activity and Mobility due to Chronic Conditions. Washington DC, US Government Printing Office, 1972, Series 10, No 96

55. Hay DJ, Wantman MJ: Selected chronic conditions: estimates of prevalence and of physician services, New York City, 1966. The City University of New York, Report Number RB/M 8/69, 1969

56. Butler RN: Dr. Butler calls for research role. Senior Citizen News 4:4, 1976
57. Goldfarb AI: Integrated psychiatric services for the aged. Bull NY Acad Med 49:1070, 1973
58. Fann WE, Wheless JC: Depression in elderly patients. South Med J 68:468, 1975
59. Judge TG: Drugs and dementia. Br J Clin Pharm 3:81 [Suppl 1], 1976
60. Rudd TN: Prescribing methods and iatrogenic situations in old age. Gerontol Clin (Basel) 14:123, 1972
61. Dostoyevsky F: The Brothers Karamazov (1880). New York, Modern Library, p 382
62. Scharer LK, Boehringer JR: Home Health Care for the Aged: The Program of St. Vincent's Hospital, New York City. New York, The Florence V. Burden Foundation, 1976
63. Gilkes JJH, Shavill DE, Wells RS: The premature aging syndromes. Br J Dermatol 91:246, 1974
64. Hayflick L: The cell biology of human aging. N Engl J Med 295:1302, 1976
65. Bouvier L, Atlee E, Mc Veigh F: The elderly in America. Population Bull 30:3, 1975
66. US House of Representatives, Select Committee on Aging: Problems of the Elderly in Syracuse, NY. 94th Congress, Second Session, October 13, 1976, p 8
67. Bild BR, Havighurst RJ: Senior citizens in great cities; the case of Chicago. Gerontologist, 16:8, 1976
68. Hodder E: The Life and Work of the Seventh Earl of Shaftesbury, KG. London, Cassell and Co, 1886, Vol 1, p 180
69. May JW: Orientation to self (editorial). Ann Intern Med 82:277, 1975
70. Rosow I: Old age: one moral dilemma of an affluent society. Gerontologist 2:182, 1962
71. Freuchen P: Book of the Eskimos. New York, World, 1961
72. Kanin G: Remembering Mr. Maugham. New York, Atheneum, 1966
73. Shakespeare W: *As you Like It*. Act II, Scene 7

       All the world's a stage,
       And all the men and women merely players;
       They have their exits and their entrances;
       And one man in his time plays many parts,
       His acts being seven ages. At first the infant,
       Mewling and puking in the nurse's arms;
       Then the whining school boy, with his satchel
       And shining morning face, creeping like snail
       Unwillingly to school. And then the lover,
       Sighing like furnace, with a woeful ballad
       Made to his mistress' eyebrow. Then a soldier,
       Full of strange oaths, and bearded like the pard,
       Jealous in honor, sudden and quick in quarrel,
       Seeking the bubble reputation
       Even in the cannon's mouth. And then the justice,
       In fair round belly with good capon lin'd,
       With eyes severe and beard of formal cut,
       Full of wise saws and modern instances;
       And so he plays his part. The sixth age shifts
       Into the lean and slipper'd pantaloon,
       With spectacles on the nose and pouch on side;

His youthful hose, well sav'd, a world too wide
For his shrunk shank; and his big manly voice,
Turning again toward childish treble, pipes
And whistles in his sound. Last scene of all,
That ends this strange eventful history,
Is second childishness and mere oblivion;
Sans teeth, sans eyes, sans taste, sans everything.

74. Rees WD, Lutkins SG: Mortality of bereavement. Br Med J 4:13, 1967
75. Kahana E: Emerging issues in institutional services for the aging. Gerontologist 11:51, 1971
76. US Department of Commerce, Bureau of the Census: Census of Population, 1970 Subject Reports PC (2)-4E: Persons in Institutions and Other Group Quarters. Washington DC, US Government Printing Office, July, 1973
77. Kastenbaum R, Candy S: The four percent fallacy. Int J Aging Hum Dev 4:15, 1973
78. US Department of Health, Education, and Welfare, Health Resources Administration: Unpublished data from 1973–1974 National Nursing Home Survey. March, 1975
79. Karcher C, Linden L: Family rejection of the aged and nursing home utilization. Int J Aging Hum Dev 5:231, 1974
80. Many nursing home residents needn't be there, study shows. Aging 233–234:14, 1974
81. Markson E, Levitz G, Gognalons-Caillard M: Elderly and the community: identifying unmet needs. J Gerontol 28:503, 1973
82. Dunlop B: Need for and utilization of long-term care among elderly Americans. J Chronic Dis 29:75, 1976
83. Tobin SS, Hammerman J, Rector V: Preferred disposition of institutionalized aged. Gerontologist 12:129, 1972
84. Kistin H, Morris R: Alternatives to institutional care for the elderly and disabled. Gerontologist 12:139, 1972
85. Hylander E, Hansen NE, Karle H, et al: Determining the needs of the elderly and the chronically disabled. N Engl J Med 294:110, 1976
86. Williams TF, Hill JG, Fairbank ME, Knox KG: Appropriate placement of the chronically ill and aged. JAMA 226:1332, 1973
87. Droller H: Does community care really reach the elderly sick? Gerontol Clin (Basel) 11:169, 1969
88. Berg RL, Browning FE, Hill JG, Wenkert W: Assessing the health care needs of the aged. Health Serv Res 5:36, 1970
89. American Public Health Association: Home health services: a national need (position paper). Am J Public Health 64:179, 1974
90. Smith R, Brand F: Effects of enforced relocation on life adjustment in a nursing home. Int J Aging Hum Dev 6:249, 1975
91. Kasl S: Physical and mental health effects of involuntary relocation and institutionalization on the elderly: a review. Am J Public Health 62:377, 1972
92. Rodstein M, Savitsky E, Starkman R: Initial adjustment to a long-term care institution: medical and behavioral aspects. J Am Geriat Soc 23:65, 1976
93. Lawton MP: Social ecology and the health of older people. Am J Public Health 64:257, 1974
94. Aldrich CK, Mendkoff E: Relocation of the aged and disabled: a mortality study. J Am Geriatr Soc 11:185, 1963

95. Leiberman J: Institutionalization of the aged: effects on behavior. J Gerontol 24:330, 1969
96. Blenckner M: Environmental change and the aging individual. Gerontologist 7:103, 1967
97. Brickner PW (ed): Care of the Nursing Home Patient. New York, Macmillan, 1971, p 1

CHAPTER 2

GOALS

Home health care programs will succeed only if there is clarity of purpose and method. Goals must be established which express the needs of both the patients and members of the staff, and the community at large must perceive that the general good is served.

Empty theorizing is pernicious. Goals must be directed toward the needs of real people, and planning must be for the long term. A sudden burst of enthusiasm does not provide sufficient motivation. Patient needs are complex and chronic, with a high proportion of medical disorders. Emotional, social, and economic problems are present as well.[1-10]

Goals include:

1. For the patients—staying out of institutions, in their own homes, at maximum independence.
2. For the staff—professional fulfillment and personal satisfaction.
3. For the community—helping families stay together, decreasing the number of patients in nursing homes, and saving public money.

THE PATIENTS

The only thing I'm worrying about is keeping out of a nursing home.
—92-year-old woman, Chelsea–Village Program patient

Goal: Stay Out of Institutions, in Own Home, at Maximum Possible Level of Independence

People generally prefer to live in their own homes, not in institutions. Positive and negative factors are involved in this preference.[11-16]

Older people have positive feelings about their own homes because there they are in a familiar environment. They can eat, watch television, sleep, and rise on their own schedule. They can keep the light on late, find the bathroom in the dark. Independence is limited only by degree of frailty.

The patient is a 76-year-old woman. Another agency had suggested that the patient was unsafe at home and should be placed in an institution.

PATIENT: Why should I go to a nursing home? You see my shrine over there? When I wake up at night, I sit in my rocker and say my rosary. When I feel like it, I can go to the kitchen and make myself a cup of tea. (She looked around her sparsely furnished apartment.) Do you see this furniture and this rug? They're *mine*, and I worked hard for them. Why should I give them up? No. I will have no part of a nursing home.

Dr. Robert Butler has pointed out:

When we talk about housing, we are really addressing the concept of ''home'' and what this means to the elderly. The place where one lives is . . . connected with who one is and how one expresses this sense of self. Many older people also associate home with autonomy and control. . . .[17]

Negative feelings toward institutions are common among older people. A recent study of the elderly in Florida showed that 85 percent of the aged people surveyed wanted to live out their remaining years at home. In regard to institutions, ''most of those out preferred to stay out. Many of those recently in wanted out.''[18] In another survey older people were asked to state the place they considered best to live. Eight in ten preferred their own home.[19]

We received the following letter from a nursing home patient in Iowa who had read about the Chelsea–Village Program:

Dear Sir:

I have been trying to get out of this Nursing Home for eight months. They won't let me out. I am 93½-years-old.

I have to find someone I can trust to mail these letters. They took my SSI check away from me. I borrowed the money for these stamps.

I wish I had never come here. This is an awful life in here. I don't want to stay here the rest of my life. I want to be at home. Can live cheaper and be happier.

These negative attitudes are based on reality. We now recognize that some of the effects that we previously thought a consequence of aging are actually produced by forced change of environment.[20-21]

For an older person to resist the forces that press for institutionalization requires courage and determination and the willingness to be unpopular with health workers who think they know best.[15, 22, 23]

From a hospital physician's discharge summary included in the chart of a 77-year-old woman:

Patient was extremely difficult to manage. She would refuse to get out of bed. She constantly complained of the cold. It was with a great deal of difficulty that she accepted physiotherapy. She was finally induced to try a walker. It was felt that she had exhausted the maximum benefit of hospitalization, and transfer to a nursing facility was advised. She rejected this and chose to sign a release to go home.

This statement describes how the supine, helpless, and aged patient was able to achieve her own goals and to outwit the erect, controlling, and vigorous physician through a prolonged campaign of passive aggression.

THE STAFF

Physicians, nurses, social workers, and others employed in these programs face a particularly difficult set of problems in working with disabled aged people. Team discussions and self-analysis are needed in order for staff members to be properly motivated and directed.[13, 24-26]

Without adequate preparation for this work, we run the hazard of developing projects which we cannot sustain, of offering promises to patients which we cannot fulfill. If we create unrealizable expectations, we simply add to the problems already faced by our homebound aged patients.

Questions for staff discussion and analysis include:

1. Why do we want to work with older people, people generally considered of low value by the society around us?
2. How will we react to patients who are suspicious of our motives and who are antagonistic to us as individuals; who reject us verbally and at the same time ask for help by their actions? Can we tolerate the ambivalence of the patient?
3. Can we work in dirty, infested living quarters; can we bear examining and talking to foul-smelling, confused, recalcitrant people?
4. How will we tolerate the scorn or amusement of our professional peers, who may accuse us of wasting our time on unsalvageable people, of being inefficient, of taking important health resources away from patients who are younger and for whom the yield is greater?[27-31]

Unless we can face these questions and develop our own answers, our contributions to our patients will be short-lived. We won't last.

Health workers are trained to cure people, and satisfaction comes from making people healthy. In working with the homebound aged, however, we must be prepared to accept unusual professional goals.[32, 33] Our patients are unlikely to be cured and, in fact, have a high death rate.

Instead, satisfaction derives from pride in meeting the needs of others in unusually difficult circumstances, pleasure in helping patients realize urgent personal wishes, and the gratification of working in a program which fulfills significant social-medical needs of the community.

The following material is from the records of a Chelsea–Village Program staff meeting:

ATTENDING DOCTOR: You sought out this job. You really wanted this kind of work. Why?

IRMA STAHL (Social Worker): My last student placement was really the thing that determined the area of social work I wanted to work in. . . . I had worked with several different types of people—young, old, juvenile delinquents, a variety—and I really enjoyed working with older people.

ATTENDING DOCTOR: If I understand what you're saying, the essence of your answer is that you have enjoyment on a personal level. You *enjoy* working with older people.

MS. STAHL: That's true.

ATTENDING DOCTOR: In my own thinking about this whole matter, I somehow divide the kinds of satisfactions into two groups: a personal one as a human being and a professional satisfaction, which is different. Do you agree?

MS. STAHL: Yes. There are a number of professional goals that I see here. One is that we're working with a group of people that other professionals hadn't been focusing on. They weren't, to the best of my knowledge, a group that social workers were anxious to work with. These people were sort of left out.

Also, I have found satisfaction in the fact that you can do small things for old people, things that make a difference to them, and the appreciation is very great. You can see results. They're in a position where an action you take will benefit them. It's very different from working with another group of people.

This very point, that we can do something for these patients that is practical and offers virtually immediate tangible beneficial results, is no defense against the strongest professional criticisms we receive. These criticisms of home health care programs center on the effort involved in working with aged people, because the problems of this group are not

26

remediable, in the long run. Because the patients are old and sick, the benefits of our services are likely to be brief.

Therefore, we must answer the question: why are we wasting money, time, and professional skills by focusing upon disabled older patients when they might better be spent on people whose life span is going to be longer?

The answer of professional health workers to this kind of inquiry is, simply, that we are not judges. If we perceive somebody to be in need of help, we offer to help. Whether they are going to die next week is not relevant.[33]

The opportunity to have contact with this kind of medical program may permit important professional growth. A medical resident went with one of our teams to see patients because the regular physician was suddenly not available. His reaction:

I had looked at this project as a hearts-and-flowers program, a kind of fruitless do-goodism. I participated the first time because of moral pressure. On that occasion I suddenly found that I felt like the great healer, bringing my art to the dregs of the earth.

I stayed with the program and found that exhilaration fluctuated with feelings of despair. The gratitude of the patients, because I am willing to help them, makes me feel good. Their bad living conditions make me upset. I admire their courage.

I feel that this experience has been invaluable to me personally—to recognize that our field is not limited to the intensive care unit.

At the highest level of professional maturity lies our ability to understand that the patients' interests and prerogatives come before our own. It may take years of training and experience before we can accept without anger or humiliation the fact that patients may know better than we do what is right for them. Participation in these programs provides a fine opportunity for learning how to temper arrogance with humility.

A woman, now 104 years old (and with a form letter of congratulation from President and Mrs. Nixon on her centenary to prove it), was sent to a nursing home from a hospital three years ago. This transfer was arranged by the social service department, on advice of physicians who felt she would be unsafe at home. The patient disliked the institution and was able to recognize that she would prefer to return home. She so informed old friends from the neighborhood, who found her a nearby apartment. Homemaking help was obtained from the city. Our program supplied health services. For the last two and a half years she has lived independently in her apartment, a rare example of a return to the community from a chronic care institution and a result of the patient's initiative.

Goal: Personal Satisfaction

Self-understanding is necessary for success in work with disabled older people. A resolution of feelings about parents and grandparents is required, along with a degree of equanimity about dying and death.[28,32,34] The simple desire to do good is not likely to be a sufficiently strong motive force.

A 22-year-old registered nurse read about our program in a professional journal and asked to work with us. She intended to pursue a career involved with medically abandoned people.

Her motives were genuine, and her professional abilities in the first six months with us were considered superior. She tolerated poor working conditions well. At length, however, the fact that her patients rarely improved, and that several with whom she had developed a relationship died, disturbed her. She brought a birthday cake to a patient one day but found he had killed himself. She became depressed, resigned, and is now working in an inpatient service.

The ultimate personal satisfaction comes in learning that we receive more from our patients than we can ever give to them.

From the records of a Chelsea–Village Program staff meeting:

ATTENDING DOCTOR: Barbara, what is there about this job that seems so important to you personally?

BARBARA RUETHER (Coordinator): I don't have any family. I didn't have any grandmother; I didn't know my parents, and I didn't grow up with anybody old. In my previous job at a drug company I tried to work on an idealistic basis. I felt that whatever I did was related to a person, and that whatever happened on this piece of paper, and with this drug, was going to happen to a human being. However, after years in the industry, I suddenly felt that I was shoving pieces of paper around and becoming more and more distant from people—so I quit.

Because I was unemployed, I was asked to take care of the mother of a friend. This woman was 78 years old and had just recently been discharged from the hospital, extremely weak, didn't even think she was going to make it. I came down every morning, and I spent the entire day with her, trying to help her eat, trying to make her respond, trying to make her feel like living. And gradually over two months' time, she came to herself.

In sitting with her in the afternoons, when some of her elderly friends would

28

come to visit, and in just talking to her, I came to realize what a beautiful human being she is. She was fascinating to me. We developed a great friendship. I learned a lot of things about the neighborhood, and I learned a lot about myself in talking to her.

But the astonishing thing was that underneath this frailty, and all the aging process, *she*, that young girl, was still there.

And I realized that I had never really thought about this before, that they're the same people they were years ago.

THE COMMUNITY

The quality of a civilization is gauged by how it cares for its elderly.

For individuals and agencies in the community, the development of home health care programs for older people is a goal of high priority.[10,11,13-15,18,19,35-49] Programs of this nature serve the humane purpose of permitting older people to remain independent in their own homes and also save money for the larger community because home health care is less expensive than institutional care.[11-15,18,43,50-59] An effective home health care program obviously fulfills significant needs of older people. In addition, family members can be helped to sustain older relatives safely at home. Public authorities have a decrease in the number of nursing home patients whom they must support. The political establishment saves money in its health budget and can, with honesty, take the position of being both sensitive and thrifty. The taxpayer benefits when public health costs fall.

Goal: Help Families Stay Together

While many of our homebound aged people are alone, about 40 percent live with a family member or have a close connection.[60] It is often easier for the family to deposit the patient in an institution than to make the effort of organizing care at home; but the feelings of guilt are unpleasant. There is also the awareness that as the older person is manipulated by the younger one, so may the same course develop in the next generation. Children observe how parents treat grandparents.

Home health care programs can provide the resources which help families sustain older people at home. However, we must also recognize that home maintenance may at times not be in the best interest of family and patient.

A 72-year-old man was homebound with chronic pulmonary disease and cor pulmonale. He did not speak English. We communicated through his wife.

29

In the year before his participation in the program, he had been hospitalized five times for acute respiratory failure. He regularly required admission to the intensive care unit, and intubation.

The patient's refusal to take his medication and follow his diet at home was the basic difficulty in this case. He lacked the willpower. Cowed by the patient's authoritarian behavior, his wife was unable to insist that he follow the medical regimen. Our role, in addition to providing medical care, was to support and guide the wife in her attempts to have the patient follow the treatment plan.

The patient was kept out of the hospital over an eight-month period through this program, but relations between the couple were increasingly unpleasant. The situation was suddenly altered by the wife's hospitalization. The patient was sent to a local nursing home, for temporary care. On the wife's return, however, he refused to leave. He loved the nursing home. It gave him a freer life. The wife visited daily, the brief contacts were pleasant, and their relationship improved.

Goal: Decrease the Number of Patients in Nursing Homes

As Kistin and Morris have pointed out:

There is mounting and consistent evidence that many elderly and handicapped persons are placed in nursing homes and other institutions not for medical reasons but because essential services to maintain them in their own homes are lacking.[44]

Home health care programs for the aged provide these services and are effective in keeping people out of nursing homes.[15,18,19,44,45,49,56,61-65] For example, we estimate that in the first year of the Chelsea–Village Program we maintained at home 70 patients who would otherwise have required institutional placement, for a total period of 420 months.

Once a program has been established, most patients can be sustained at home. The Massachusetts Department of Public Health claims that only 21.4 percent of patients who are entered into a home care program subsequently require institutional care and that "the amount of business passing between nursing homes and home health agencies is surprisingly small in either direction."[65]

A similar analysis, performed by the Baltimore Bureau of Patient Care, is concerned with the likelihoood of keeping mentally impaired elderly out of institutions.

After the social and medical evaluations are completed, the social worker and physician make recommendations to the patient and family. In most instances, it is possible to resolve for the patient and his family a workable plan which allows

30

the patient to remain in his own home. . . . To effect this . . . involves a combined, interdisciplinary approach and careful discussions with the patient and his family.[66]

Goal: Save Money

Home health care is cheaper than nursing home care (Chap 15). [1,12,14,15, 43,44,50,51,54,55] In New York City the present reimbursement rate for Medicaid patients in nursing homes, the minimum rate available, is greater than $800 per month. The costs of care at home for appropriate aged homebound people is about half this amount, and this includes the value of rent, food, clothing, telephone, medications, professional health services, and the help of community agencies.

CHELSEA–VILLAGE PROGRAM CASE REPORT

The patient is an 82-year-old woman living alone on the fourth floor in a two-room, walk-up apartment. She was referred to us by a superintendent. She is restricted to her home by severe osteoarthritis of the hips and spine. She also has essential hypertension. Her income is limited to social security payments. This patient's only resource for food and social contact was a neighbor and friend who had died recently.

The medical issues are not complex, consisting of medication for pain and hypertension, reassurance, and monthly visits. However, additional services have been required for successful home maintenance. Our social worker has arranged for a meals-on-wheels program to deliver a hot meal each day and for homemaker services from the New York City Department of Social Services for once-weekly shopping, cooking, and cleaning. This patient has been sustained at home for the last 16 months, as she wishes, instead of in a nursing home.

Her living and health costs are as follows:

	MONTHLY COSTS ($)	SOURCE OF PAYMENT
Rent, utilities	71	Patient
Food (including Meals-on-Wheels)	80	Patient
Telephone	6	Patient
Drugs, supplies	10	Patient
Other expenses	10	Patient
Chelsea–Village Program costs	108	Chelsea–Village Program budget
Homemaker	160	New York City
Total	445	

31

REFERENCES

1. Shanas E: Measuring the home health needs of the aged in five countries. J Gerontol 26:37, 1971
2. Rosen HJ: Modern health care delivery for the aged: a program in total health maintenance. J Am Geriatr Soc 20:505, 1972
3. Brody SJ: Evolving health delivery systems and older people. Am J Public Health 64:245, 1974
4. Akhtar AJ, Brie GA, Crombie A, et al: Disability and dependence in the elderly at home. Age Ageing 2:102, 1973
5. Gardiner R: The identification of the medical and social needs of the elderly in the community. Age Ageing 4:22, 1975
6. Harris R: Breaking the barriers to better health care delivery for the aged. Gerontologist 15:52, 1975
7. Cohen ES: Integration of health and social services in federally funded programs. Bull NY Acad Med 49:1038, 1973
8. Hobman D: Practical care of geriatric patients. A. An old person's view of health services. R Soc Health J 1:21, 1975
9. Daniels RS, Kahn RL: Community mental health and programs for the aged. Geriatrics 23:121, 1968
10. Quinn JL: Triage: coordinated home care for the elderly. Nurs Outlook 23:570, 1976
11. Trager B: Home care: providing the right to stay home. Hospitals 49:93, 1975
12. Chapin SE: Home care advocated for the aged and chronically ill. Geriatrics 23:40, 1968
13. Sherwood S (ed): Long-term care: A Handbook for Researchers, Planners, and Providers. New York, Spectrum, 1975
14. Markson E, Kwol A, Cumming J, et al: Alternatives to hospitalization for psychiatrically ill geriatric patients. Am J Psychiatry 127:1055, 1971
15. Rossman I: Alternatives to institutional care. Bull NY Acad Med 49:1084, 1973
16. Kutner B: The calculus of services for the aged. Can Med Assoc J 98:775, 1968
17. Butler R: Why Survive? Being Old in America. New York, Harper and Row, 1975, p 103
18. Bell WG: Community care for the elderly: an alternative to institutionalization. Gerontologist 13:349, 1975
19. Markson E, Levitz G, Gognalons-Caillard M: Elderly and the community: Identifying unmet needs. J Gerontol 28:503, 1973
20. Lawton MP: Social ecology and the health of older people. Am J Public Health 64:257, 1974
21. Laverty R: Nonresident aid-community versus institutional care for older people. J Gerontol 5:370, 1950
22. Walton M: An old person living alone in the community. Gerontol Clin (Basel) 10:358, 1968
23. Baker MJ: The reasons and cure for dehumanization in nursing homes. Hosp Community Psychiatry 25:173, 1974
24. Flynn JP: The team approach: a possible control for the single service schism—an exploratory study. Gerontologist 10:119, 1970
25. Roth ME, Tarnopoll I: Organization of a coordinated home care program in Erie County, New York. Public Health Rep 82:639, 1967
26. Gaitz CM: The coordinator: an essential member of a multidisciplinary team delivering health services to aged persons. Gerontologist 10:217, 1970

27. Darnborough T, Ingram GIC, Gwynne AL, et al: Case conference: does the end justify the expense? J Med Ethics 1:187, 1975
28. Comfort A: On gerontophobia. Med Opinion Rev 3:30, 1967
29. Another generation gap: physicians vs. the elderly. Mod Hosp 122:42, 1974
30. Cyrus-Lutz C, Gaitz CM: Psychiatrists' attitudes toward the aged and aging. Gerontologist 12:163, 1972
31. Cohen M, Rusalem H: Homebound rehabilitation: preparing the way. J Rehabil 41:31, 1975
32. Strank RA: Caring for the chronic sick and dying: a study of nursing attitudes. Nurs Times 68:166, 1972
33. Carpenter JO, Wylie CM: On aging, dying, and denying. Public Health Rep 89:403, 1974
34. Kastenbaum R: On death and dying: should we have mixed feelings about our ambivalence towards the aged? J Geriatr Psychiatry 7:93, 1974
35. Testoff A, Levine E: Nursing care supplied to older people in their homes. Am J Public Health 55:541, 1965
36. Ryder CF, Stitt PG, Elkin WF: Home health services: past, present, future. Am J Public Health 59:1720, 1969
37. Raskind MA, Alvarez C, Pietrzyk M, Westerlund K, Herlin S: Helping the elderly psychiatric patient in crisis. Geriatrics 31:51, 1976
38. Lenzer A: Home care: the patient's point of view. Hospitals 40:64, 1966
39. Richter L, Gonnerman A: Home health services and hospitals. Hospitals 48:113, 1974
40. Griffith JR: A home care program for a small community. Hospitals 36:58, 1972
41. Kelman HR, Muller J: The role of the hospital in the care of the ambulatory chronically ill and disabled patient after discharge. Am J Public Health 57:107, 1967
42. Herz KG: Community resources and services to help independent living. Gerontologist 11:59, 1971
43. Royle GA: Practical Care of the Geriatric Patient. C. Community care of the elderly, can we get it right? R Soc Health J 95:28, 1975
44. Kistin H, Morris R: Alternatives to institutional care for the elderly and disabled. Gerontologist 12:139, 1972
45. Berg RL, Browning FE, Hill JG, Wenkert W: Assessing the health care needs of the aged. Health Serv Res 5:36, 1970
46. Hylander E, Hansen NE, Karle H, et al: Determining the needs of the elderly and the chronically disabled. N Engl J Med 294:110, 1976
47. Kahana E: Emerging issues in institutional services for the aging. Gerontologist 11:51, 1971
48. Kahana E: The humane treatment of old people in institutions. Gerontologist 13:282, 1973
49. Home health services: a national need. Position paper. Am J Public Health 64:179, 1974
50. Silver GA, Cherkasky M, Weiner H: The home care program in a general hospital. In Linn L (ed): Frontiers in General Hospital Psychiatry, New York, International Universities Press, 1961
51. Yeager R: Hospital treats patients at home. Mod Health Care 4:29, 1975
52. Morris R: The development of parallel services for the aged and disabled. Gerontologist 14:14, 1974
53. Lepping H, Kjeer S: A Study of the Noninstitutional Care of the Elderly. Minnesota, School of Public Health, 1974

54. Lang SL, Ritchie MT: "Home" for aged. NY State J Med 73:1698, 1973
55. Wilson D: Love and common humanity could save health care dollars. Can Med Assoc J 95:28, 1975
56. Soloman N: Keeping the elderly in the community and out of institutions. Geriatrics 28:46, 1973
57. Bryant NH, Candland L, Loewenstein R: Comparison of care and cost outcome for stroke patients with and without home care. Stroke 5:54, 1974
58. Houghton L, Martin AE: Home vs. hospital: a hospital-based home care program. Health Social Work 1:88, 1976
59. McCarthy E: Comprehensive home care for earlier hospital discharge. Nurs Outlook 24:625, 1976
60. Brickner PW, Janeski JF: The Chelsea–Village Program—A Four Year Report. New York, Saint Vincent's Hospital, 1977
61. Libow LS, Caro FG, Lidta M: Symposium: delivery of geriatric community care. Gerontologist 14:286, 1974
62. Dunlop BD: Need for and utilization of long-term care among elderly Americans. J Chronic Dis 29:75, 1976
63. Tobin SS, Hammerman J, Rector V: Preferred disposition of institutionalized aged. Gerontologist 12:129, 1972
64. Williams TF, Hill JC, Fairbank ME, Knox KG: Appropriate placement of the chronically ill and aged. JAMA 226:1332, 1973
65. Clients of home health agencies. N Engl J Med 293:1261, 1975
66. Leonard K, Kelly AM: The development of a community-based program for evaluating the impaired older adult. Gerontologist 15:114, 1975

CHAPTER 3

HOW TO ESTABLISH A PROGRAM

The program requires a central core of motivated people. This small group must focus upon the following points:

1. Site of the program
   The importance of a hospital base
   Convincing hospital administration to accept the program
   Hospital funding
   Hospital–neighborhood relationships
   Fulfillment of hospital's founding principles
   Why present hospital home care departments do not serve the purpose

2. Obtaining staff
   Professional staff
   Nonprofessional staff
   Job descriptions

3. Creating a community relationship
   Planning
   Identifying community organizations
   Finding the patients
   Personal liaison and direct service to patients
   Money and politics

SITE OF PROGRAM

Importance of a Hospital Base

For the best chance of success, the program should be based in a hospital.[1-10] Only a hospital has the full range of resources needed to care properly for homebound aged people, with their complex set of problems. These resources include physicians, both those who provide medical care on a regular basis and those with special skills; nurses and social workers, both those who are interested in case work and those who can deal with community organizations.

The hospital has a personnel department experienced in obtaining professional and nonprofessional staff members, and screening them.

Hospitals also provide inpatient beds, which are immediately available as needed. A close relationship to the inpatient service is essential for proper care of people who are sought out and found to be seriously ill. It is fatuous to attempt diagnosis and treatment without prompt and easy access to the full range of medical services.

Furthermore, hospitals have an already existing, highly developed relationship with other community and government agencies, exceedingly important to the creation of a network of care;[11-17] and hospitals usually have a good name and reputation. This point is a critical one for case finding and effective fund raising.

The hospital-based program is capable of being comprehensive; has a good chance of fulfilling the objectives of helping elderly people remain independent at home; is likely to function in a sustained manner over a prolonged period; and, therefore, does not create unrealizable expectations among patients.

Free-standing programs, no matter how substantial, are unlikely to fulfill these criteria. At one extreme are projects started by good-hearted community volunteers, frustrated by the apparent disinterest of established institutions in problems of aged people. Characteristically, these projects, and similar ventures such as free clinics, health projects for skid row men, and venereal disease centers for homosexuals, have with few exceptions demonstrated limited staying power. Most have failed; and the failures are due not to lack of need but to inadequate community base, the inherent evils of volunteerism, the ephemeral nature of government and other funding sources, and/or failure to provide adequate back-up support through affiliation with major health care institutions.[9, 18-24]

At the other end of the spectrum are programs of long standing and fine repute. Good examples are Visiting Nurse Service associations, found throughout the country, and settlement houses with senior citizens' projects. The services offered to older people by these agencies are characteristically of high quality and value but are not sufficient by themselves to meet the needs of the homebound aged. More is required than nurses' visits, homemaker services, socializing, and trouble shooting.

Hospitals serve a variety of constituencies, commonly including people both rich and poor, a racial mix, young and old. People from the local neighborhood may perceive the hospital as a primary source of care. Others from farther away may look to it as a tertiary agency, offering complex subspecialty services.

Hidden, medically unreached people are another constituency, one whose needs may be forgotten while the institution struggles to find means of caring for the acutely ill. It is common knowledge that the interest, motivation, and dollars of hospital administrations are particularly focused upon the needs of inpatients. Ambulatory care and community health problems take second place or are ignored.[25-29]

In order to attract the attention of hospital administrators to the needs of homebound aged people, they must be shown how hospital-based programs for these patients benefit the institution.

Hospital Funding

The hospital administration will be asked for financial support at the start of the program. This support will be either in the form of permission for professional staff members to offer their services during regular paid time or the actual employment of physicians, nurses, social workers, and others to work full time in the program. Because many urban hospitals, both governmental and voluntary, are in financial difficulties, the hospital administration may react negatively to this request.

It is important to make clear that the negative reaction is shortsighted. The cash and/or personnel costs can be balanced against other factors. The following kind of memorandum may help.

BIG APPLE HOSPITAL
HOME HEALTH MAINTENANCE PROGRAM FOR THE AGED

Cost Justification Analysis

Pertinent questions have been raised regarding the cost justification to the institution of establishing a hospital-based home health care program for the aged. In light of the present financial difficulties of the hospital, and because the program will use expensive assets of the hospital (the time of professional staff members who volunteer for this work), these questions deserve an answer.

A. Costs to the Hospital of Personnel Time, Per Week, including 10 Percent Fringe Benefits

Physician (house staff) time (8 hours)	$ 65.00
Nursing time (8 hours)	50.00
Social service time (8 hours)	60.00
Professional staff supervision (15 hours)	120.00
Costs per week	*$295.00*
Estimated costs for 1 year	*$15,340.00*

B. Assets to the Hospital
   1. Funds Raised, and Cash Benefits Therefrom

   The program staff has been successful in raising grants from private philanthropic agencies. These funds are sufficient to pay the salaries of a coordinator, and a driver–community worker and to pay for the cost and maintenance of a vehicle.

   Big Apple Hospital receives 15 percent of the grants (that portion used for salary) for overhead expense. The cash income to the hospital from this source will be $3,000.00 in the first year.

   2. Occupancy of Hospital Service Beds

   Patients seen by personnel of the home health care program will require hospitalization in 20 percent of cases yearly, based on the experience of similar programs elsewhere. These people, when hospitalized, are generally seriously ill. It is our opinion that many of our patients would have died at home if not found by our program.

   Hospital gross income and anticipated gross income from this bed utilization is $136,000.00 per year. Of this sum, at least $102,000.00 (or 75 percent) is net incremental income. This sum of $102,000.00 is money that the hospital would not have gained were it not for the home health care program.

   The question is asked: Would not some of these patients have been hospitalized at Big Apple Hospital even if the Home Health Care Program did not exist? The answer is that, in almost every case, these patients were failing at home, *with no apparent recourse to any form of medical care,* until we arrived. Almost all of these hospital admissions are the direct result of our intervention, and would not have taken place without the program.

SUMMARY:

The Hospital donates, in paid time of professional staff, about $295.00 per week, to the home health care program. Donated time per year is, therefore, valued at:

   $15,340.00

The hospital receives:

   $3,000.00

per year in grant overhead. The hospital has received, or will receive:

   $102,000.00

38

in incremental net income from necessary bed utilization through the first 12 months of this program.

Hospital–Neighborhood Relationship

During the inner-city turmoil of the late 1960s and early 1970s, hospitals were often placed on the defensive by community groups because, as institutions, they were part of the established society, a society seen by some people as being insufficiently responsive to local needs.[30-34]

Many hospitals have had to face a new network of relationships with community agencies, political groups, and activist individuals, simply to survive in a combative environment. More recently, the need for community support has assumed the force of law. For hospitals to achieve stability and needed growth, local approval has been mandated by government [32, 35, 36]

The legal basis for community power over hospitals includes the Office of Economic Opportunity legislation (1964),[37] the 1968 guidelines for the O.E.O. Neighborhood Health Centers,[38] the Model Cities bills (1966),[39] the Partnership for Health Program,[40] the New York State law creating the Health and Hospitals Corporation of New York City,[41] and its interim policy guidelines.[42] Other legislation to the same effect is the New York State Ghetto Medicine Law (1968)[43] and its guidelines,[44] federal guidelines for the establishment of family health center programs,[45] the 1970 Amendments to the Hill-Burton Act,[46] Public Law Number 92–603 (forming the Comprehensive Health Planning Agency), the state laws mandating changes in the Blue Cross programs,[47] and the provisions for consumers in the laws creating the Health Systems Agencies.[48]

These laws are implemented through such documents as the "Manual for Review and Comment," Department of Health, Education, and Welfare, May, 1973, central health planning standards and guideline, state hospital codes, and implementation plans at various levels of government.

Obviously, it is difficult for a hospital administrator to understand and work effectively in this maze of legislation. This comment is doubly valid when we realize that the health industry is in a constant state of change, and so are the laws and manuals which control it. Having the community as an ally may be of ultimate value.

It is for this reason that hospital administrators now recognize that the health, sometimes the very survival, of their institutions depends on good community relationships. The development and support of home health care programs for the aged present an unusually favorable opportunity for

39

a hospital to work with its neighbors. The most helpless people in the community benefit directly, and the hospital is perceived as humane and responsive in an environment which is increasingly negative toward established institutions.[8, 31, 49-52]

Fulfillment of Hospital's Founding Principles

For financial benefit and for reasons of community relations, hospital administrators may recognize that establishment of a home health care program serves the self-interest of their institutions. We would be too cynical, however, if we deny to administrators their share of humane impulses. Almost all hospitals have founding purposes which speak directly to the needs of homebound aged people. Voluntary hospitals commonly have a religious origin, public hospitals (city, county, state, or federal) a mandate to care for people who need help, often those who have no other source of care.

In both instances, administrators may be able to recognize that the hospital is fulfilling a basic founding purpose through the establishment of a home health care program and that they are the key to bringing their own institutions back to the fulfillment of first principles.

Why Present Hospital Home Care Programs
Do Not Serve the Purpose

Traditional home care programs of hospitals serve the valuable purpose of shortening hospital stays. Typical home care patients are discharged with the expectation that nursing and rehabilitative services provided at home will speed their return to normal function.[3, 4, 6, 53-62] With a few exceptions[63-65] these programs are limited to short-term care and to people who have been inpatients. These restrictions make traditional home care useless for aged, homebound patients, who require long-term services, are usually unconnected to hospitals, and are unlikely to return to full activity.

It is not feasible for traditional home care departments of hospitals to be transmuted into effective home health care programs:

1. Limitations in Medicare and Medicaid laws and in Blue Cross plans [4, 55-57, 59-61, 66, 67] prohibit adequate physician participation.
2. The maintenance of chronically disabled patients in the program is discouraged.
3. Home care department staff members occasionally utilize other agen-

40

cies for patient support but are not particularly directed toward planning and coordinating the network of services required to sustain people safely at home over a long time span.

OBTAINING STAFF

We start with the assumption that there is a nucleus of individuals motivated to begin the program. A nurse, doctor, and social worker, creating the first team, make the ideal nucleus.[68-72] Around them coalesces a staff, drawn irresistibly (we hope) by the opportunities for service which fulfill personal and professional goals.

Professional Staff

It is the task of the initial team to recruit further professional members. This is done in part by talking about the program, by individual discussion, and by speaking at staff meetings. More important than talking, however, is action. Once the team has obtained administration support, started visiting patients in their homes, providing services, and functioning together, inevitably others will become interested.[73]

Health workers tend to be either pragmatists or idealists.[74] They are likely to stress either the science or the art, the mechanical or the humanistic elements, in their respective fields.[75] It is difficult to do both well.

Physicians find it hard to correlate the behavioral aspect with the physical. Understanding of the total patient, mind and body, is fraught with uncertainties and is, therefore, an uneasy path for the doctor to take. He tends to follow the more certain path of the chemical sciences. . . .[76]

Doctors, nurses, and social workers are present in a reasonable supply in most hospitals. Within a large enough pool of talent, the best of the humanistically oriented will seek out opportunities to work in this kind of program.

From a Chelsea–Village Program staff conference:

ATTENDING DOCTOR: Chris, you started recently. Could you give us some idea of what it was that made you want to work in this department, what your own preconceptions of it were, and what your present realizations of it are?

CHRISTINE VITARELLA (Nurse): As you know, I've worked as a nurse on hospital floors for many years. After a while you get yourself into a rut there,

41

involved mostly in the technical things. You can't help it. But really, for a long period of time, I wanted to get involved in some sort of total patient care. Realistically, you can't do that on a hospital floor. You try; everybody hopes to, but it can't be done.

After I heard about the [Chelsea–Village] program—and how the doctor and the social worker and the nurse go into the home and see the total picture of the patient and meet the total needs—I felt this was interesting and a really good chance to get involved.

ATTENDING DOCTOR: In the modest amount of time you've been able to spend in the program so far, how does it stack up?

VITARELLA: It's beautiful. Here every patient is an individual. . . it's Mr. Brown, and you see him as Mr. Brown. This is his home, his social environment. This is his medical problem. But he's a person. You see him as a human being.

In the hospital, you see the patient as a diagnosis: he's a "cardiac." That's a mortal sin in nursing school, to let that attitude develop, but it happens.

Nonprofessional Staff

Employees at the nonprofessional level, including, for instance, the coordinator, driver, and homemaker, may be recruited in part from presently existing hospital staff. This source of personnel will be useful at the beginning of the program if the administration agrees. However, as the case load increases, full-time employees will be needed. Here we will review how to obtain workers who fulfill expectations. Finding money to pay these salaries is discussed in Chapter 16.

1. Use the personnel department in recruitment, but insist on a separate interview and the right to power of final decision about hiring.
2. In the interview with the prospective employee, spend time discussing the philosophy and the practical application of the program. Emphasize the point that aged people are involved, that the working environment may be dirty and insect-ridden, that you are seeking employees with an unusually high level of motivation to help others. An employee with a restricted image of the job will not be a success in a home health care program for the aged. The patient comes first.

An intern walking through a hallway passed by an elderly patient just as the patient slipped from under his restraints in a wheelchair and slid gradually to

42

the floor. The patient was supine but uninjured. The intern looked for help and spied a nurses' aide.

INTERN: I wonder if you could give me a hand picking up this patient.
AIDE: Oh, Doctor, I can't do that. It's not part of my job.

3. Review the job requirements in detail, but emphasize the spirit in which the work is done. The job description is a useful personnel device. We emphasize the point in the job description that all employees are expected to perform "clearly unrelated assigned duties as needed." An understanding that all program employees will be asked to serve patients as needs become apparent is essential. The job description is a guide but not a Bible or legal code to be construed strictly. It is instead an outline within which the employee is free to serve the patient.

4. Have a trial period. Good personnel practice demands this. Observe the new employee in direct contact with aged patients. Look for empathy and understanding, the ease with which the employee tolerates the physical slowness of the patient, bad smells, cockroaches, urinary and fecal incontinence, confusion. Be wary of the potential employee who uses an aged person as an object of derision, scorn, contempt, who is short-tempered or impatient, who is overly sweet and gushing, or who takes the job as an emotional vent.[77,18]

Job descriptions of the Chelsea–Village Program coordinator, community health aide, and driver are included in Chapters 4, 13, and 12, respectively.

5. Seek out indigenous people to fill jobs. Employees who reside in the area of the hospital know the geography, speak the language of the district (literally or figuratively), and are likely to have entree to neighborhood organizations and groups useful in case finding and service.

6. The employment of older people within the program is an attractive concept and should be considered. Always remember that the purpose of the program and of the employee is to serve the patient. To hire an older person deliberately, in order to make a point, is fine as long as the patients do not suffer. An older person could make a good coordinator but is not likely to be effective as a driver or homemaker. Heavy manual work is required in these jobs. Older people can make an important contribution in friendly visitor projects and telephone

43

reassurance services, which are complementary to home health care programs.

CREATING A COMMUNITY RELATIONSHIP

The effectiveness of the program is dependent upon a close relationship between the staff and community organizations and people.[17, 79-87] It is a consistent truth, and of particular importance in this kind of service, that no hospital-based medical program working in the community will succeed without mutual respect between the hospital and its neighbors. Further, hospital people must develop an understanding of the community in which they work, its social and economic network, its politics, and its power sources.

Before starting the program and throughout its course, the initiators must discuss the concept, and its plans and implementation, with every community agency and individual having a potential interest in health and/or aged people. This widespread continuing discussion and review serves the following important purposes.

Planning

Planning sessions with community agencies provide not only the appearance, which is important, but also the reality of a combined program, in which the hospital and its neighborhood are partners for the common good.

An essential element in making the program work is the creation for each patient of a network of services which provide a safe home situation. This network must consist in part of assistance provided by a number of community-based groups which have no intrinsic connection with the hospital. Planning the program with these groups provides opportunity to exchange practical ideas which avoid redundancy and inefficiency, names, phone numbers, addresses, hours of operation, methods and systems of handling urgent developments, entree into the government bureaucracy.

The following list of organizations is included as a guide, subject to local variation:

Government Agencies (Federal, State, County, City)
 Antipoverty programs
 Welfare offices
 Department of health

44

Office for the aging
Police department
Fire department
Planning board
Social Service Agencies
Visiting nurse service
Office of Economic Opportunity programs
Religious and charitable agencies
Local volunteer programs, such as friendly visitors, telephone reassurance
Committees of political organizations
Settlement houses
Local medical society
Other hospitals
Fraternal groups
Ethnic organizations
United Fund
Charitable organizations as appropriate, e.g., cancer, arthritis, multiple sclerosis
Hospital
Social service department
Home care department
Emergency room
Outpatient department staff
Individuals
Economic Organizations
Local chamber of commerce
Unions
Individuals
Hotel managers
Superintendents
Community activists, busybodies, gossips, and know-it-alls
Potential patients—including people attending senior citizens' centers[88]

Finding the Patients

The classic homebound aged person is so isolated and unknown to the community that he may never be found. In order to help these patients, strenuous effort must be given to methods of case finding. By involving large numbers of community people and groups in the planning process,

45

the additional purpose is served of utilizing the community as the major resource for referral of people who need assistance.

Most of the potential patients are hidden from view, since they are physically disabled by definition (homebound) and commonly lack friends and relatives. It takes the development of a high index of interest within the community before the problem is recognized.

Of course, it is essential that people referred to the program for assistance are visited promptly by the team. Nothing will destroy the hospital–neighborhood relationship more effectively than the appearance of ignoring a referral. This not only injures the patient but embarrasses the person making the referral and casts doubt upon the reliability of the program staff. Do not announce a starting date until you have a professional health team ready to go.

Personal Liaison and Direct Service to Patients

Aged people referred to the program are often suspicious of the professional staff, fearful that in some way permitting hospital people into the house will result in forced institutionalization. Because of these fears, the community person who makes the referral may be crucial in bringing together the patient and the team. The neighbor, hotel manager, superintendent, or other local person who knows the patient personally can bridge this gap of anxiety.

Beyond this, the community friend, as a volunteer, may provide direct assistance that really counts, as illustrated in this Chelsea–Village Program case report.

The patient is a 73-year-old woman referred to our program by a neighbor. She lives in a single-room, walk-up apartment. At our first contact she was homebound by right-sided heart failure with massive fluid retention. She was confused, apparently senile, and habitually defecated in kitchen pots scattered around the room rather than in the available toilet. Medical treatment of her cardiac disease was met through our program by administration of digitalis, diuretics, and potassium. Our staff arranged to see that she took her medication daily. Twenty-two pounds of edema fluid was lost.

Her need for socialization and human contact was met by the devoted interest of a community resident who began visiting her at our suggestion. He appeared every day, helped her to clean her apartment, and required her to eat, wash, and groom herself.

His demonstration of interest altered the patient's behavior strikingly. Her confusion faded as her life became more structured. She is now clean and uses the bathroom in the traditional manner. Her state of heart failure has improved sufficiently to allow her to leave her apartment. She participates in activities at a local senior citizen's center and is an active and happy person.

Money and Politics

Local organizations are not likely to be a source of immediate cash for the program, but in grant applications the support of community agencies and people is essential. This support will be forthcoming if the community is genuinely involved in the planning and conduct of the program.

Evidence of a wholehearted partnership between the hospital and its community serves to:

1. Firm up those elements within the hospital administration and staff who give money and moral support to the program and help them resist factions within the institution that may be antagonistic.
2. Strengthen requests to philanthropic agencies for money. People who give money away feel, with justice, that it should not be wasted. Proof that the program has extensive community support indicates that the planners are intelligent and that the likelihood of success is high.
3. Meet official and unofficial requirements of government. Officially, many sources of money within government require that the "community," or "consumers," be part of program planning and control. [32,36,89] Unofficially, it is wise to recognize that government employees at all levels, both elected and appointed, tend to respond to the voice of the voter. The community consists of many individuals who vote. If local people and agencies are solidly behind the program and are able to express themselves clearly and yet with a sensible amount of subtlety, forces in government will tend to react favorably. Of course, it helps if the request for funds has intrinsic merit. Since the programs meet the wishes of the patients and the community and are cheaper than nursing homes, they are attractive and winning to government.

REFERENCES

1. Libow LS: A public hospital-based "community care system." Gerontologist 14:289, 1974
2. Goldman F, Fraenkel M: Patients on home care: their characteristics and experience. J Chronic Dis 11:77, 1970
3. Lenzer A: Home care: the patient's point of view. Hospitals 40:64, 1966
4. Richter L, Gonnerman A: Home health services and hospitals. Hospitals 48:113, 1974
5. Griffith JR: A home-care program for a small community. Hospitals 36:58, 1972

6. Kelman HR, Muller J: The role of the hospital in the care of the ambulatory chronically ill and disabled patients after discharge. Am J Public Health 57:107, 1967

7. Houghton L, Martin AE: Home versus hospital: a hospital-based home care program. Health Social Work 1:88, 1976

8. Sammond PH: Hospital–community cooperation brings care to senior citizens. Hospitals 50:117, 1976

9. Buford JA: Neighborhood health centers need back-up. Hospitals 49:43, 1975

10. Mims RB, Thomas LL, Conroy MV: Physician house calls: a complement to hospital-based medical care. J Am Geriatr Soc 25:28, 1977

11. Kovner AR, Katz G, Kahane SB, Sheps CG: Relating a neighborhood health center to a general hospital: a case history. Med Care 7:118, 1969

12. Rawlinson HL: Planning home care services. Hospitals 49:66, 1975

13. Sillen, J, Parker B, Mitchik E, Feldshuh B, Frosch W: A Multidisciplinary Geriatric Unit for the Psychiatrically Impaired in Bellevue Hospital Center. New York, Bellevue Geriatric Evaluation and Service Unit, Psychiatric Division, Bellevue Hospital Center, 1972

14. Trager B: Home care: providing the right to stay home. Hospitals 49:93, 1975

15. Wilson EH: The integration of hospital and local authority services in the discharge of patients from hospitals. Hospitals 48:113, 1974

16. Rioux C: Health and social services under the same roof. Can Nurse 71:24, 1975

17. Colorado Community Care Organization for the Aged and Disabled: Application for a Demonstration Program Grant Submitted by the Colorado Department of Social Services, Denver, Colorado, Aug 11, 1976

18. One city's controversial plan to give seniors a fair shake on health. Am Med News 17:11, 1974

19. Brickner PW, Greenbaum D, Kaufman A, O'Donnell F, O'Brien JT, Scalice R, Scandizzo J, Sullivan T: A clinic for male derelicts. Ann Intern Med 77:565, 1972

20. Stoeckle JD, Anderson WH, Page J, Brenner J: The free medical clinics. JAMA, 219:603, 1972

21. Gibson CD: The neighborhood health center: the primary unit of health care. Am J Public Health 58:1188, 1968

22. Geiger JH: The neighborhood health center. Arch Environ Health 14:912, 1967

23. Gillespie GM: Project Head Start and dental care—one summer of experience. Am J Public Health 58:90, 1968

24. Hoekelman RA: A 1969 Head Start medical program. JAMA 219:730, 1972

25. Bodenheimer TS: Patterns of American ambulatory care. Inquiry 7:26, 1970

26. Bellin LE: How to make ambulatory care start ambulating. In American Hospitals Association: Reshaping Ambulatory Care Programs. Chicago, 1974, p 3

27. McMahon JA: Hospitals must adapt to changing community perceptions. Hospitals 49:37, 1975

28. Roemer MI: From poor beginnings, the growth of primary care. Hospitals 49:38, 1975

29. Ottensmeyer DJ: Ambulatory care: old attitudes, old habits must change. Hosp Med Staff 4:1, 1975

30. Gocke TM, Neiman SL: The provision of ambulatory care in an urban nonuniversity setting. Arch Intern Med 134:158, 1974

31. Downey GW: Ghetto needs: doctors, dollars, and dedication. Mod Hosp 122:39, 1974

32. Cunningham RM: The newcomers don't come quietly. Mod Health Care 3:11, 1975

33. McKnight JL: Hospitals must work to change image. Hospitals 49:72, 1975
34. Phillips DF: Hospitals vs. communities: the Grant Hospital experience. Trustee 28:30, 1975
35. Kresky B: Ambulatory care: impact of changing concepts on planning for facilities. NY State J Med 74:562, 1974
36. Christensen DB, Wertheimer AI: Consumer action in health care. Public Health Rep 91:406, 1976
37. Economic Opportunity Act of 1964, Pub L No 88–452, 78 Stat 508 (codified in scattered sections of 42 USC 1970). Economic Opportunity Amendments of 1966, Pub L No 89–794, 80 Stat 1415 (codified in scattered sections of 20, 42 USC). Economic Opportunity Amendments of 1967, Pub L No 90–222, 81 Stat 672 (codified in scattered sections of 3, 42 USC)
38. Guidelines: The Comprehensive Neighborhood Health Services Programs, Washington DC, Office of Economic Opportunity, March, 1968
39. Demonstration Cities and Metropolitan Development Act of 1966 (Model Cities Act) Pub L No 89–794, 80 Stat 1255 (repealed)
40. Comprehensive Health Planning and Public Health Services Amendments of 1966, Pub L No. 89–749, 80 Stat 1180, 42 USC Sect. 242q–243, 246, 247a note. Partnerships for Health Amendment of 1967, Pub L No 90–174, 81 Stat 553 (codified in scattered sections of 42 USC—some sections repealed and eliminated by subsequent legislation)
41. An act in relation to the creation of the New York City health and hospitals corporation and providing for the power and duties thereof. Ch 1016, 1969 NY Laws 1591 (McKinney's)
42. Interim Policy and Guidelines for Community Boards of New York City, Health and Hospitals Corporation, 1970
43. An act to amend the public health law in relation to the provision of medical care in public health facilities (Ghetto Medicine Law) Ch 9967, 1968 New York Laws 1946 (McKinney's)
44. Guidelines: Implementations of the Ghetto Medicine Law (Schedule A), The City of New York, Department of Health, June, 1972
45. Guidelines: Family Health Center Program, Washington DC, US Department of Health, Education, and Welfare, January, 1972
46. Medical Facilities Construction and Modernization Amendments of 1970, Pub L No 91–296, Title 1–120, 42 USC Sect 291 Note
47. An act to amend the public health law in relation to providing appropriate emergency financing for ambulatory and emergency service rendered by voluntary hospitals, Ch. 1061, 1974 New York Laws 1726 (McKinney's). An act to amend the public health law in relation to the inclusion of losses from ambulatory and emergency services in hospital payment rates and making an appropriation therefor, Ch 1062, 1974 Laws 1727
48. National Health Planning and Resources Development Act of 1974, Pub L No 93–641, Sect 1503, 1512, 1524, 42 USC Sect 300k–3, 3001–1, 300m–3 (Suppl V, 1975)
49. Brickner PW: Is there a discipline of community medicine? Am J Med, 60:936, 1976
50. Brickner PW: The homebound aged—a medically unreached group. Ann Intern Med 82:1, 1975
51. Brickner PW: The outlook for ambulatory services. Hosp Prog 56:64, 1975
52. Beaudry ML: Broadening the institution's health care base. Hosp Prog 56:66, 1975

53. American Hospital Association: The Hospital and the Home Care Program. Chicago, 1972
54. American Medical Association, Committee on Community Health Care: Statement on Home Health Care. Chicago, American Medical Association, 1973
55. Trager B: Home Health Services in the United States. Washington DC, US Government Printing Office, 1972
56. Blue Cross Association: Policy Statement on Home Health Care, Chicago, Blue Cross Association, April 1974
57. US Social Security Administration: Directory of Medicare Suppliers of Services, 1st ed, Washington DC, US Government Printing Office, 1967
58. Joint Commission on Accreditation of Hospitals: Accreditation Manual for Hospitals. Chicago, 1973
59. Providers of services and independent laboratories. Federal Health Insurance for the Aged. Code of Federal Regulations. Title 20, Chapter III, Part 405, HIR–15 (6–68). Washington DC, US Department of Health, Education, and Welfare, 1973
60. Blue Cross of Greater New York Coordinated Home Care. New York, Blue Cross Association, May 1974. Home Health Services Medicare Bulletins. Blue Cross–Blue Shield, through March 10, 1976
61. US Department of Health, Education, and Welfare, Home Health Agency Manual. HIM–11 (6–69) Revised. Washington DC, US Government Printing Office, 1974
62. McCarthy E: Comprehensive home care for earlier hospital discharge. Nurs Outlook 24:625, 1976
63. Mumford D, Bogdan I, Hoyt E, et al: Home health care for the aged. Ann Intern Med 83:125, 1975
64. Hainer JW, King S: Care for the homebound aged. Ann Intern Med 82:717, 1975
65. Lockwood JA: Medical care for the elderly. Ann Intern Med 83:741, 1975
66. Ryder CF, Stitt PG, Elkin WF: Home health services—past, present, future. Am J Public Health 59:1720, 1969
67. Dunn A: USA—Home health care. Nurs Times 71:1082, 1975
68. Sherwood S (ed): Long-term Care: A Handbook for Researchers, Planners, and Providers. New York, Spectrum Publications (Halsted Press), 1975. A medical perspective of team care.
69. Roth ME, Tarnopoll I: Organization of a coordinated home care program in Erie County, New York. Public Health Rep 82:639, 1967
70. Flynn JP: The team approach: a possible control for the single service schism—an exploratory study. Gerontologist 10:119, 1970
71. Kinoy SK: Home health services for the elderly. Nurs Outlook 17:59, 1969
72. McHugh JC, Chughtai MA: The importance of team work in geriatric care. Nurs Times 71:140, 1975
73. Twain M: The Adventures of Tom Sawyer (1876). In: The Family Mark Twain. New York, Harper, 1925, pp 292–95
74. Crawshaw R: Humanism in medicine—the rudimentary process. N Engl J Med 293:1320, 1975
75. Mechanic D: Medical Sociology: A Selective View. New York, Free Press, 1968. p 23
76. Cope O: Man, Mind, and Medicine. Philadelphia, Lippincott, 1968, p. 17
77. Jacoby S: Waiting for the end: on nursing homes. New York Times Magazine, March 31, 1974, p 13
78. Miller MB: Decision-making in the death process of the ill aged. Geriatrics 26:105, 1971

79. Royle GA: Community care for the elderly: can we get it right? R Soc Health J 95:28, 1975

80. Leonard LE, Kelly AM: The development of a community-based program for evaluating the impaired older adult. Gerontologist 14:289, 1974

81. Quinn JL: Triage: coordinated home care for the elderly. Nurs Outlook 23:570, 1975

82. Brody SJ: Comprehensive health care for the elderly: an analysis. Gerontologist 13:412, 1973

83. Hobman D: Practical care of geriatric patients. A. An old person's view of the health services. R Soc Health J 1:21, 1975

84. Cohen ES: Integration of health and social services in federally funded programs. Bull NY Acad Med 49:1038, 1973

85. Bell WG: Community care for the elderly: an alternative to institutionalization. Gerontologist 13:349, 1973

86. Beverly EV: Unique organization helps seniors declare, win, and keep their independence. Geriatrics 30:114, 1975

87. Herz KG: Community resources and services to help independent living. Gerontologist 11:59, 1971

88. National Council on the Aging, for the Office of Economic Opportunity: Community Organization, Planning, and Resources and the Older Poor. Technical Assistance Monograph No. 1 Match SK (ed). March, 1970

89. Epperson GW, Juedeman RF: Accounting to the community. Hospitals 49:83, 1975

CHAPTER 4

HOME HEALTH CARE IN OPERATION

The Chelsea–Village Program (CVP) of Saint Vincent's Hospital is a prototype health care program for homebound, isolated, aged people.[1-4] This chapter uses the CVP as a case history, in which the origin, conduct, and results of the program are discussed and analyzed. This material may be useful in the development of other programs, although there is no suggestion that precise replication is necessary or wise. Each program should meet the particular needs and circumstances of its hospital and community.

Statistical data about the CVP and our patients are located in the Appendix.

GENESIS OF THE CONCEPT

Observation in our own hospital emergency room, in the 1960s, led us to realize that certain groups of people characteristically are brought in too late for treatment, either moribund or dead on arrival. The first such group that we recognized was residents of welfare hotels, primarily middle-aged, alcoholic men. We established a clinic in the largest of these hotels, with physicians from the hospital and nurses from the Visiting Nurse Service of New York as staff members.[5, 6]

These men generally were too indifferent, frightened, or angry to seek needed health care through local hospitals or physicians. Our experience included care for men who would not permit themselves to be properly treated and for whom disability seemed to be preferable to good health, and, it seemed, men who would rather die in the hotel than make the

52

effort to get treatment elsewhere. We found that many of these men had short attention spans, an antiestablishment orientation, a low level of tolerance for standing in lines, and they were put off by the regimentation of the hospital.[7]

We learned that, badly damaged as these men were by their sociopathic behavior, the older among them were the worst off. They suffered the combined burdens of a deteriorated style of life and the physical consequences of aging.

Based on this understanding, we took another look at our own community and realized that aged people, particularly those who were homebound and alone, were a second medically unreached group. While we can say of the first group—alcoholic derelict men—that they *will* not participate in the health care system, we can equally well say of homebound aged people that they *cannot*. They are barred from the system by their own disabilities.[3]

INITIAL PLANNING

In our planning for creation of health services for this group we benefited from lessons learned in the hotel project. When health workers try to reach isolated patients away from the hospital base, they must think beyond the purely medical aspects of disease. An understanding of the community in which they work, its social and economic problems and its politics, is essential for success.[8-14] An appreciation of how the hospital works, the duties and abilities of its people, where to look for support, how to contend with opposition, is equally important.

In the summer of 1972 we started planning the program. It may seem in retrospect that we were highly organized and functioned with machinelike precision. In fact, we were uncertain about our means and unclear about our ultimate goals. We had the benefit of strong motivation and considerable past experience in community health work.

We made up a preliminary list of problems:

THE PATIENTS We knew that their difficulties would be complex and multifaceted,[15-21] that the patients would be isolated and hard to find.

PROFESSIONAL STAFF The organizers included two physicians, a social worker, and a nurse. We would make the first health team and would not have to depend on others to initiate the program. However, more staff members would be essential, and we would need assistance from several hospital departments.[22-26]

53

HOSPITAL ADMINISTRATION We required administrative assistance. We hoped for participation by professional staff members on regular paid time, requiring hospital approval. We would need space, a telephone, and we would need the good will and moral backing of the institution so that we could put forward the program as a part of the hospital. We feared, otherwise, that we might be looked at as odd do-gooders rather than as serious health workers.

COMMUNITY PEOPLE AND AGENCIES We knew that community support would be needed in order to integrate our program into the regular work of other community projects[12, 14, 27-29] and to seek out the patients. We would have to find and talk with recognized community groups and agencies and also look for individuals, such as hotel managers and building superintendents.

We felt that it might be difficult to get the attention of these people.

MONEY We planned to start the program in a small way, with hospital staff and no money. We did not know whether we might need money later or, if so, how much. We knew that no significant sum was available from patients because most were impoverished, and we knew that reimbursement from Medicare and Medicaid would not be forthcoming. These laws do not permit hospitals to bill for care outside the walls of the institutions.[30-33]

We had no prior experience in raising grant money and deferred that matter temporarily.

SOLVING PLANNING PROBLEMS

We dealt with these issues by talking. We spoke with representatives of every community agency we could find, all three police precincts, and the two settlement houses in our area, fire stations, the offices of the three congressmen whose districts merge here, city and state politicians, Office of Economic Opportunity programs, senior citizens centers, every church and synagogue, local planning boards, block associations. We found a universal understanding of the need and of willingness to help.

We approached our hospital administrators at a time when financial stress upon the voluntary hospital system in New York City was severe and getting worse. Administration's reaction was favorable, and to the present the hospital continues its support. It takes an unusual administration to recognize the imperatives of this kind of program, but this response from the Sisters of Charity of Saint Vincent de Paul who run Saint

54

Vincent's Hospital is a realistic application of the founding spirit of the institution. It was created in 1849 to care for the sick poor.

We met with directors of clinical departments of the hospital, with house staff, and with nursing and social service. Here, ability to respond to our request for voluntary participation depended on existing demands upon time and on staffing schedules.

We had excellent response from resident physicians, especially in the most important area of internal medicine. Social service participation was moderate, largely because of personnel shortages. Nursing reaction was limited, but we overcame this problem through good fortune. One of the Sisters, a registered nurse, has devoted full-time to the program from the start.

We had large group meetings with hospital and community representatives. These sessions served to introduce our ideas widely through the hospital and our geographic area, resulted in agreements with other voluntary and governmental agencies to participate in care of our patients, and helped to create the atmosphere of interest and expectation necessary for case finding of these hidden patients. The meetings also pointed up certain problems and areas of uncertainty.

EXCERPTS FROM RECORDS OF PRELIMINARY PUBLIC MEETINGS

MRS. RODRIGUEZ (Democratic District Leader):   Why has the North Chelsea Houses' tenants' organization not been contacted?

A: We are first concentrating on organizations in south Chelsea, nearer the hospital. We will expand our services to north Chelsea as soon as possible.

MRS. FRIEDMAN (Golden Ring Club):   Will you continue to serve your patients, or refer them to other agencies?

A: We will do whatever seems in the patient's best interests, but we intend to make full use of all community agencies.

DR. GREENBAUM (Medical Resident):   I question whether physician's time will be used efficiently. Perhaps other professional personnel should be used for the initial house contact.

A: We feel the doctor's presence is necessary. We must accept the fact that this will not be an efficient program in the sense of numbers of patients seen per professional hour. All or most of our cases will be frightened people with massive social and/or medical problems.

MRS. FRED (Senior Citizen's Center):   Our communicators attempt to reach our members who are homebound, but in many cases even they are unable to make contact because they are not admitted or the location is unsafe.

A: We expect to be relatively safe because we will be in teams of three people.

Getting the person's confidence may be more of a problem. We plan to combine persistence with sensitivity.

OFFICER FLORIDA (Local Police Precinct): Can you handle emergencies?

A: We do not have the ability to deal with emergencies. We see this as a program to help people with chronic, complex problems. For disastrous or acute situations, it is best to call 911 and get an ambulance.

Ms. HEALY (St. Vincent's Hospital Social Worker): Do you plan to limit patients strictly by age?

A: We see this mainly as a program for elderly people, but we will not be rigid, and if a younger person in our area is homebound and in need of help, we will take the patient on.

LEARNING ABOUT OUR COMMUNITY

Through the process of meeting and talking, we gathered important information about the Chelsea and Greenwich Village areas which our hospital serves, information which we needed to make the program work.

Chelsea is primarily a lower middle class residential area, housing about 80,000 people. There are pockets of severe poverty and 30 welfare hotels. About 6,500 people live in housing projects. Chelseaites include a mixture of immigrant populations. The area has many second- and third-generation Irish and English, with substantial numbers of people whose origins are Italian, German, and Greek. The area is about one-third Hispanic (Puerto Rican and from many countries in Central and South America). Many of the Jewish residents are retired garment workers, living in housing built by the International Ladies Garment Workers Union. The area is about 5 percent Black.

Greenwich Village houses about 75,000 people and is more widely split along economic lines. There are expensive attractive brownstone houses, areas designed for artists (SoHo), street people, including adolescents attracted to the area from all over the country by Greenwich Village's Bohemian reputation, welfare hotels, and the monolithic ethnic enclaves of Little Italy and Chinatown.

About 14 percent of the local population is age 65 or over.[34, 35]

THE START

At length, when talking and analysis were clearly no longer a substitute for action, we declared a starting date. Our initial home visit, January 17, 1973, was made with a team of doctor, nurse, and social worker walking to the patient. We had no paid professional or nonprofessional staff, no

56

money, no vehicle. We had the formal support of our hospital, a telephone extension in the department of community medicine, widespread goodwill throughout the community, cool clear weather, pure hearts, and our first patient.

We learned by doing, following basic precepts. Our stated purposes were to help our patients (1) remain in their own homes and community, (2) out of institutions, (3) in the best possible state of health, and (4) at the maximum possible level of independence.

Our early cases demonstrated the viability of our concept and at the same time revealed problems and questions we had not anticipated and which demanded solutions and answers.

Would We Receive Sufficient Referrals?

During the first few weeks we were off to a sputtering start. Referrals were few. We feared, of course, that our preparations were inadequate, that nobody was paying attention.

The misery of a child is interesting to a mother, the misery of a young man is interesting to a young woman, the misery of an old man is interesting to nobody.
—Victor Hugo, *Les Miserables*[36]

It was encouraging that the early referrals were from a variety of sources (Chelsea Action Center, Visiting Nurse Service, police department, Saint Vincent's emergency room, Saint Vincent's social service department).

Within a month we had more patients than we could handle with the initial team. The next concern was . . .

Would We Be Able to Recruit
Sufficient Professional Volunteers?

Physicians on the house staff responded in adequate numbers to the need. These doctors were encouraged by their directors to volunteer during the regular work day if patients under their care were covered by other house officers. This plan worked. By the end of the first month five physicians were regularly involved.

Nursing services were given totally by our Sister, as noted above.

Social service staff was in shortest supply. The Department was low on personnel, and each case represented considerable expenditure of time. Individual social workers accepted cases, but we never achieved adequate social work coverage through the volunteer approach. This point was an

57

important factor in our recognition that we would have to make the effort to raise money for salaries.

Could We Balance Staff against Demand for Service?

At first, we had periods when staff volunteers exceeded, in time available, the number of cases referred to us. This was followed by a surge of referrals that left us struggling to find a way to meet the need. We feared loss of credibility.

This stormy course settled down gradually, as we became responsible for more patients and as more staff members became available on a regular basis. This kind of imbalance is inevitable at the start of a program. It must be expected in a situation where the number of potential patients is uncertain and the sources of referral are so various.

Could We Resolve Complex Problems?

CHELSEA–VILLAGE PROGRAM CASE REPORT

F.P. is an 89-year-old man, living alone, known to the program for two years. Shortly prior to our intervention he had been hospitalized twice for generalized weakness, dyspnea, and malnourishment. He insisted upon returning home when he improved.

A neighbor referred the patient to us at a point when the process of deterioration was starting again.

Medical evaluation showed that Mr. P. had emphysema and chronic bronchitis with limited exercise tolerance, sufficient only to care for himself at a minimal level. In discussions with the social worker and nurse, Mr. P. made it clear that he was depressed, because he was alone and afraid of death. During the first few months of our relationship he called the ambulance eight times and was brought to the hospital emergency room in a state of panic, but with reassurance that he was not dying, he was willing to go back home.

We established medical treatment of his lung disease with appropriate drugs. Through regular visits, the nurse helped Mr. P. plan a method of remembering the proper doses and intervals. The social worker spent time talking with Mr. P. about his fears. She also obtained a homemaker who was willing to work at night, the time of greatest anxiety, and who prepared a substantial dinner, kept the apartment clean, did necessary shopping.

This combination of practical service, control of disease, and personal attention has been effective in keeping Mr. P. comfortable and cheerful in his own

58

home. Over the last 22 months there have been no hospitalizations or ambulance calls.

Could We Learn to Screen Referrals?

We had distributed the phone number of our program throughout the community, and during the regular work day it was answered indiscriminately by anyone at hand in the office of the department of community medicine. Patents referred to us were occasionally accepted without adequate thought, and we learned quickly, the hard way, that certain requirements had to be met.

GEOGRAPHIC   The public transportation network in our area is effective on the north-south axis but poor going east and west. One day it took the team an hour to reach a new patient on the East Side of Manhattan. More rigid geographic rules were instituted, which continue to apply, even though we now have a vehicle and a driver. We learned that there are practical limits to the ability of a single program to serve a large area.

WILLINGNESS OF PATIENTS TO RECEIVE US   People have rejected our help for various reasons.

CHELSEA–VILLAGE PROGRAM CASE REPORT

Mr. O'Brien [name slightly changed] is a 99-year-old man who was referred to us by three different community organizations during the early months of the program, but on each occasion there was no answer to our knock on the door.

   One day our nursing Sister, who had known him several decades earlier, caught up with the patient hobbling painfully and slowly along the street.

SISTER: Mr. O'Brien, how come you're never home when we come to see you?
MR. O'BRIEN (peering closely at the speaker):   You're from Saint Vincent's Hospital?
SISTER: Yes.
MR. O'BRIEN: Saint Vincent's Hospital is full of spics, kikes, wops, and niggers—and I don't want to have anything to do with you!

A more common cause of rejection is the patient's fear of the large institution and its power to manipulate the individual, to force the patient into the hospital or a nursing home.

59

This concern is understandable. Consider the reputation of health professionals for feeling and acting as though they have the right to decide the patient's fate.[37]

In some cases we have succeeded in quieting fears through persistent and kindly attention; sometimes through the intervention of a relative, friend, or community person known and believed by the patient; and sometimes we do not succeed.

It is our good fortune that our nursing Sister is generally known and trusted in the community and is in a position to solve many of these difficult human issues.

HOMEBOUNDEDNESS   We visited a patient, self-referred by telephone, only to find no answer to our knock. As we started to go back downstairs, we were met by the patient walking up, rather briskly, and carrying two shopping bags full of groceries.

PATIENT: Oh, I'm so sorry you got here before me. I hope I didn't keep you waiting.
TEAM MEMBER: We thought you called for help because you couldn't get out and needed a doctor.
PATIENT: Oh, no. I'm out all the time, but it's easier if you come to me. I don't like the bother of the clinic.

RELATIONSHIP TO OTHER PHYSICIANS   We received a referral from a hotel manager. An elderly man appeared to be doing poorly. Our first visit revealed the patient to be in heart failure. We did an electrocardiogram, took blood for basic laboratory studies, and started him on slow digitalization.

The next day we received a telephone call from a local doctor.

PHYSICIAN: Mr. —— is my patient. I go to see him once a week. How dare you usurp my authority. You are guilty of trying to steal my patient. I'm reporting you to the county medical society and the AMA.
SECRETARY: I'll tell the boss.

We realized that the physician was correct. We had been injudicious or, worse, foolish. We had not appreciated that this potential conflict would arise.

The doctor was placated with an apologetic letter, and we withdrew from the case.

As a result of these experiences we created an intake card, and referrals are now accepted only if they meet these criteria: the patient is geographically accessible, homebound, willing to receive us, and lacks access to medical care.

We construe accessibility and homeboundedness as liberally as possible, so that no one is turned away arbitrarily.

The data on the card is used to assign priority to new referrals (Fig. 4–1).

GROWTH

Within three months it was clear that we needed permanent staff members and that this would require money and a budget.

Three nonprofessional employees and a half-time social worker were appointed.

Nonprofessional Staff

COORDINATOR In addition to the standard secretarial aspects of the job, this employee is trained to receive and make an initial evaluation of referrals, to handle calls from patients, relatives, and agencies, to make appointments for visits, and to know when to ask for advice and where to find it. See Figure 4-2 for job description.

DRIVER The need for increased efficiency required the employment of a driver and the purchase of a vehicle, a large station wagon. The primary function of the driver is to transport the teams from place to place, but he has also been taught how to move our disabled and wheelchair-bound patients when trips are necessary. He has learned how to take EKG's and to perform this function for the program in our patients' homes.

Our driver knows the intricate street layout of Greenwich Village and is fluent in Italian and Spanish, as well as in English.

Further discussion of the driver's function and the subject of transportation is found in Chapter 12.

HOMEMAKER We needed our own homemaker because of delays in obtaining services from the New York City Department of Social Services—Homemaker Division, and because some patients are simply ineligible for these services. Our program is free of red tape, and our homemaker can be at work in a patient's home without delay. Furthermore, she is not restricted by agency rules to a precise number of hours she must stay with a patient, the number of patients she can see in one

61

```
Name: _____   Date _____  Sex _____

Address: _____  Age _____

Apt. no. _____  Phone _____

Person calling: _____

Phone no. of caller: _____  Org. _____

Do you know if other organizations are helping? _____

If so, which _____

Translator needed? _____  Language: _____

Will outside agency provide this? _____

Community liaison (who will be present) _____

_____

Date and time of appointment: _____

_____
```

```
Nature of Problem:




```

FIG. 4-1.   Front (top) and back (bottom) of card for new referrals.

Job Summary: Coordinates activities of program personnel. Develops and maintains statistics relevant to program. Maintains liaison with related health and welfare agencies, patients, families.

Responsibility: Under the supervision of the Administrative Assistant of the Department of Community Medicine,

1. Coordinates the activities of program personnel; makes sure all duties are performed.
2. Maintains contact by phone with patients.
3. Schedules patient appointments.
4. Maintains patient charts and program records.
5. Processes applications for Medicaid, equipment, homemaker services, etc.
6. Develops and maintains statistics relevant to program.
7. Maintains liaison with related health and welfare agencies.
8. Performs various secretarial and clerical tasks: types letters, answers phone, maintains files, etc.
9. Performs related assigned duties.
10. Performs clearly unrelated assigned duties as needed.

Skill: High school graduate with two years of college or at least four years of work experience.
Bilingual: Spanish, Italian, or Hebrew, as well as English.
Ability to work with people.

Effort: Sits, stands, moves about. Normal activity.

Working Conditions: Good.

FIG. 4-2. Job description for coordinator of the Chelsea–Village Program.

day, or the duties she can perform. She, in fact, combines the functions of the typical homemaker, housekeeper, and home health aide.

Further discussion of homemaker functions is found in Chapter 13.

Professional Staff

A half-time social worker was hired in the third month and was able to carry a case load of about 35 active patients. By combining the efforts of this employee with the volunteer time already available, we kept pace with the growth rate for another year.

By the third year we had two full-time social workers in the program. See Chapter 7 for detailed discussion of social worker functions.

Money and Budget

We now faced the need for cash and a financial plan, and succeeded in raising the needed funds from small- and medium-sized philanthropic agencies. A detailed discussion of fund-raising methods and cost analysis is found in Chapter 16.

PATIENTS AND CASES

We are closely involved with our patients and their daily life problems. As a result, we are usually able to view them as individuals rather than as cases. Occasionally, our language may reveal professional narcissism, the sense that we are more important than the patient, but we struggle against this tendency. We resist separating patients into categories; each person is clearly distinct and different. There is no typical case. For the sake of this discussion, however, we have selected examples from our files that may have a general application.

A REJECTING PATIENT—ULTIMATELY RESPONSIVE

The patient (now deceased) was an 84-year-old woman referred to us by a local settlement house.

First Visit—Doctor's Note
An obese, snappy, very aged w♀, sitting in chair with elephantine legs (maximum edema up to knees). Requests that we not talk down to her or speak of her as senile. Uses no Rx. Ambulates poorly with walker. Floor thick with urine, feces, and cockroaches.
Px: 4-plus pitting edema to knees. Patient refuses further examination.
Plan: Furosemide 40 mg every other day. Return one week.

Second Visit—Social Worker's Note
Mrs. V. was eating chocolate when we arrived. She is not amenable to answering questions. Would not even discuss the possibility of buying a portable commode. She has $12,000 in the bank that she is very reluctant to spend, but this makes her ineligible for Medicaid.

Fifth Visit—Nurse's Note
Patient permitted us into the apartment, but we were not allowed to examine her. I asked her to go into hospital for treatment of edema. She won't.
   The patient insisted on hobbling to stove—offered me a cup of coffee. Three cockroaches in cup. I said, "No thanks. I just had breakfast." Mrs. V., "Oh, you shouldn't have done that. You know I always offer you something."

Eighth Visit—Doctor's Note
Both legs have infected ulcers. Still trying to hospitalize. Took a furosemide tablet with Pepsi-Cola.

The patient agreed to enter the hospital the next day. Treatment of edema and leg ulcers was moderately effective. The apartment was thoroughly cleaned, and the patient was able to return home with a homemaker.

AN ACCEPTING PATIENT—PROLONGING INDEPENDENCE

The patient, an 89-year-old immigrant from England, was formerly a captain in the Connaught Rangers, a division of the British Army disbanded in 1922, at the founding of the Irish Free State. The Captain established a successful business life in the United States. He reached his 90th year living in modest circumstances, with a roommate of the same age who was bedridden.

The Captain cared for his friend, and we gave health services. The Captain himself became homebound by arthritis and the onset of diabetes mellitus.

For the next 23 months our team and community agencies combined to provide resources which permitted the roommates independence. The Captain particularly was alert and enjoyed freedom of mind, as this poem demonstrates. His opinions are his own:

Some Thoughts On My Ninetieth Birthday

Today I've lived for ninety years
Through peace and war, through joy
  and tears.
I thank the Lord that I was born
While law was law and men were
  strong.
And when our virtuous womenfolk
Regarded wedlock as no joke.
And didn't think it a disaster
To obey their husband, lord and
  master,
And knew they came from Adam's
  rib,
A thing unknown to Women's Lib.
When man looked man right in the
  face
And honest work was no disgrace.
Now "work" is called a dirty word
And loss of sweat is thought absurd.
Children driven mad by dope,
Deprived of health and faith and hope.
Another thing that's very sad
The Nation has gone money-mad.
For those who want to get rich quick
A nice jail sentence does the trick.
For they're no sooner in than out
Folk pay to hear what it's about.
And all the so-called intellectuals
Are lesbians or homosexuals.
Statesman, so-called, of Nixon school
Think every honest man a fool.
Statesman, forsooth, crook politicians
Foul nursing homes, striking
  physicians,
Dishonest judges, crooked cops,
Rape, mugging, murder never stops.
I hope to see in '76
That politicians and their tricks,
Both petit larceny and grand,
Are all in jail or Switzerland.

In due time the roommate died. The lease of the apartment was in the roommate's name. The Captain was threatened with eviction, and we were forced to place him in a nursing home.

C.B. is a 67-year-old woman referred to us by a distant relative. Miss B. had worked in an office until age 65. She then retired, became a recluse, and spent her time eating.

First Visit–Doctor's Note, April 2, 1974
Patient was able to open door for us but tripped, fell, and couldn't get herself up. It took us 15 minutes to figure out how to lift her—it was like trying to pick up a massive bag of jelly.

Obesity is present to a remarkable degree. In addition, 3-plus edema. Pulse—160, irregular rhythm. BP—cuff not big enough. EKG—rapid atrial fibrillation.

The patient agreed to hospitalization. It required four men from the ambulance company to carry her downstairs. Weight recorded in the hospital was 335 pounds. After five weeks' hospitalization, she returned home under our care, weighing 280 on a medical regimen of digitalis, diuretics, insulin for newly discovered diabetes mellitus, and a sodium-restricted 1,200 calorie diabetic diet.

Over the next 15 months, under our close observation, the patient's weight fell steadily, and her medical disorders remained stable.

Doctor's Note, August 14, 1975
Weight—196. Patient goes out once a week. Able to climb stairs without assistance.

Miss B. agreed to help in our program by providing telephone reassurance to another patient each day.

Social Service Note, January 30, 1976
Patient reverting to inactive status in our program. Improved and no longer needs us. About to start a trip on a freighter through the Panama Canal to California, fulfilling a lifelong ambition.

CASE CONFERENCES

Weekly Chelsea–Village Program staff meetings are used for planning, review, and resolution of complex problems, and team communication and coordination.

IRMA STAHL (Social Worker):   I want to present the case of Paulette G. today. She is a Polish Jewish woman, now 80 years old, who is a victim of Nazi persecution.

She lives with her daughter, an extremely anxious woman in her late 40s. She is out of work, and the two of them live on the mother's Social Security and SSI payments, a total of $195 per month.

My main concern now is that the daughter's hysterical behavior is harming the mother. I don't know how to work with the daughter so we can help the mother.

DOCTOR: Give us some medical information about the mother.

STAHL: She's a short, obese woman who is limited to bed and chair, with some use of a walker. We know that she has ASHD, diabetes, and severe arthritis. She is also confused. She clings to her daughter.

The daughter is unrealistic about goals. She wants her mother to be what she calls "a real person"; she wants her to be the way she was before. She should be walking around, and she shouldn't be sick, and her mind should be clear, and she shouldn't be old. She feels her mother should be completely well.

DOCTOR: What does the daughter do that makes working with her so difficult?

STAHL: She has succeeded in manipulating a large number of community agencies into participating in the case, and now we face conflicting authority, cross orders of all kinds, and the mother sits in the middle of this storm getting no better. Our program is involved, and so is the social service department of another hospital. Also, the Visiting Nurse Service and Jewish Family Service have been calling. Do we belong in this case at all? With all these people involved, no one is able to exercise proper supervision. The daughter receives advice and medication from various doctors and then disregards all the orders. She has called me regularly and demanded emergency visits. When I go, she isn't there to answer the door. Her only consistent reaction is that she refuses to consider a nursing home for her mother.

DOCTOR: She's ambivalent. Still, there are parts of the daughter's attitude that I like, even though she's exceptionally difficult. I like the fact that she can't tolerate the idea of her mother's going into a nursing home. Do you know if they were in a concentration camp?

STAHL: I think they may have been.

DOCTOR: Well, it may be a critical historical fact. If the daughter is in her late 40s and she went through this whole process at the time. . . . I don't know what experiences you all may have had with people who survived concentration camps, but often it simply destroys them. The daughter's behavior strikes me as being characteristic. And what would this have done to her own relationship to her mother? She may perceive her mother as a person who somehow managed to save her.

STAHL: She indicated that she thought her mother had.

DOCTOR: Therefore, she might not be able to tolerate the idea of having her mother put away in a nursing home. The similarity between that and the concentration camp is all too obvious.

SISTER TERESITA (Nurse): I don't know this patient, so maybe I have a clearer view of this confused situation. It seems to me that we are in danger of focusing on the daughter's behavior, rather than on our real objective, the welfare of the mother. I see the daughter's conduct as a violent but disorganized effort to keep her mother with her. If we can get the daughter's confidence, so she relies primarily on us, maybe we can hold them together and meet everybody's main wish: to keep the mother safe, medically stable, and out of a nursing home.

Through this discussion we worked out a plan of action. We simplified matters by calling off the other agencies. By direct and frequent contact with the daughter, we succeeded in calming her fear that she was about to lose her mother by death or institutionalization. As the daughter became less agitated, the mother improved and was less confused. So far, they are together.

THE DYING PATIENT

Our patients are old, and many of them are ill. Death is common. Patients and their families often make it clear to us that death at home is preferred to hospitalization. For this to be feasible, both physical and psychological preparation is necessary.

Physical arrangements to provide adequate comfort for the patient are simple[38-43] and depend mainly upon the presence of a willing friend, relative, or employee to share the living quarters or to be nearby. Emotional issues are more complex.

People who are informed that they have a limited life expectancy react in different ways. Some seem to be able to cope adequately with the psychic pain that may come in the form of anger, depression, fear, or inappropriate guilt. They adjust emotionally to the point that they are able to live the final weeks and months of their lives with inner tranquility. Other patients seem unable to handle the pain.[44]

Impending death can be a time of great stress and unhappiness for everyone involved. But this is not inevitable. People can learn to face death, come to terms with it, and be at peace.[45-50]

It is important to remember that the patient's wishes come first. The challenge lies in trying to understand what the patient truly wants. Dr. Elisabeth Kübler-Ross has made clear[51] that the conspiracy of silence among patient, family, and staff about the fact of approaching death is cruel. The patient usually understands that death is near but cannot men-

68

tion it to anyone because it is a dirty secret. The family will not talk about it. They are afraid to. The staff does not want the emotional burden either.[52,53] It is almost always true that people are relieved and feel better if the subjects of death and dying can be discussed with sensitivity, freely and openly, and if emotion can be expressed.

Some patients suffer more from abrupt emotional isolation and unwitting rejection than from their illness itself. Many feel appreciative, not only because they have time to make confessions, either sacramentally or informally. The opportunity to discuss their feelings helps subdue irrational fears and guilt sentiments associated with thoughts of death.[54]

Patients sometimes feel that any feelings they may express are a burden to their family. This Chelsea–Village Program case report is relevant.

A.D. was a 70-year-old woman dying of cancer, being cared for by her husband and her son at home. The bed was moved into the large kitchen, where she would be in the heart of all family activities. Dear relatives and friends visited regularly, but the patient's impending death was never discussed. On the day of the Chelsea–Village Program team's last visit Mrs. D.'s poodle was nearby. After the doctor and the nurse had finished examining the patient, the social worker picked up the dog and sat by her bedside. Mrs. D. said she had no patience with the dog any more, and started to weep. She said, "I'm feeling very lonesome. I just hate to be leaving my family behind. They look so sad. Thank you for letting me cry and for letting me talk."

Members of the family must be prepared, as well as the patient. The following material from a Chelsea–Village Program staff conference concerns an 80-year-old man nearing death from carcinoma of the esophagus, cared for by his two sisters, ages 78 and 81.

F. RUSSELL KELLOGG (Fellow, Community Medicine): Mr. R. keeps asking what is wrong with him. The sisters don't want him to know. They are under a lot of strain both because of the physical effort of taking care of him and because he's dying.

SISTER TERESITA: We have told them that there are alternatives if they can't continue with him at home, but they want to go on.

ATTENDING DOCTOR: What are the physical facts of the case?

KELLOGG: He needs help urinating, so both sisters are up all night. They try to feed him, but his appetite's gone and he has trouble swallowing. He's becoming cadaveric. The aide washes him. But his main worry has to do with the nature of his illness, why he's not getting better. That's all he talks about. As

69

far as the sisters are concerned they really feel he shouldn't know. They are very threatened by his knowing.

IRMA STAHL: The sisters have to be worked with and brought to the point of allowing him to be talked to and supporting the discussion.

ELLEN QUIRKE (Social Worker):   Let me interrupt a moment. What about the patient's right to know? He's the one who is asking the questions, "What is wrong with me? Why am I so weak? Why don't I get better?" Granted, the sisters are frightened or angry because he has cancer, he's dying, and they feel responsible to care for him. They may feel that telling him the truth will place an additional burden on them they can't bear. But still, it's his right to know.

ATTENDING DOCTOR: I think that's absolutely true. We should never forget that our first purpose is to aid the patient, not the family. The patient's needs come first. We tend to get diverted by the people who are the more vigorous ones, who are able to confront us with their wishes, like his sisters. But we have to get past that and understand what the patient's needs are. If he's saying that, one way or another, he wants to know, he wants to have more information about himself, I think we ought to find a way of doing it.

The social worker and the nurse had several meetings with the sisters, and feelings of anxiety were discussed. They recognized at last that the strain would be decreased by talking openly with their brother. But first, the doctor spoke frankly with him about dying. His response was, "I know. Take care of my sisters."

REFERENCES

1. Brickner PW, Janeski FJ: The Chelsea–Village Program: Four-year Report, January 18, 1973–January 17, 1977. Chelsea–Village Program, Department of Community Medicine, St. Vincent's Hospital, 153 West 11th Street, New York, NY 10011
2. St. Vincent's sends MD's into the home. NY Med 30:305 September, 1974
3. Brickner PW, Duque T, Kaufman A, Sarg M, Jahre JA, Maturlo S, Janeski JF: The homebound aged, a medically unreached group. Ann Intern Med 82:1, 1975
4. Brickner PW, Janeski JF, Duque T, Stahl I, Ruether B, Kellogg F, Madeira S, Stall J: Hospital home health care program aids isolated homebound elderly. Hospitals 50:117, 1976
5. Brickner PW, Greenbaum D, Kaufman A, O'Donnell F, O'Brian JT, Scalice R, Scandizzo J, Sullivan T: A clinic for male derelicts, a welfare hotel project. Ann Intern Med 77:565, 1972
6. Brickner PW, Kaufman A: Case finding of heart disease in homeless men. Bull NY Acad Med 49:475, 1973
7. Stephens J: Society of the alone: freedom, privacy, and utilitarianism as the dominant norms in the SRO. J Gerontol 30:230, 1975
8. Griffith JR: A home health care program for a small community. Hospitals 36:58, 1962

9. Wahl D: The Volunteer Protective Service Board: A Framework for Action. RATE Program, Family Service Association of Greater Fall River, 101 Rock St, Fall River, Mass 02720

10. Bell BD: Mobile medical care to the elderly: an evaluation. Gerontologist 15:100, 1975

11. Garetz FK, Peth PR: An outreach program of medical care for aged high-rise residents. Gerontologist 14:404, 1974

12. Wilson EH, Wilson BO: Integration of hospital and local authority services in the discharge of patients from a geriatric unit. Lancet 2:864, 1971

13. Kaplan J: Appraising the traditional organizational basis of provoding gerontological services. Gerontologist 7:200, 1967

14. Knowelden J: Information for community planning and coordination of long-term care services. Med Care 14:78, 1976

15. Brody SJ: Comprehensive health care for the elderly: an analysis—the continuum of medical, health and social services for the aged. Gerontologist 13:412, 1973

16. Rosen HJ: Modern heatlh care delivery for the aged: a program in total health maintenance. J Am Geriatr Soc 20:505, 1972

17. Hobman D: Practical care of geriatric patients. A. An old person's view of the health services. R Soc Health J 1:21, 1975

18. Cantor MA, Mayer M: Health and the inner city elderly. Gerontologist 16:17, 1976

19. Clark M: Patterns of aging among the elderly poor of the innercity. Gerontologist 11:58, 1971

20. Carp FM, Kataoka E: Health care problems of the elderly in San Francisco's Chinatown. Gerontologist 16:30, 1976

21. Shanas E: Measuring the home health needs of the aged in five countries. J Gerontol 26:37, 1971

22. Leonard LE, Kelly AM: The development of a community-based program for evaluating the impaired older adult. Gerontologist 15:114, 1975

23. Bell WG: Community care for the elderly: an alternative to institutionalization. Gerontologist 13:349, 1973

24. Caro FG: Professional roles in the maintenance of the disabled elderly in the community: a forecast. Gerontologist 14:286, 1974

25. Raskind MA, Alvarez C, Pietrzyk M, Westerlund K, Herlin S: Helping the elderly psychiatric patient in crisis. Geriatrics 31:51, 1976

26. Kinoy SK: Home health services for the elderly. Nurs Outlook 17:59, 1969

27. Kovner AR, Katz G, Kahane SB, Sheps CG: Relating a neighborhood health center to a general hospital: a case history. Med Care 7:118, 1969

28. Libow LS: A public hospital-based geriatric "community care system." Gerontologist 14:289, 1974

29. Kutner B: The calculus of services for the aged. Can Med Assoc J 98:775, 1968

30. Trager B: Home health services and health insurance. Med Care 9:89, 1971

31. Henry LH: Caring for our aged poor: the medicare gap. New Republic 164:17, 1971

32. Medicare: Program of Health Insurance for the Aged and Disabled. Social Security Act, Title XVIII, 42 USC 1395 et seq.

33. Medicaid: Grants to States for Medical Assistance Programs. Social Security Act, Title XIX, 42 USC 1396 et seq.

34. Extracted from: Facts for Action, Sept 1971. New York City Office for the Aging, 250 Broadway, New York, NY 10007. Source: US Bureau of the Census, 1970

35. Community Planning District Profiles, Part I: Population and Housing, Sept 1974. New York City Planning Commission, 2 Lafayette Street, New York, NY 10007

36. Hugo V: Les Miserables. Winston JC (ed). Saint Denis, p. 283. Originally published 1862

37. Miller MB: Decision-making in the death process of the ill aged. Geriatrics 26:105, 1971

38. Green BR, Irish DP: Death education: preparation for living. Cambridge, Mass, Schenkman Publishing Co, 1971, p. 7

39. Malkin S: Care of the terminally ill at home. Can Med Assoc J 115:129, 1976

40. Gibson R: Supporting the patient at home. Br Med J 1:35, 1973

41. Wilkes E: How to provide effective home care for the terminally ill. Geriatrics 28:93, 1973

42. Kobrzycki P: Dying with dignity at home. Am J Nursing 75:1312, 1975

43. Keywood O: Care of the dying in their own homes. Nurs Times 70:1576, 1974

44. Carey RG: Living until death: a program of service and research for the terminally ill. In Kübler-Ross E (ed): Death: The Final Stage of Growth. Englewood Cliffs, NJ, Prentice-Hall, 1975

45. Cassel EJ: The Healer's Art. Philadelphia, Lippincott, 1976

46. Domning TT, Stackman T, O'Neille P, et al: Experiences with dying patients. Am J Nurs 73:1058, 1973

47. Gilmore AJ: The care and management of the dying patient in general practice. Practitioner 213:833, 1974

48. Kyle D: Terminal care. J R Coll Gen Pract 21:382, 1971

49. Hancock S, Saunders C, Anderson WF, et al: Care of the dying. Br Med J 1:29, 1973

50. Hockey L: Dying at home. Nurs Times 72:324, 1976

51. Kübler-Ross E: On Death and Dying. New York, MacMillan, 1969

52. Epstein C: Nursing the Dying Patient. Reston, Va, Reston Publishing Co, 1975

53. Cull JC, Hardy RE: The Neglected Older American. Springfield, Ill, Thomas, 1973, p. 114

54. Feifel H: The meaning of death in American society. In Green BR, Irish DP (eds): Death Education. Cambridge, Schenkman Publishers, 1971, pp 9–10.

SECTION TWO
Professional Services

CHAPTER 5

THE NURSE

with Sister Teresita Duque, R.N.

Nurses have suffered more than other health workers from a stereotyped and, therefore, limited view of permissible functions and duties. In the last several years, these restrictions have been questioned.[1-8] Nurses have developed the ability to function as partners and team members of doctors and other workers in the service of patients.[9-14] These nurses, we must emphasize, are not trying to be doctors but instead are developing expanded roles as nurses. They are fulfilling new opportunities appropriate to their training and experience.

This expansion has developed naturally from previous nursing functions. It is worth noting that when the first district nursing associations were formed in the 1880s, their objectives included care for the sick poor in their own homes instead of in hospitals.[15] Elizabeth Walker points out that:

Public health nurses have always carried out many practices which are only now becoming recognized as legitimate functions for nurses. In most public health agencies . . . nurses have traditionally functioned in a relatively independent manner, with physician collaboration.[8]

Examples include rural public health nurses, nurse specialists in psychiatry, and nurse midwives. We now recognize that nurses in home health care programs for the aged also have substantial opportunity for expansion of responsibility and of personal growth.

Nurses working in these programs are concerned with patient screening and case evaluation, independent nursing practice, traditional nursing duties, team membership, and teaching of peers and students.

PATIENT SCREENING AND CASE EVALUATION

Efficient use of health care teams requires in many instances that new referrals have a screening visit. This need holds true particularly for patients whose requirements for assistance are not clear to the program coordinator from information supplied by telephone. The nurse is likely to be well qualified for decision making and able to balance patient needs with the ability of the program to meet those needs.

CHELSEA–VILLAGE PROGRAM CASE REPORT

M.C. is an 83-year-old woman living in a senior citizens' hotel, out of contact with relatives, referred to us by the manager. She has been highly suspicious of people who attempt to help her and, as a result, has alienated her remaining friends as well as workers from social agencies.

She was in a state of chronic congestive heart failure but did not have proper medical care because of her distrust of doctors and hospitals.

After the initial evaluation, the patient would accept follow-up visits only from the nurse. As a consequence, full medical care and responsibility for this patient, including interval physical examination and control of digitalis and diuretic therapy, has fallen upon the nurse. Regular discussions are held with a physician who functions as an outside consultant. The patient has thrived under this regimen.

Further, the nurse is able to distinguish, on a screening visit, those patients who are too ill to wait for a team visit, and who may require immediate hospitalization.

CHELSEA–VILLAGE PROGRAM CASE REPORT

M.S., an 89-year-old woman, was referred by a relative in another state who had heard about the program. The patient was described on the telephone as an "alert, independent woman who is adamant that she will not enter a hospital." The relative was concerned that the patient, living alone, was becoming dirty and malnourished. The only community contact was the elevator man in the patient's building.

The patient was willing to receive a visit from the nurse, who found the home situation to be unstable. The patient was too weak to get out of bed, incontinent of urine and feces, but intellectually intact.

The nurse and the patient were able to hold a rational discussion. This resulted in the patient's acceptance of hospitalization because of her stated confidence in the nurse and the promise that the patient would be returned to her own home.

In the hospital, a diagnosis of marked hypothyroidism was established. Treatment was effective, and the patient was able to come back to her own home, under a network of care, where she survived for another six months.

The development of case evaluation as a nursing function in the

76

Chelsea–Village Program has resulted in increased ability to use staff time efficiently. In the first year of the program, 17 percent of our referrals were ultimately considered to be inappropriate. This figure has fallen to 4 percent of the patients accepted into the program in the fourth year.

INDEPENDENT NURSING PRACTICE

As independent health workers in home health care programs, nurses can utilize their own abilities, skill, training, and background for the benefit of patients, and in ways not necessarily shared by other professionals.

Home health care nurses offer to the team clinical common sense and judgment, composure in the face of trouble, and a readiness to do anything to help the patient, without false pride.

Opportunity for nurses to provide continuing direct patient care abound in this kind of program. Patients may find themselves feeling particular empathy with the nursing member of the health team, often because of amorphous fear of the physician; or the nurse may be qualified by experience to handle particular kinds of medical problems better than other team members and will, therefore, direct the treatment.

CHELSEA–VILLAGE PROGRAM CASE REPORT

A 65-year-old man living in a welfare hotel was bound to his room by a massive leg ulcer caused by venous stasis, trauma, and neglect.

Earlier, when he was physically able to do so, he had visited emergency rooms and clinics of several hospitals for advice, but had never followed through on treatment.

The ulcer involved the entire anterior and lateral surface of the left leg below the knee. Exuberant granulation tissue made the circumference three times that of the right leg. When the patient was first seen, purulent, foul-smelling drainage was marked, despite any benefits rendered by the maggots found in the lesion.

The patient accepted visits from the nurse, and over a 10-month period she provided consistent treatment with warm antiseptic soaks, sterile dressing, and oral antibiotics. This plan was effective in healing the ulcer.

Patient attitudes are obviously of critical importance.[16, 17] Patients do not always accept the nurse as a decisive factor in giving care, but this negative view can often be overcome in time. In the example of a medical clinic, for instance, patients receiving care from nurses had fewer broken appointments and offered less criticism of services than did those receiving traditional clinic care.[18]

Situations occasionally occur in which the patient insists that the physician be in charge, as follows.

NURSE: How are you feeling today, Mrs. B.? I'd like to check over your medications with you.

PATIENT: I'm glad to see you, dearie, but I think it would be better to wait for the doctor.

We do not feel that it is the function of our program to force our preconceived ideas about professional interrelationships upon our patient. We choose to follow the patient's wishes.

In accepting a more independent function than that of the traditional model, nurses must face up to possible conflicts with other health workers and with fellow nurses.[19-22]

This material is from the records of a Chelsea–Village Program staff meeting:

LAURA STARITA (Coordinator): I think part of the reason it [independent nurse function] has worked in our program is that our first nurse [Sister Teresita] has not been submissive to the doctors. The doctors really look to Sister for her opinion. She lets it be known when she thinks something should be done.

JAMES JANESKI (Social Worker): I'm quite satisfied that Sister is not submissive!

SISTER TERESITA (Program Nurse): The house staff doctors have never acted as though they were the boss, so I have not had to defy them in any way. It's a pleasure to work with them. I can't even think of one who would say, "I'm the doctor."

F. RUSSELL KELLOGG (Fellow in Community Medicine): Our reason for this attitude is that the program draws a certain type of physician, who is secure enough to accept this situation. On the other hand, for the physician who really feels the need to be in control, this kind of egalitarianism is threatening.

SISTER TERESITA: The doctors we have attracted to the program are not the traditional ones.

ATTENDING DOCTOR: Sister, do you, as an individual, feel that you are the coequal of the doctors in the program? Or superior, perhaps?

SISTER TERESITA: I have never felt, even as a nursing student, that I could just say, "I don't know anything, I just work here." I think a nurse who has an intelligent question gets an intelligent answer. In this program I feel, obviously, that I have a right to express myself, that I'm not in any way less than others.

CHRISTINE VITARELLA (Program Nurse): In the past, when I was a ward nurse,

78

I never had a problem with house staff on the floors. If I had an opinion, they would respect it. If I wanted to do something a little more medical, and not nursing, they would respect it.

My big problem came from the nursing staff. When there was a conflict, it was made clear to me that I should just do what I was told to do. There were many times on the floor when I stepped over the boundary line. If something needed to be done, I would do it. I'd say a little prayer that my nursing supervisor wouldn't walk in because, according to the system, I would get my head handed to me if she saw me plugging in an IV on someone who really needed an IV, when the house staff was too busy on the floor. I had created that kind of rapport with many of the house staff. I really didn't see myself as the secretary picking up the orders.

Independence has its limits. We recognize that nurses may require the supervision of a physician, that notes must be countersigned, and prescriptions and orders must be written by the doctor. However, nurses can earn increasing responsibility under supervision and ultimately provide substantial direct patient care.[23-26]

TRADITIONAL NURSING PRACTICE

Nursing practice, as we know it today, had its origins in the 1850s and 1860s. Concern grew about the plight of sick and wounded soldiers in military hospitals[27-31] and the condition of the sick poor among immigrants crowded into city slums. "A social consciousness which was characterized by idealism and humanitarianism was gaining momentum among various groups of people, particularly the better educated women: this idealism was the overriding impetus contributing to the development of nursing."[15]

In important ways, nursing functions in home health care programs follow these traditions. The overriding concerns are idealistic and humanitarian. Nurses in the 1970s are involved, as they have always been,[32] in patient education, diagnosis and treatment of disease, and psychological support.

Patient Education

Nurses in these programs must have the skill and patience to teach medical self-care to aged people. Typical problems include learning to give insulin injections, testing urine for glucose, understanding diets, organizing the medication schedule, and use of contact lenses following cataract surgery.

79

Nurses characteristically have worked in this field and are well qualified by training and experience to do so.[33, 34]

In 1970, of 700,000 registered nurses at work in this country, 10 percent were involved in public health programs. There are approximately 700 Visiting Nurse Services, employing more than 7,000 nurses full- or part-time.[35] These professional health workers are all engaged, to some degree, in patient education.

In home health care programs, however, there are extra difficulties. The patients, because they are old and sick, may be unusually clumsy, not understand clearly, continually make errors, or fail to follow through. The nurse must have a high level of kindness and persistence and not perceive repeated failure by the patient as a personal affront.

This material is excerpted from the Chelsea–Village Program Chart of G.B., a 78-year-old Cuban man.

7/10/73   Previously known to Saint Vincent's Hospital clinic. Now homebound. History of renal insufficiency, cardiac disease of unknown cause, Parkinson's disease. Patient unable to understand his medications. Speaks only Spanish, with Sister Teresita.

7/17/73   Patient still unclear about Rx. Serum digoxin level: "trace." Needs homemaker services.

10/16/73   Probably taking Rx correctly. Bottles labeled clearly for him.

11/8/73   Patient called. "Feet feel funny." Urgent. Sister noted no signs of edema or inflammation. Told him to soak his feet in evenings.

1/9/74   Patient called Sister. Can't find Rx. Sister brought him his pills.

1/15/74   Patient called. Constipated. Given MOM by Sister.

1/30/74   Patient has stopped all his Rx because he believes they caused constipation. Explanations. Edema of legs noted. Started Rx again.

2/25/74   Finally seems to be taking Rx as prescribed.

7/31/74   Stable, but confused about Rx. Bottles color-coded for him.

9/27/74   Claims to be taking meds, but Sister questions this. New physical findings—reducible right inguinal hernia.

1/12/75   Hernia painful, can't reduce. Hospital admission necessary. Patient refused until Sister confirmed the need.

1/30/75   Patient returned home two days ago. Had uneventful hernia repair.

5/30/75   Pulse rate 36 today. EKG—heart block. Told patient he needed readmission. Refused until Sister confirmed need.

6/10/75   Patient returned home today. Stable. Reviewed medications. He appears to understand.

6/11/75   Urgent call to Sister. Pacemaker "feels funny." On arrival patient opened door, completely undressed. He said, "Excuse me a minute," went into his bedroom, closed door. Then called out to Sister, "Come in." He was lying on his bed, still nude. Sister said pacemaker looked OK.

9/24/75   Said he had chest pain last night. *Doctor:* What did you do for it? *Patient* (in Spanish): Oh, I did what Sister always tells me to do. I took two aspirins and warm milk, and the pain went away.

1/23/76   Urgent call. Diarrhea. When we got there, patient said he felt all better. Says he took two aspirins and warm milk, the way Sister always tells him, and the diarrhea stopped.

10/11/76   Urgent call for Sister. Patient can't find medications.

And so on. Possibilities for patient error are infinite:

Patient B.H., a 75-year-old immigrant from Eastern Europe, had difficulty communicating in English. She was supposed to take six aspirin tablets daily, and one digoxin tablet, but reversed the dosages. After 10 days she felt ill. She was admitted to the hospital with digitalis intoxication (nausea and yellow-green vision).

Treatment of Disease

Nurses can carry out diagnostic and/or treatment plans for particular diseases without regular and immediate doctor supervision.[36-40] Examples include blood pressure recordings to sustain or exclude the diagnosis of hypertension and treatment of leg ulcers or chronic dermatoses that require repetitive procedures, such as soaks or application of Unna boots.

CHELSEA–VILLAGE PROGRAM CASE REPORT

A.S., a 70-year-old woman, was referred to our program by a building superintendent. She had been sent home from another hospital after pinning of a fractured hip, bedbound, with an eight-hour, seven-day homemaker. Our physical exam revealed prominent decubitus ulcers of both heels, which eliminated the possibility of walking.

Our nurse reviewed the problem in the home with a surgical consultant. A plan for treatment was evolved, which included careful debridement, soaks, dry dressings, and foot elevation, controlled by the nurse. The homemaker was able to work closely with the nurse, and the treatment plan was carried out meticulously.

81

The ulcers healed, and the patient graduated from bed to walker to cane. She became able to care for herself, and finally the homemaker was no longer needed. The patient, while homebound, is independent.

Psychological Support

Our patients are usually chronically ill, depressed, facing an uncomfortable and uncertain future. They need to develop confidence in the treatment program and a sense of trust in the health worker in order to persist in their own care. Discouragement sets in easily, and the nurse, by training and by professional image, is in a particularly good position to help. It is part of our understanding of the word "nurse" to assume that she provides emotional support to the patient.[41-46]

This material from a Chelsea–Village Program staff conference makes the point.

SISTER TERESITA: Mrs. M., an 83-year-old lady referred to us by the home care department, has been in the hospital twice, earlier this year, for leg ulcers. Skin grafts didn't take, and finally she refused further surgery. Also, she knows she has a growth in her breast, which she won't allow anyone to look at. She went home. At first, home care and the visiting nurse provided physical therapy, replacement of Unna boots, and dressings. After about six months, Medicare questioned why she was being kept on home care for so long, so home care had to say "goodbye." And as they said "goodbye" to her, the visiting nurses said they could no longer keep going and changing the dressings for some financial reason. That left the patient to us.

Tony (the surgical consultant) and I went there, and she was very surprised. She said, "I thought everyone had given me up." We reassured her that, even though the other groups *had* to because of other pressures, we would continue to visit her.

She is seriously disabled, and she lives alone in her apartment. But she's a very determined lady—and she wants to stay there. She will be doing her best to remain in her own home.

ATTENDING DOCTOR: Does she have a phone?

SISTER TERESITA: She's not willing to have one because she's extremely deaf. She does have a hearing aid, which she manages to put away in her drawer because it bothers her. Communicating with Mrs. M. is very difficult. Tony tells her his instructions very clearly, and she looks at me and says, "What did he say?" Me, she hears! Because she has very limited money—and because she refuses to spend what she has on supplies—we had to go back to primitive ways. When we ran out of her 4 by 4's, we boiled an old white sheet and cut it

82

up for dressings. She put them on herself. They are probably just as good as the other dressings. For the past few months she has been stable, in a precarious way.

A sophisticated nursing approach to this patient has no value. In order to help her meet her own goal of staying in her own apartment, we have given her human contact and basic understanding.

The nursing functions exemplified by this case are straightforward. Any nurse could fulfill them. They concern bandages and dressings and how to keep clean.

In addition, in this case, the nurse had an even more important therapeutic value: she was the primary patient contact, the person who kept the patient attached to the human race. She translated for the doctor because the patient would listen only to the nurse, she was the patient's confidante, she was the part of the health care system that the patient trusted.

This kind of psychological support grows naturally from the nurse's opportunities in the home health care program. The nurse is the worker most likely to know everyone in the program and most likely to be present on every home visit. While each health worker, including doctors and social workers, has an overriding relationship with some of the patients, the nurse has a consistent contact with all of them, and for some she is the dominant force.

THE NURSE AS TEAM MEMBER

Nurses, generally, have been conditioned to accept a passive position in the planning and conduct of health services.[7]

The nurse, because of the history of nurse-physician professional interrelationships, may be reluctant to speak up, to express ideas in team conferences and in the patient's home, to accept her share of responsibility. This viewpoint is not satisfactory for the nurse who is a member of a health care team. All members must contribute energy, intelligence, and imagination to the team's work[47, 48] and, even more important, have the motivation to support associates in difficult patient care situations. A team is greater than the sum of its parts.

Team development (discussed in depth in Chapter 8) requires particular attention to nurse-doctor relationships and means of resolving team conflicts.

In the health care team, doctor and nurse must correct habits which may have developed during training and on inpatient services.

Bates points out that:

As doctors and nurses change their patterns of working together, they inevitably face differing expectations of each other's behavior. They must resolve at least some of these differences if this new relationship is to survive. For many, the battles and the peacemaking have been lonely processes, worked through in relative isolation from colleagues and fraught with significant discomfort.[19]

The battle must first be fought in our own minds. Willingness to share problems and responsibilities obviously must grow from each of us. Next, each of us must be prepared to accept others as professional associates. We must be able both to share authority and to receive advice.

The team, in its first tentative form, is welded into an effective unit by direct care of patients—and by team conferences.

The team conferences, in the Chelsea–Village Program, have shown that nurse–doctor conflicts are a potential problem, to be worked through, and that nurse–social worker relationships must be created in toto. Nurses and social workers commonly fail to have any contact in traditional health care locations, such as hospitals.

ATTENDING DOCTOR: Do you see any differences in your relationships with doctors and social workers in this program, compared to your work on the floors?

CHRISTINE VITARELLA: I didn't have much relationship with the social workers. To me, they got patients their checks and handled discharge planning, to home or a nursing home. That's where it ended.

Since I've been here, I've begun to understand their role a little bit more. It's more than paper work, or helping somebody into the program, or getting them money. It's meeting all the needs of the person. And in our conferences, when we review patients' problems, I may throw in a bit of medical feedback, Ellen or Irma [social workers] may give us some social information, and together we'll work out an approach to the problem.

ATTENDING DOCTOR: What about your relationship to physicians?

VITARELLA: I feel that I've always had a rapport with the house staff, on the floors and in this program.

ATTENDING DOCTOR: Do you feel that the simple fact of establishing a rapport is going to achieve for you what you want in your work with a doctor? Let me be specific. The relationship between nurses and doctors has been described as similar to that of boss to servant. The doctor writes the orders, the nurse carries them out. The nurse will not take the initiative. And, as a rule, with all the rapport in the world, that's the way the inpatient services function.

VITARELLA: From what I've seen of Sister Teresita I've got a lot to learn from her about being a full member of a team.

ELLEN QUIRKE (Social Worker): I think Sister Teresita is a primary factor in the development of our teams. She knows every patient and sees them all regularly. She's very alert to social needs when she goes into a home and reports the needs to me if I'm not with her.

JAMES JANESKI (Social Worker): Do you see any conflict?

QUIRKE: No.

JANESKI: I think there is a clearer connection between Sister Teresita and the social workers than there is between her and some physicians. I think that some of the doctors have trouble with Sister taking such a dominant position. They are not used to a nurse doing that. They want to put her back into place.

SISTER TERESITA: Jim, I understand what you're saying. It hasn't been too often, but occasionally I sense a doctor's reaction by a facial expression or a shrug of the shoulders. For instance, when I suggest changing medication—I'm extremely careful in the way that I do it—the doctor may look at me and seem to be asking, "Where did you get the authority to bring up that question?"

For some nurses, full professional, personal, and intellectual satisfaction comes from expanded opportunities in nontraditional programs, such as the Chelsea–Village Program and others.[5, 6, 9, 12, 13] These health care settings provide the chance for working in ways that overcome the contradictions that some writers[49, 50] have seen between what nurses are taught and what they are permitted to practice.

Kinlein[51] points out the following disturbing characteristics of some traditional nursing programs:

1. The notion of defined limits to learning, as evidenced in comments such as, "You don't need to know *that* to nurse." She stresses that there should never be any boundaries to acquisition of knowledge, for student nurses or anybody else.
2. The emphasis on preventing error without a coequal effort to bring about good health through positive effort.
3. Responsibility without authority.

Nurses and nursing students should have the opportunity first to observe and then to participate under guidance in home health care programs.[52] Through the process of seeing nurses in action, in health teams, as coequals in status and authority with other health workers, nurses can set wider career goals. Attitudes are established in clinical situations which permit learning by doing.[53]

It is important that people in training have models to emulate. It is just as true of nursing students as of medical students that they "need to be with someone who is not merely talking about but actually delivering comprehensive health care—and who is sufficiently competent and confident in this role to merit their respect and admiration."[54]

Nursing students assigned to the Chelsea–Village Program have felt that this opportunity enables them to develop a sense of independence in nursing judgment, to acquire new methods of communication, and to broaden their understanding of disease entities and their effects on the total person.[24]

SUMMARY

Independent, skilled nurses, motivated and self-confident enough to work as coequal team members with doctors and social workers, are essential to the success of these programs.

Nurses who are submissive perpetuate the status of the physician as dominant, but when nurses understand their options and know how to establish leadership when it is appropriate, the team is made to work. The patients benefit.

REFERENCES

1. Brickner PW: Expanded roles for nurses: the view of a physician. In Changing Role of the Hospital and Implications for Nursing Education. Dept. of Diploma Programs, National League for Nursing, New York, 1974
2. Brickner PW, Bolger AG, Boyle MT, Duque T, Holland P, Janeski JF, Kaufman A, Madden PM: Outreach to welfare hotels, the homebound, the frail. Am J Nurs 76:762, 1976
3. McGivern D: Baccalaureate preparation of the nurse practitioner. Nurs Outlook 22:94, 1974
4. Kubala S, Clever LH: Acceptance of the nurse practitioner. Am J Nurs 74:451, 1974
5. Judge D: The new nurse: a sense of duty and destiny. Mod Health Care 2:21, 1974
6. Judge D: The coming battle over nurse practitioners. Mod Health Care 1:29, 1974
7. Catellier E: Nursing: putting the pieces together. Hosp Prog 56:76, 1975
8. Walker AE: Primex: the family nurse practitioner program. Nurs Outlook 20:28, 1972
9. Brickner PW, Duque T, Kaufman A, Sarg M, Jahre JA, Maturlo S, Janeski JF: The homebound aged: a medically unreached group. Ann Intern Med 82:1, 1975
10. Brickner PW, Janeski JF, Duque T: Hospital home health care program aids isolated, homebound elderly. Hospitals 50:117, 1976

11. Brickner PW, Janeski JF, Rich G, Duque T, Starita L, La Rocco R, Flannery T, Werlin S: Home maintenance for the homebound aged. Gerontologist 16:25, 1976
12. Brickner PW, Greenbaum D, Kaufman A, O'Donnell F, O'Brian JT, Scalice R, Scandizzo J, Sullivan T: A clinic for male derelicts: a welfare hotel project. Ann Intern Med 77:565, 1972
13. Burnett I, Walsh GF: Caring for single room occupancy tenants. Am J Nurs 73:1752, 1973
14. Tomes EK: Expanding the nurse's role. Urban Health 5:31, 1976
15. Tinkham CW, Vorhies EF: Community Health Nursing: Evolution and Process. New York, Appleton-Century-Crofts, 1972
16. Spitzer WO, Sackett DL, Sibley JC, et al: The Burlington randomized trial of the nurse practitioner. N Engl J Med 290:251, 1974
17. Bergman R, Hellman G: Community nursing services as perceived by posthospitalized patients. Am J Public Health 59:2168, 1969
18. Lewis C, Resnick B: Nurse clinics and progressive ambulatory patient care. N Engl J Med 227:1236, 1967
19. Bates B: Doctor and nurse: changing roles and relations. N Engl J Med 283:129, 1970
20. Bates B: Physician and nurse practitioner: conflict and reward. Ann Intern Med 82:702, 1975
21. Lewis HL: Nurses: how much like doctors? Mod Health Care 3:45, 1975
22. Theiss BE: Investigation of the perceived role functions and attitudes of the nurse practitioner role in a primary care clinic. Milit Med 141:85, 1976
23. Burton LE, Smith HH: Public Health and Community Medicine for the Allied Medical Professions, 2nd ed. Baltimore, Williams & Wilkins, 1975
24. Greenridge J, Zimmern A, Kohnke M: Community nurse practitioners—a partnership. Nurs Outlook 21:228, 1973
25. Scott JM: The changing health care environment: its implications for nursing. Am J Public Health 64:364, 1974
26. Schulman J, Wood C: Experience of a nurse practitioner in a general medical clinic. JAMA 219:1453, 1972.
27. Skrovan C, Anderson ET, Gottschalk J: Community nurse practitioner: an emerging role. Am J Public Health 64:847, 1974
28. Christy TE: Nurses in American history: the fateful decade, 1890–1900. Am J Nurs 75:1163, 1975
29. Austin AL: Nurses in American history: wartime volunteers, 1861–1865. Am J Nurs 75:816, 1975
30. Friedman R: Stephen Smith and health of immigrants, 1850–1865. NY State J Med 76:2050, 1976
31. Berman JK: Florentia and the Clarabellas—a tribute to nurses. J Indiana State Med Assoc 67:717, 1974
32. Dock LL: Lillian D. Wald: our first public health nurse. Nurs Outlook 19:659, 1971
33. Ruddick-Bracken H: The district nurse as health educator. Nurs Times 69:1187, 1973
34. Wilson A: Nursing and eye problems of the aged. Sight Sav Rev 41:171, Winter, 1971
35. Facts About Nursing: A Statistical Summary, 1970–1971 Edition. New York, American Nurses Association

36. Stollerman GH: Nurse practitioners and the treatment of sore throats. JAMA 227:1303, 1974
37. Merenstein JH, Rogers KD: Streptococcal pharyngitis: early treatment and management by nurse practitioners. JAMA 227:1278, 1974
38. Greenfield S, Friedland G, Scifers S, et al: Protocol management of dysuria, urinary frequency, and vaginal discharge. Ann Intern Med 81:452, 1974
39. Runyan JW: The Memphis Chronic Disease Program. JAMA 231:264, 1975
40. Clark AB, Dunn M: A nurse clinician's role in the management of hypertension. Arch Intern Med 136:903, 1976
41. McRae CF: Public health nurse in home management of patient with chronic lung disease. JAMA 236:1747, 1976
42. Wilkiemeyer DS: Affection; key to care for the elderly. Am J Nurs 72:2166, 1972
43. Kalisch BJ: What is empathy? Am J Nurs 73:1548, 1973
44. Davitz LJ, Davitz JR: How do nurses feel when patients suffer? Am J Nurs 75:1505, 1975
45. Robinson S: Home visits to the elderly. Am J Nurs 74:908, 1974
46. Hutchins MH: The geriatric patient: "help me" Nurs Clin North Am 6:795, 1971
47. Gardner HH, Ouimette R: A nurse-physician team approach in a private internal medicine practice. Arch Intern Med 134:956, 1974
48. Brunetto E, Birk P: The primary care nurse—the generalist in a structured health care team. Am J Public Health 62:785, 1972
49. Cleary DM: A nonstrike for patient care. Mod Health Care 3:43, 1975
50. Mundinger MO: Primary nurse—role evaluation. Nurs Outlook 21:642, 1973
51. Kinlein ML: Independent nurse practitioner. Nurs Outlook 20:22, Jan, 1972
52. Williams GO: The Elderly in Family Practice: An Evaluation of the Geriatric Visiting Nurse. J of Fam Prac 5:369, 1977
53. Flexner A: Medical Education in the United States and Canada. New York, Carnegie Foundation, 1910, p 59
54. Wray JD: Undergraduates and graduate education in community medicine. In Lathem W, Newbery A (eds): Community Medicine. New York, Appleton-Century-Crofts, 1970, Chap 12

CHAPTER 6

THE PHYSICIAN

Physicians must participate fully as members of health care teams in order for homebound aged patients to receive adequate diagnosis and treatment. Doctors working in these programs provide general medical care to patients under a set of unusual circumstances and have the opportunity to achieve the highest form of professional fulfillment: the direct application of intelligence, skill, and compassion for the benefit of sick and helpless people.

The basic purpose of home health care programs for the aged is to help older people sustain an independent life at home. The patients are, by definition, disabled. They are subject to a wide variety of physical and psychological stresses, as well as the problems of poverty, poor housing, and isolation. Consistent physician participation in teams with nurses and social workers is essential for the success of this work.

VALUE TO THE DOCTOR

Apparently, few physicians are capable of dealing with large numbers of chronically ill persons with sustained enthusiasm. If this is true, what is the possible explanation? The physician, like all people, needs to maintain his self-esteem. [this] is lowered when he does not see clear improvement resulting from his efforts. . . . The chronically ill patient is not likely to express gratitude to the physician for his help. Adding to this is the physician's lack of understanding of the complex changes going on within the chronically ill person. The physician is aware that there are many social-psychological complications, but since he does not understand them, it adds to his discouragement.

—Ewald W. Busse[1]

All physicians are busy. It requires a high level of motivation for people in training, or in practice, to make time available for participation in home health care services.[2-5]

What benefits do doctors derive from their efforts? The following comments from a Chelsea–Village Program staff conference speak to this point.

ATTENDING PHYSICIAN: What good does it do you, in your development as a physician, to work in this kind of program?

JEFFREY STALL (Medical Resident): I think it does three things. It gets me out of the hospital and out of the structured part of the training program, both of which give me a very parochial view of medicine. Also, it introduces me to homebound old people, an opportunity I wouldn't get any other way. This is important because I intend to practice internal medicine, and I need this experience. And, number three, it gives me humility—it teaches me about old people and their problems and what I can and can't do as a doctor.

F. RUSSELL KELLOGG (Fellow in Community Medicine): The perspective in the hospital is limited. When we take care of a patient inside the institution, it's hard to look beyond the hospital environment. In this program we see the patients in the outside world, and we interact with the reality of their eating habits, their living space, their filth, their neighbors, their connections with people around them—or their lack of connection. This is valuable to me, because people live in the real world. They don't live in the hospital all the time.

NANCY ROISTACHER (Medical Resident): In the hospital I have a tendency to look at patients on paper. I see a lab result, and add medicines here, and add a test there. I've learned in this work that it isn't always necessary to do just that in order to care for patients adequately. Some of my patients who are living in their own environment are getting along very well. I find there's not such a great need to correct everything on paper if they're functioning well as people. There's a great old man I've seen up on Greenwich Avenue who has slight swelling of his legs. In the hospital situation I would give him a diuretic, but this would make him miserable at home because he can't get to the bathroom easily. At home, I just have him elevate his legs, and he's doing fine.

KELLOGG: That's really true! I've experienced it. In the hospital we focus on the academics of medicine because we're in training. We think of patients in terms of numbers and quantities. In the program we have less numerical material to work with. Our focus is on the patient as a functioning individual. We can try to keep this focus in the hospital, but we get caught up in academics.

ROISTACHER: Some things are practical in the hospital that cannot be done at home.

MARC SHERMAN (Fellow in Community Medicine): I had a chance to work in the outside world, and now I'm back in the inside world again. As house officers, we're unrealistic about illness. We tend to think that if the patient isn't having a myocardial infarction and in cardiogenic shock, he doesn't belong in the hospital, and that ends our concern. But most illness is not that way. This is not necessarily what you see when you become a doctor in the real world. In this program we're very much in that world.

90

ATTENDING DOCTOR: The value of this work to me is the opportunity it gives for fulfillment of deep personal and professional goals. I'm able to pay back to the society I live in some of the debt I feel for being given the chance to be a doctor. And also I find a lot of gratification in knowing that my skill and experience are useful to helpless old people who might otherwise be dead or in a nursing home—and who don't want to be. I'm really happier when I'm working in this program than in any other part of my professional life.

Doctors often find it hard to work with chronically ill patients and with old sick people whose prognosis is poor. The patients complain. They are frightened. They may be unrealistic, uncooperative, and antagonistic. The circumstances of examination may be poor. And yet doctors must learn how to work with and to help these people if they are to become complete physicians.[3, 6-9] As Oliver Cope notes[5]: "There will always be an art to the practice of good medicine, because it can be assumed that there will always be a limit to what is known with certainty and beyond that limit the physician will have to grope his way. Try he must, as best he can, for he has no other alternative."

IMPORTANCE OF THE DOCTOR

Physicians have particular capabilities which are needed in this form of health service. They function within a network of professional and organizational relationships that provide essential strengths for the program. These resources include: (1) relationship to the hospital, (2) diagnostic skill, (3) understanding the potential for treatment, (4) understanding psychiatric symptoms, and (5) emotional support of the patient.

Relationship to the Hospital

A full range of health services must be available in order for patients to receive proper treatment. Therefore home health care programs must be based in hospitals. Doctors on hospital staffs, at the level of house officer, fellow, and attending physician, are the critical resources for success of the program. To paraphrase Willie Sutton,[10] go to hospitals to staff the programs, because that's where the doctors are.

ADMITTING PATIENTS   The admitting process at hospitals is likely to respond favorably to requests for patient admissions from its own physician staff members for the same kind of patient it would otherwise reject.

Free-standing agencies, on the other hand, commonly do not have doctors on their staffs and lack the capability to admit patients under their

91

care who become seriously ill. They may face rejection by hospital emergency rooms and admitting offices because they are not an integral and respected part of the hospital proper.

The characteristic problem is exemplified in this extract from a Chelsea–Village Program chart:

Miss —— from the Visiting Nurse Service called. She referred this patient to us because she thinks he needs admission, and she was refused by the local hospital on the East Side. She told them that the patient was a 94-year-old louse-ridden, confused, malnourished, impoverished man, coughing up blood, who was quite helpless. They told her that they had no beds, and they didn't accept that kind of patient anyway.

It is quite possible for hospital personnel—from admitting office staff through aides, clerks, administrative officers, and doctors, social workers, and nurses—to perceive such a patient as a challenge rather than as a burden. This may require personal reappraisal of the reasons for entering the health field and a refocusing of attention upon the ultimate goal: to give help to sick, disabled people.

DISCHARGE OF PATIENTS   The home health care program offers benefits to doctors in terms of discharge planning. For program patients admitted for acute illness, there is assurance that the patient will be received back into the home health care process and not create a discharge problem. In addition, when hospital doctors become aware of the program, they will use it as a source of care for certain of their own patients who fit the criteria. In the Chelsea–Village Program about 8 percent of the patients are referred by physicians.

Occasionally such patients fall under our care because their physicians will not make house calls. More often, however, the doctor recognizes that the medical-social complexities of the case are extreme and require more time and a wider variety of professional skills than he or she can bring to the case.

This material from the charts of Chelsea–Village Program patients makes the point:

Patient A.L.—Doctor's Note
66-year-old woman, uterine cancer with metastases throughout abdomen. Referred by attending doctor for terminal care support, since chemotherapy had reached limit of usefulness.

Patient B.D.—Coordinator's Note
Dr. —— called and asked if we could see this patient. He has been taking care of her for several years. She is now 86, deaf, with urinary incontinence. Her

heart failure is controlled with medication. She is living in the Scotland Arms Hotel (senior citizens' residence) and doesn't like it. Keeps calling doctor to ask his help in moving. He doesn't know what to do. Asks us to take over.

CONSULTANTS   A hospital-based program has access to a wide variety of consultants. Subspecialists do not, of course, participate in giving home health services routinely, but they can be very important in particular cases. The skills of urologists, surgeons, psychiatrists, dermatologists, and others are occasionally vital in diagnosis and patient management.

PATIENT MANAGEMENT   Skill in managing complicated chronic medical issues is often necessary, as the following Chelsea–Village Program case reports make clear.

C.M. is an 84-year-old woman, alone, but with interested neighbors, homebound by general debility and weakness. Early in her course with the Chelsea–Village Program she developed purulent drainage from her right first toe. Surgical consultation was arranged.

Diagnosis
Peripheral arterial disease, with gangrene of the toe tip. The surgeon visited the patient weekly over a 15-month period in an attempt to control gangrene. He utilized wet and dry dressings, Unna boots, and elevation. The area of necrosis remained limited to tip of toe for 8 months. Subsequently it spread, gradually but inexorably, to include the entire toe and a portion of the foot. Amputation was at length considered inevitable, but the patient refused. The surgeon performed debridement regularly in the home for 2 more months. The patient at length permitted amputation by the consultant, who had gained her confidence through the prolonged period of regular attentive care. She is now returned home in satisfactory condition, in a wheelchair, with a homemaker.

The surgeon's particular experience and skill were essential in the management of this patient's health problem, and probably the key to her ultimate return home.

In the following case, psychiatric judgment and knowledge of psychotropic drugs were of critical importance in helping the patient.

R.P. is a 69-year-old woman, referred by the Visiting Nurse Service. At the time of our first visit she had been bedbound for 22 months, under the continuous care of her aged husband. The stated cause of the patient's problems was "weakness" and "drainage from the pelvis." She felt depressed by fear of cancer and also by the fact that her son had "joined the Hare Krishna." Over the 22 months she said she had lost about 50 pounds.

Physical examination was unrevealing except for vaginitis and obesity, with-

93

out evidence of weight loss. The gynecologic problem was treated successfully, and the discharge ceased, but the patient remained depressed and in bed. A psychiatric consultation was arranged in the home.

Diagnosis
Mild organic brain syndrome with depressive features and somatic preoccupation. The patient was placed on doxepin HCl (Sinequan). Within two weeks she was up, cleaning the house, cooking, visiting neighbors, and attending the hospital clinic. One week after this, the husband died suddenly, but the patient was unperturbed and continued her new way of life.

DIAGNOSTIC SKILL The physician's ability to make clinical diagnoses is clearly essential to proper patient care in these programs. Homebound aged people often have multiple disorders, compounded by social disabilities. It takes considerable medical skill to penetrate through the distracting elements and understand the basic disease process.

Table 6–1 lists the primary medical cause of homeboundedness in the first 466 Chelsea–Village Program patients. The medical truism that the commonest disorders occur most often is apparent here, but occasionally, and unexpectedly, cases appear that offer a major diagnostic challenge, as indicated in the following Chelsea–Village Program case report.

R.N. is a 78-year-old woman, referred by her husband because of demented behavior for several weeks. The patient is confused, hallucinating, and spends her days shouting, crying, and striking at him, even though she is confined to a wheelchair. Past medical history included:

1976 (6 months prior to the first Program visit): Left cerebral infarction, with marked right hemiparesis. The patient has been in bed and wheelchair from this date.

1972: Total left hip replacement, with four units of blood during surgery, followed by hepatitis.

1965 to date: Diabetes mellitus, with one episode of ketoacidosis and coma 10 years ago, now controlled by diet.

1963: "Dermatomyositis," diagnosis established by electromyographic studies and muscle biopsy. Patient has been free of muscular symptoms for past 10 years.

Her treatment regimen: diabetic diet, prednisone, 5 mg twice daily since 1965 for treatment of "dermatomyositis," Darvon (propoxyphene hydrochloride) for pain, and Dalmane (flurazepam hydrochloride) for sleep.

94

TABLE 6-1
Medical Causes of Homeboundedness

DISABILITY	NUMBER OF PATIENTS
Orthopedic Disorders	121
Arthritis	52
Previous fractures	32
Paget's disease of bone	2
Amputation(s)	9
Osteogenesis imperfecta	1
Other orthopedic	25
Neurologic Disease	52
Cerebrovascular accident (stroke)	32
Parkinson's disease	5
Multiple sclerosis	3
Peripheral neuropathy	2
Other neurologic	10
Medical Disorders	198
Chronic pulmonary disease	27
Cardiac disease	37
Alcoholism—chronic	9
Obesity	6
Anemia	3
Peripheral vascular disease	12
Generalized debility and weakness	43
Blindness	7
Malignancies	20
Lung (7)	
Breast (2)	
Gastrointestinal tract (7)	
Prostate (4)	
Other medical	34
Psychiatric-Psychological Disorders	59
Chronic organic brain syndrome	29
Mental retardation	4
Psychosis—acute or chronic	12
Anxiety	5
Other psychiatric	9
Other	12
Not Homebound	24
Total	466

The likely possibilities for etiology of the patient's symptoms included cerebral arteriosclerosis, cerebral vasculitis from collagen disease, drug-induced psychosis. Other considerations were complications of poorly controlled diabetes mellitus or unappreciated liver disease, but these were promptly ruled out. It was clear that Mrs. N. had underlying cerebral arteriosclerosis. The stroke was obvious evidence. This did not explain her recent development of psychotic behavior, however.

Attention was focused upon the adrenal steroids as a possible cause,[11-13] although she had been on the same homeopathic dose for 13 years. When this point was discussed with the husband, he confessed that he had recently raised his wife's prednisone dosage to 60 mg daily, on the theory that it would help her walk again. In his youth he had spent one year in medical school and felt qualified to make decisions about medication. The patient was weaned from prednisone, and the psychosis cleared.

This case demonstrates the point—obvious, but needing regular re-emphasis—that a careful history is the key to good medicine. Mrs. N.'s situation also serves as a reminder that the use of medication in aged people is hazardous, not only from unexpected side effects but also because drugs may not be taken correctly.[14-18]

Understanding the Potential for Treatment

Through training and experience, doctors are able to make major decisions about patient care when other health workers may hesitate or over-react. These decisions often relate to the wisdom of staying at home versus transfer to the hospital, evaluation of signs and symptoms, and use of medications.

The following Chelsea–Village Program case report is an example.

G.S. is a 65-year-old ex-government employee, forced into retirement by a cerebrovascular accident and significant residual right hemiparesis. He has been under the care of the Chelsea–Village Program for the past 2½ years, living in a residential hotel, moving around slowly with a walker. Treatment of hypertension with standard drugs had been effective until prominent peripheral edema was noted one year ago, associated with mild exertional dyspnea. The blood pressure had risen from the range of 140/90 to 210/110. There was no other change in the physical examination. Electrocardiogram showed only an increase in left axis deviation. Blood count, serum electrolytes, and tests of kidney function were normal.

Decisions about the use of medication and the need for hospitalization were made by the physician, in consultation with other team members, and the patient, who wanted to remain home if at all possible. A simple change in antihypertensive drugs, sodium restriction, potassium supplementation, and addition of digitalis to the regimen provoked a prompt fall in the blood pressure. Peripheral edema decreased. It has been considered safe to keep the patient out of the hospital on this regimen, to date.

Without the presence of a physician in this case, no possibility of adequate treatment in the home existed. An unnecessary hospitalization would have resulted.

Understanding Psychiatric Symptoms

THE PROBLEM WITH "SENILE" The challenge of proper diagnosis in patients presenting psychiatric symptoms is considerable. It is vital to avoid thinking of all aged and confused people as "senile."

The word *senility* implies a permanent loss of intellectual function due to aging. Labeling a patient as senile permits us, as health workers, to put that person away, either in an institution or, more figuratively, out of our minds as no longer worthy of serious consideration.

In fact, this viewpoint is often incorrect, leads us into diagnostic error, and is clearly pernicious to the interests of our patients. It would be wise to eliminate "senile" from the medical vocabularly and to stop generalizing about psychiatric symptoms in older people.[19, 20]

A wide variety of correctible medical and psychologic disorders are known to produce changes in affect, behavior, and/or memory. Older people are no more immune to organic disease than is any other age group.

ACUTE ORGANIC BRAIN SYNDROME The symptoms of memory loss, intellectual failure, change in affect, and confusion about time, place, and person can be produced by many diseases. It is particularly important that this be understood in dealing with older people because of our tendency to stereotype the patients and to assume that advanced age itself is responsible. Furthermore, these symptoms, especially when acute in onset, are often reversible.[21-26]

According to the American Psychiatric Association, organic brain syndrome is a "mental condition characteristically resulting from diffuse impairment of brain tissue function from any cause."[27-28] We must seek out that cause.[29-31] The etiology of acute organic brain syndrome in the aged is summarized in Table 6–2.

97

TABLE 6–2
Etiology of Acute Organic Brain Syndrome in the Aged

Vascular	Neoplasm
Strokes, both major and petty	Both primary and metastatic
Arteritides, such as collagen disease	
Partial occlusion of major vessels,	Nutritional
such as carotid arteries	Malnutrition, including avitaminoses
Trauma	Alcoholism
Fat emboli from skeletal fractures	
Subdural hematoma	Toxic
	Poisons
	Medication
Infection –	
Brain abscess	Metabolic
Meningitis	Liver, kidney, thyroid disease
Paresis	Diabetes mellitus

Particularly noteworthy problems in this group of patients are chronic subdural hematoma, malnutrition, drug reactions, chronic organic brain syndrome, depression, and psychosis.

CHRONIC SUBDURAL HEMATOMA   Older people can be frail and unsteady. They fall and sustain head injuries, often without external evidence. Subdural hematoma may result and produce symptoms gradually, over a period of months. This is an insidious process, which can result in death, and yet it is curable if it is considered and treated.

CHELSEA–VILLAGE PROGRAM CASE REPORT

A.S. was a 75-year-old woman, homebound by a previous fractured hip with nonunion and poor surgical result. She had a homemaker eight hours per day and used a walker. The patient fell frequently, however, because of generalized weakness and inability to use the walker securely. Over a period of three months, the patient became increasingly somnolent and uncommunicative, although she would eat and follow directions. She was hospitalized. No evidence of trauma was found. The fundi were not seen clearly because of cataracts. She died within a week. Autopsy showed a large organizing frontal subdural hematoma.

MALNUTRITION   Peculiar dietary habits are commonplace in aged, disabled people living alone. This is a result of inability to shop, lack of money, loss of desire for proper self-care, and poor or absent teeth.

A.W. is an 88-year-old woman found living alone in a single-room building since the death of her husband six months previously. She was referred by the Visiting Nurse Service because she was hallucinating. Physical examination revealed an emanciated, dirty, aged woman, with a diffuse erythematous rash and bleeding gums. It was apparent that she suffered from diarrhea. Her major complaint to us was that her neighbor came through the keynole at night and sat on top of the refrigerator staring at her. Careful history made it clear that she was living on coffee, condensed milk, sugar, jam, and lettuce, provided at her request by the superintendent. The diagnosis of malnutrition, with the probability of combined vitamin deficiencies (pellagra, scurvy), was obvious.[32-35]

The patient refused hospitalization and any tests but permitted a change in her diet. She was placed on a Meals-on-Wheels program and homemaker assistance. On this regimen all aspects of the problem improved, her delusions and diarrhea ceased, she gained weight and is no longer homebound.[14, 36-39]

DRUG REACTIONS   A review of the drugs being taken, whether or not they are as prescribed, and the dosage schedule can offer important diagnostic information,[21, 40] as is made clear in the case of patient R.N., cited earlier in this chapter. In addition, even though medication may be taken correctly, aberrant side effects can be a problem in aged people, as illustrated below.

L.R. is a 98-year-old woman, completely intact mentally although slowed down physically, who requested medication for relief of anxiety. She was given phenobarbital, 15 mg four times daily. On this regimen, her agitation increased to an intolerable level. The phenobarbital was cut, and her symptoms abated.

CHRONIC ORGANIC BRAIN SYNDROME   Changes in behavior which occur gradually, without underlying medical disease, are less likely to be correctible.[21, 31, 42] Diffuse physical changes within the brain have been found in these patients at autopsy.[24, 42-45] As Jack Weinberg points out[21]:

Early features are errors in judgment, decline in personal care and habits, an impairment in capacity for abstract thought, a lack of interest, and apathy. Many emotional reactions are possible, depression, anxiety and irritability being the most frequent. A loosening of inhibitions can be an early sign. As deterioration progresses, medical symptoms proliferate, and the traditional signs of organic dysfunction become more evident. Hallucinations may be present, especially at night. Rambling, incoherent speech and fabrication are frequent signs. Sleeplessness and restlessness are common. The patient may wander away from home.

Paranoid tendencies may be exacerbated or appear for the first time. Occasionally, one may even see manic and hypermanic states.

These patients can be difficult to work with. The health workers involved must use the maximum in sympathy, tact, and maturity, because they are likely targets for the patient's delusions.

DEPRESSION   Somatic signs and symptoms of weight loss, insomnia, anorexia, and constipation are signposts of depression. The physician should be alert to this point and—*once organic disease has been eliminated*—act, because depressions are often treatable illnesses.

Reactive depression is common in older people,[22, 24, 45, 46] understandably based on the loss of health and of loved ones, the financial problems and loneliness that often occur, concern over incapacity and helplessness, and that potent factor, the fear of impending death. To the extent that these factors can be corrected through the skill of the health workers, medication, and counseling, reactive depression may clear.

The more serious psychotic depression, with the threat of suicide, is also a treatable disease.[22, 23, 47, 48] Physicians must act in these cases with a sense of urgency. The suicide rate among the aged is high.[49, 50] Psychiatric advice should be obtained,[22] and hospitalization may be required.

PSYCHOSIS   Home health care programs are likely to be involved with the care of patients who have clear-cut psychoses, particularly in areas of the country where state mental hospital patients have been discharged into the community.[51-56] Because of their bizarre behavior patterns, patients draw widespread attention, and often there is no health care resource available beyond these programs. State hospital doors are closed, and the psychiatric sections of acute care hospitals may resist receiving these patients because reimbursement will not be forthcoming.

Chronic schizophrenic patients are among the least malleable and cooperative of all the homebound aged. They will not listen to reason, as we interpret it, because they are involved in a pattern of reasoning all their own.

The following material is abstracted from the chart of a Chelsea–Village Program Patient:

Physician's Note
This patient, a 60-year-old man, gives a history which is unclear. He apparently has been in a state mental hospital and also has been seen in a local emergency room or clinic.

100

He was referred to us by the Visiting Nurse Service of New York. We find him living in an 8-by-10 foot room in the Hotel Pearl. Numerous ashtrays are piled high with cigarette stubs. The patient is unwashed and is thin but appears to be in basically good health, based on the superficial physical exam permitted. He says that a clinic doctor told him that he could not let water touch him for one year from the date of visit. He couldn't have an erection for 3½ years from that date, either. The patient says he was told at a clinic last year that the six or seven packs of cigarettes he smokes per day were inadequate to sustain his blood pressure and that he should be smoking one carton daily. However, he cannot afford the cigarettes, or food either, for that matter, because he is not able to make the $35 per day to which he is entitled through begging. By law every person he accosts on the street through panhandling is required to give him 25 cents. Since most of them don't, he is legally permitted to call them lice, finks, and perverts, which he does, loudly.

Because he has no money for food, he is legally entitled to receive free meals in any restaurant. The restaurants do not cooperate, even though by law they are required to set aside 21 percent of their money to feed people like him.

The patient says he is a member of the government of Greenwich Village, but he remains a very unpopular person, he says, because he speaks explicitly to people on the street who do not give him the money to which he is entitled.

Our psychiatrist consultant felt that the patient should be hospitalized. He refused, moved from the Hotel Pearl, and has been lost to contact.

Demented behavior may produce a situation which is hazardous, especially when the patient is isolated and physically helpless. In rare instances, it is necessary to exercise control against the patient's wishes, always with the intention of helping the patient regain independence as quickly as possible, as noted in the following Chelsea–Village Program case report.

S.P. is a 91-year-old woman living alone, known to the Program for three years. She has become increasingly resistant to working with the health team to keep herself clean and nourished. Within the last year she fell and fractured her hip and received severe burns from spilling hot coffee on herself. When she assaulted her homemaker with an icepick (to no avail), psychiatric advice was obtained. The patient has refused to allow homemakers to continue helping her because "they are stealing from me and abusing me."

Today she indicated through a locked door that she could not get up to let us in. We obtained a key from the manager. The apartment was quite cluttered, smelled of urine. The patient was lying on a couch and couldn't get up.

She was alert; her mood was anxious, angry, and depressed; her affect, labile and inappropriate. She had ideas of reference as well as paranoid persecutory delusions about who we were and why we were there. She was not oriented to time or place. She voiced assaultive intent and implied indirectly that she would like to die. She said she needs help but refuses to accept it when offered.

Legal steps were taken to bring the patient to the hospital.

Emotional Support of the Patient

Old disabled people suffer from the normal human frailties of anxiety, fear, frustration, but in a magnified form. Not only do they often live a life of isolation, with constant difficulty in carrying out daily activities, but must face as well the fact of bodily deterioration and impending death. Doctors can do more than make diagnoses and treat illness. By demonstrating a kindly, persistent, and genuine interest, the doctor can create an atmosphere of equanimity and assurance, and provide a degree of peace of mind, which is of enormous importance to the well-being of the patient, and even lead to physical improvement.

Listening to the patient, taking the time to understand truly what is being said—and what is left unsaid—is an essential component of psychologic support. Glib reassurance is valueless. Behaving as though the patient is an inert object is pernicious.

The following material from a Chelsea–Village Program staff conference is pertinent:

ELLEN QUIRKE (Social Worker): I remember a situation on the Rehab ward at Jacobi Hospital. It was my first assignment as a student. There was a young man sitting in bed, a paraplegic. The doctors came by on rounds and were talking about this boy, right by his bed, as though he weren't there. I couldn't believe it. They talked right over his head and never addressed him.

ATTENDING DOCTOR: Physicians are the worst offenders in degrading patients this way, and for reasons that are obvious. First of all, the patients are passive. They're in bed, in a physically inferior position. The doctors are standing up. Also, the fact that the patient is ill and the doctors are supposedly the source of cure is a factor. It's easy to slip into a situation in which the doctor feels, or at least acts, all powerful, and the patient is absolutely emptied of all stature. I've participated in this. It takes a long time to be self-confident enough to recognize the hideousness of this form of behavior.

Ignoring the patient is bad enough, but I've seen worse. When I was a medical student, we had a professor of medicine, a courtly man, a gentleman from Virginia, who looked like the epitome of a great teacher. He was leading ward rounds one day, typical rounds with lots of house officers and students, quoting of recent journals, presentation of cases at the foot of the bed. Suddenly a patient managed to speak up and intrude into the discussion of his own case.

102

He said, "Doctor, doctor, please, can you just tell me what's wrong with me?" The professor turned to the patient and said, "I'm afraid you have a mighty bad cancer." I could see the hope and fight drain out of the patient.

Help for an old, anxious person requires taking ample time.[36, 57, 58] Without this, we fail our patients.

This point is exemplified by N.G., a widow of age 75, well known to the outpatient department of St. Vincent's Hospital, in this Chelsea–Village Program case report:

Mrs. G. has severe arthritis but managed to walk, with difficulty, and remain independent. She was referred to the Chelsea–Village Program by a clinic nurse after she failed to keep several appointments. On the first visit she complained of generalized body itching, without evidence of insect bites or any other lesion, but could not explain why she was now homebound. On the second visit, however, she asked to speak privately with the physician. After 15 minutes of circumlocution, she blurted her fear that she had cancer of the breast "because that's where the itching started."

Careful physical examination failed to reveal any suggestion of a breast mass, and the patient was so informed.

Itching was relieved by use of a humidifier (the air was dry from steam heat). Mrs. G., who had in essence been paralyzed by fear, has returned to medical care in the clinic, where she has remained stable for the last three years.

In this case the physician's concentrated attention was helpful, but it is also possible to do it wrong. Professional arrogance can lead us away from proper understanding of the patient, as noted in this Chelsea–Village Program staff conference abstract:

ATTENDING DOCTOR: I'd like to discuss E.S., because she is having difficulty accepting us. As you know, she's 92 years old, homebound, deaf, virtually blind. She used to travel to her physician on the East Side, but now she can't make it. She was accustomed to having the best and paying for it. She's no longer in a position to do that either.

Her major complaints are generalized weakness and fecal incontinence. I think she was having substantial trouble accepting this kind of disability. She's a highly intelligent, intellectually intact, very aged, and quite helpless person. She's the one who said to us when we first saw her, "The only thing I'm worrying about is keeping out of a nursing home."

I've seen her three times. We have attempted to concentrate on the possibility of improving her eyesight and hearing. I decided that the best place to get an evaluation was here in the hospital clinic. We would get her here, pick her up, bring her back home. The process of arranging this was underway when the problem became evident. Who received the call?

BARBARA RUETHER (Coordinator):   Her friend called and said that Mrs. S. did not want to go to our clinic, that she would not keep her clinic appointments, that she was not interested in our services, and that we should send a copy of our records to her old doctor.

DOCTOR: Where did we go wrong? We obviously didn't understand her wishes properly. Have you had a chance to talk with her further?

IRMA STAHL (Social Worker):   Yes. Was there any previous indication that she perceived our program as charity?

DOCTOR: Not outwardly.

STAHL: I called her. She feels that this whole thing, meaning our program, is like a clinic, and she doesn't want to be involved in that sort of arrangement. And, in addition to that, she's resigned to her eye and ear problems and accepts the fact that they cannot be changed.

DOCTOR: All we've succeeded in doing is upsetting her. I'd like your opinion about why this happened. I know her best; I've seen her more often than anyone else. Obviously I am to blame for missing the point of this case.

SISTER TERESITA (Nurse):   Well first of all, we didn't appreciate her ambivalence about accepting charity. We didn't charge her, and that was a blow to her pride. We made it worse by talking about the clinic. She couldn't tolerate that. It was too painful, so she withdrew, even though she has no other logical source of care. In addition to that, you were too aggressive about getting her eyes and ears looked at. You didn't seem to be giving her a choice. You insisted that she make the effort, without understanding that she might not want to. She probably recognized better than you that her chances for improvement were poor.

You were too blunt, not sensitive enough to her particular needs, so now we've lost the chance to help her and have made her life more aggravated and upset. But I forgive you!

This failure is an example of the psychological blindness of the doctor, an inability to see the human being inside the case. Through strenuous efforts by team members we were able to reestablish a relationship with Mrs. S., but we were forced to recognize that our intervention had not necessarily been a blessing.

CHARACTERISTICS OF PHYSICIANS IN HOME HEALTH CARE PROGRAMS FOR THE AGED

Doctors working with bereft aged people have selected themselves out from their medical associates. They can be expected to have the strength to do the unusual, to recognize the needs of aged and helpless people as an opportunity for service rather than as an ungratifying chore, to look at these patients as "the most complicated and challenging of human beings,"[19] rather than as passive objects. They are doctors who have strong confidence in their own judgment and the willingness to develop team relationships with nurses and social workers.

These comments from a Chelsea–Village Program Staff conference are relevant.

ATTENDING DOCTOR: Are you getting any feeling from your friends on the house staff that you're doing something sort of silly?

F. RUSSELL KELLOGG (Fellow in Community Medicine): I think that some of the house staff respect what we're doing, some don't see it as important, and some outright resent that we bring extra work to them when we admit these patients.

JEFFREY STALL (Medical Resident): I've never really thought of *my* participation in comparison to anyone else. I've seen it as a very personal thing, as a commitment we have to these patients, to this type of service. I think the doctors in the program are people who have a volunteer spirit, who believe that the medical profession should always have a volunteer spirit, and I think those house officers who have that spirit and want to do it are basically different from those who just don't.

ATTENDING DOCTOR: What are we doing by putting this much energy into people whose longevity is so limited? What are we salvaging here? Is it an efficient use of professional staff time to work with people whose average age is 80 and are already sick, when the same amount of effort put into children's programs might have a bigger payoff? How do we answer these questions?

STALL: I think that older people are the part of the population most neglected in terms of attention and care. Even if we fail sometimes to solve their medical problems, we can help them by bringing ourselves. I think they're deserving of it.

MARC SHERMAN (Fellow in Community Medicine): *I* don't ask questions like that. I deal with what faces me. If somebody's sick, I try to help. I don't look at him while he's there and think, I'm not going to take care of what he's got; instead I'm going to run over here and take care of this kid because he's going to live longer. But that doesn't answer your question.

ATTENDING DOCTOR: It does exactly.

KELLOGG: If we look in the hospital at how much money we spend in other areas where we cannot justify the expense in terms of cost-effectiveness—cardiogenic shock, for instance. . . .

SHERMAN: Well, in that case, why run an ICU? How long are these people going to live? What is the effective output of these patients afterward? What are they good for?

ATTENDING DOCTOR: The way you put it is in tune with my way of thinking. It

105

seems like an obvious question, What are we doing with all these old people who are just going to die anyway? But when we start to define the matter more carefully, we begin to recognize that we cannot separate out one human being from another. What we can do as physicians is to help the people who need our help as best as we can. And that's the end of it.

REFERENCES

1. Busse EW: Some emotional complications of chronic disease. Gerontologist 2:153, 1962
2. Anshin RN: Emotional problems of the chronically ill. J Am Geriatr Soc 10:447, 1962
3. Another generation gap: physicians vs. the elderly. Mod Hosp 122:42, 1974
4. Editorial: attitude towards the aging. NZ Med J 78:537, 1973
5. Cope O: Man, Mind and Medicine: The Doctor's Education. Philadelphia, Lippincott, 1968
6. Gaynes, NL: A logic to long-term care. Gerontologist 13:277, 1973
7. Miller DB, Lowenstein R, Winston R: Physicians' attitudes toward the ill aged and nursing homes. J Am Geriatr Soc 24:498, 1976
8. Carpenter JO, Wylie CM: On aging, dying, and denying; delivering care to older dying patients. Public Health Rep 89:403, 1974
9. Comfort A: On gerontophobia. Med Opinion Rev 3:30, 1967
10. Sutton W, Linn E: Where the Money Was. New York, Viking, 1976
11. Brown J, Pearson CM: Clinical Uses of Adrenal Steroids. New York, McGraw-Hill, 1962, p 420
12. Thorn GW, Adams RD: Braunwald E, Isselbacher KJ, Petersdorf RG (eds): Harrison's Principles of Internal Medicine, 8th ed. New York: McGraw-Hill, 1977, pp 554–556
13. Goulding EJ: Prednisone psychosis: a nursing care study. Nurs Times 62:1093, 1966
14. Anderson F: Old and alone: a patient with special problems. Med Opinion 5:14, 1976
15. Russell B: Letter: Drugs and "dementia" in the elderly. Br Med J 4:783, 1973
16. Schwartz D, Wang M, Zeitz L, Goss MEW: Medication errors made by the elderly, chronically ill patient. Am J Public Health 52:2018, 1962
17. Libow LS, Mehl B: Self-administration of medications by patients in hospitals or extended care facilities. J Am Geriatr Soc 18:81, 1970
18. Rudd TN: Prescribing methods and iatrogenic situations in old age. Gerontol Clin (Basel) 14:123, 1972
19. Butler RN: Why Survive: Being Old in America. New York, Harper, 1975, p 225
20. Judge TG: Drugs and dementia. Br J Clin Pharmacol (Suppl) 3:81, 1976
21. Weinberg J: Geriatric psychiatry. In Freedman AM, Kaplan HI, Sandock BJ (eds): Comprehensive Textbook of Psychiatry, 2nd ed. Baltimore, Williams & Wilkins, 1975, p 2415
22. Fann WE, Wheless JC: Depression in elderly patients. South Med J 68:468, 1975
23. Gaitz CM: Mental disorders: diagnosis and treatment. In Busse EW (ed): Theory and Therapeutics of Aging. New York, Medcom Press, 1973, pp 72–82
24. Kral VA: Psychiatric problems in the aged: a reconsideration. Can Med Assoc J 108:584, 1973
25. Gianturco DT: The older psychiatric patient at Duke Hospital. In Fann WE, Maddox

GL (eds): Drug Issues in Geropsychiatry. Baltimore, Williams & Wilkins, 1974, pp 73–76

26. Moses DV: Assessing behavior in the elderly. Nurs Clin North Am 7:225, 1972
27. American Psychiatric Association, Committee and Nomenclature and Statistics: Diagnostic and Statistical Manual of Mental Disorders, 2nd ed. Washington DC, 1968
28. Magaline S: Dictionary of Medical Syndromes. Philadelphia, Lippincott, 1971
29. Goldfarb AI: Integrated psychiatric services for the aged. Bull NY Acad Med 49:1070, 1973
30. Sandok BA: Organic brain syndromes. In Freedman AM, Kaplan HI, Sandock BJ (eds): Comprehensive Textbook of Psychiatry, 2nd ed. Baltimore, Williams & Wilkins, 1975
31. Hodkinson HM: Psychological medicine: the elderly mind. Br Med J 2:23, 1975
32. Judge TG: Nutrition of the elderly. Physiotherapy 62:179, 1976
33. Corless D: Diet in the elderly. Br Med J 4:158, 1973
34. Exton-Smith, AN: Problems of diet in old age. J R Coll Physicians. Lond 9:148, 1975
35. Latchford W: Nutritional problems of the elderly. Community Health 6:145, 1974
36. Johnson AN: The physician's role in the care of the aging. Gerontologist 10:33, 1970
37. Somers AR, Moore FM: Homemaker services—essential option for the elderly. Public Health Rep 91:354, 1976
38. Berg WE, Atlas L, Zeiger J: Integrated homemaking services for the aged in urban neighborhoods. Gerontologist 14:388, 1974
39. Shinn EB, Robinson ND: Trends in homemaker-home health aide services. Abstr Social Workers 10:3, 1974
40. Libow LS: Pseudosenility: acute and reversible organic brain syndromes. J Am Geriatr Soc 21:112, 1973
41. Opit LJ, Shaw SM: Care of the elderly sick at home: whose responsibility is it? Lancet 2:1127, 1976
42. Arie, T: Dementia in the elderly: diagnosis and assessment. Br Med J 4:540, 1973
43. Corsellis JAN: Cerebral degeneration and mental disorders in later life. In Psychiatric Disorders in the Aged. London, World Psychiatric Association, 1965
44. Roth, M, Tomlinson BE, Blessed G: The relationship between quantitative measures of dementia and of degenerative changes in cerebral grey matter of elderly subjects. Proc R Soc Med 60:254, 1967
45. Wang HS, Busse EW: Dementia in old age. Contemp Neurol Ser 9:151, 1971
46. Busse EW, Reckless JB: Psychiatric management of the aged. JAMA 175:645, 1961
47. Post F: The management and nature of a depressive illness in late life: a follow-through study. Br J Psychiatry 121:303, 1972
48. Carver EJ: Geropsychiatric treatment: where, why, how. In Fann WE, Maddox GI (eds): Drug Issues in Geropsychiatry. Baltimore, Williams & Wilkins, 1974, pp 63–68
49. Benson RA, Brodie DC: Suicide by overdoses of medicine among the aged. J Am Geriatr Soc 23:304, 1975
50. Bromley DB: The Psychology of Human Aging. Middlesex, England, Pelican Books, 1966
51. Raskind MA, Alvarez C, Pietrzyk M, Westerlund K, Herlin S: Helping the elderly psychiatric patient in crisis. Geriatrics 31:51, 1976
52. Eisdorfer C: Issues in the psychopharmacology of the aged. In Psychopharmacology and Aging. New York, Plenum Press, 1973

53. Epstein LF, Simon A: Alternatives to state hospitalization for geriatric mentally ill. Am J Psychiatry 124:955, 1968
54. Lipscomb CF: The care of the psychiatrically disturbed elderly patient in the community. Am J Psychiatry 127:8, 1971
55. Windle C, Scully D: Community mental health centers and the decreasing use of state mental hospitals. Community Ment Health J 12:239, 1976
56. Kirk SA: Effectiveness of community services for discharged mental hospital patients. Am J Orthopsychiatry 46:646, 1976
57. Johnson WM: Medical management of older patients. JAMA 175:649, 1961
58. Woods D: It's time to think about a new deal for the old. Can Med Assoc J 115:60, 1976

CHAPTER 7

THE SOCIAL WORKER

with Ellen Quirke, M.S.W.
and Irma Stahl, M.S.W.

One day after finishing a home visit, the nurse and the doctor were headed toward the parked Chelsea–Village Program van. As they walked, the nurse caught sight of a frail old woman struggling at the curb to cross the street. The nurse walked over, offered her arm, and said, "Looks like you could use some help!" The woman stared at her for a moment, accepted the extended arm, and said, "Oh, thank you dear, you must be a social worker!"

In home health care programs for homebound, aged people, social workers serve two major purposes. They provide urgently needed professional services directly to patients and, because they function within a health care team, share with their co-workers the particular attitudes, skills, and techniques of social work.[1-6] Only through teamwork can the complex and multifaceted health and social needs of homebound, aged people be fulfilled.

AIMS AND METHODS

. . . the primary aim of social work practice is to enable people to command their own lives and destinies to the greatest extent possible in light of the isolating, technological, specialized and hopelessly complex world in which we live in the Twentieth Century.[7]

Traditionally the social work profession has consisted of three distinct fields: casework, groupwork, and community organization. Casework is ". . . a method of helping individuals to meet needs derived from the impoverishment of the environment or the limitations of individual capacity."[8] In groupwork, the social worker uses the group process to achieve goals. "Basic to Social Work is the use of the group as an instrument for enhancing social functioning of the individual as a social being."[9] Community organization, a more recently defined major area of concentration, is a process "whereby individuals, groups, and organizations engage in planned action to influence social problems."[10]

The practicing generic social worker integrates these three fields. Home health care programs for the aged provide social workers maximum opportunity to utilize all the methods of the profession. In the Chelsea–Village Program, we are engaged in generic social work.

We conduct our social work practice "not within the traditional boundaries . . . but across lines by asking ourselves what kinds of problems call for what kind of services and actions."[11]

THE GENERIC SOCIAL WORKER

When the Chelsea–Village Program was being organized in 1972, community organizing techniques were needed.[12] The elements we were concerned with included isolated, homebound, aged people with significant social and medical problems; St. Vincent's Hospital, a community-oriented health institution; and a politically active, socially conscious group of neighborhood people and agencies.

The organization process, described in Chapter 3, was effective. Once the program started, casework became our major concern. The setting was dynamic and flexible. In order to understand the complex needs of our clients and to help them, we were required to use a wide variety of methods. To illustrate:

Four elderly men, all of whom have had strokes, live in separate rooms at a local single-room-occupancy hotel. Each is struggling with adjustment to sudden incapacity. All are rebelling against the surroundings in which they live. Complaints about the food and about the other residents are voiced. Each man feels alone in his suffering but withdraws into his room in a state of depression.

There are several possibilities for helpful intervention. First, the social worker may involve each individual in an ongoing treatment relationship. As alternatives, there are the formation of a therapeutic group, in which the men can help each other, or of a task group, in which the patients, working together, can plan strategies to make changes in the hotel. Groups involving employees of the facility, of homemakers, or of family members may be useful. Often, a combination of these methods can be employed simultaneously.

Social casework in its broadest sense occupies most of our time. Close and consistent contact is essential to effective work with our patients.

110

This relationship is "the bond that vitalizes, warms, and sustains the work between helper and helped."[13] The point is made clear in the following Chelsea–Village Program case report.

Mrs. K. is a 65-year-old widow referred to us after she repeatedly missed clinic appointments.

A team assessment of the patient revealed medical problems, which were essentially psychosomatic, and depression.

Regular visits by the social worker eventually enabled the patient to accept needed psychiatric hospitalization. Observation and treatment were brief but effective, and the patient returned home, stabilized on an antidepressant medication. Continued social casework with Mrs. K. gradually drew from her a more positive response to our services, which were designed to increase her human contacts and her level of functioning.

We were permitted to develop a network of care: a homemaker, a friendly visitor, and St. Vincent's Hospital student nurses. The feelings of depression and the psychosomatic ailments have ceased. The patient is no longer homebound, attends the hospital outpatient department, and visits our office as a friend.

FOCUSING ON THE INDIVIDUAL

A major goal of social work is individualizing, differentiating one person from another, singling each person out from the mass. The process is especially important for older people, who are often thought of in stereotypes; and the first step is an analysis through which we try to understand the particular characteristics and problems of the individual.

Assessment

Assessment is to the practice of social work what the physical examination is to the practice of medicine.

Assessment consists of trying to understand first, what the trouble is; second, what seems to be contributing to the trouble; and third, what can be changed and modified. In each of these questions strengths as well as weaknesses in both person and situation are important considerations.[14]

In order to understand "what the trouble is," the worker tries to gather all the information pertinent to the person in his or her situation. She keeps in mind that "the specific client–situation complex must be viewed repeatedly against a series of approximate norms—of average expectancies—concerning behavior of the client and of others, concern-

111

ing pertinent aspects of social situation, and concerning concrete realities.''[15]

The worker must understand the particular pressures the individual is under, the modes of adaptation, the methods of coping, before making recommendations.

We understand our patients only by knowing their ''very particular needs, feelings, desires, physical and mental characteristics, and style of life.''[7] This Chelsea–Village Program case report makes the point.

Mrs. S. is an 84-year-old widow and former opera singer who has occupied the same small and dingy apartment for the last 60 years. Her living room serves as her bedroom, and she sleeps on a dilapidated studio couch. At one point she acknowledged that she needed a new bed. Because of Mrs. S.'s limited income the worker offered her a hospital bed which had been donated to the program. "Certainly not!" she said, "A hospital bed in my sitting room?" What would have been perfectly acceptable to someone else was out of the question for Mrs. S. In her scheme of things, comfort was not to be sacrificed for beauty even if the price was right. In fact, someone later generously donated to the Program a studio bed, upon which Mrs. S. now rests comfortably.

From Assessment to a Plan of Action

For a newly referred individual, assessment begins with these questions:

How did this patient come to be referred to us?
Who made the referral, and why?
Is he or she receptive to the team visit?
What precipitated the current need?
Has he or she sought help elsewhere?
What other agencies are involved?
What is the medical/social situation as described
   by the referring person?
Is it requested that any particular individual be present
   when the team visits the patient?

Once a patient is accepted into the Chelsea–Village Program, hospital records, if any, are obtained in order to increase our body of knowledge.

At the first visit, the social worker secures an accurate, detailed picture of the patient's living situation. The following information is vital:

How far from the hospital does the patient live?
What is the neighborhood like?

Does the building seem safe?
Does it appear cared for?
Is it structurally sound?
Is there any problem gaining entrance?
How many flights of stairs to the apartment?
Is there a working elevator?

The bulk of the assessment naturally takes place through direct discussions with the patient.

. . . the process of understanding begins with what the client sees as his problem, then moves into understanding some aspect of the client himself and some aspects of the rest of the system within which he locates his trouble—and the ways in which these facets interrelate, interact, transact, and affect each other.[15]

The particular areas which the Chelsea–Village Program social worker covers with patients include medical situation and level of functioning, emotional state and degree of alertness, environmental factors and living situation, family/relative/friend network, financial status, and involvement with other agencies.

The following assessment is typical:

Miss B. was referred to the Chelsea–Village Program by a local priest. A neighbor was to buzz the team in, because Miss B. could not be depended on to answer the doorbell. The team entered the building and found Miss B. living on the fourth floor of a walk-up apartment building. Miss B. is a friendly 80-year-old single woman, a former nurse. She received the team as "an answer to my prayers."

Medical: Mild congestive heart failure; diffuse osteoarthritis.

Functional: Unable to walk stairs; unable to carry out most activities of daily living.

Emotional: Appropriate affect; acknowledges confusion and recent memory loss; oriented to person and place.

Environmental: Poor apartment for patient because of her inability to walk stairs. Has no phone. Extremely isolated. A favorable point: rent-controlled apartment.

Living Situation: Cramped, neglected apartment, reflects patient's inability to manage alone.

Family/relative/friend network: Only relatives are two siblings living in Europe. They correspond. Has interested and helpful neighbors but no friends.

Financial: VA pension. Recently lost SSI because of failure to appear for recertification interview.

Involvement with other agencies: Church. A Brother visited her after neighbor sought help there.

Developing a Social Work Plan of Action

Immediate and long-term goals must be set for the plan of action. In Miss B.'s case the immediate goals were to (1) institute Meals-on-Wheels, (2) process a request for a homemaker, (3) utilize a Chelsea–Village Program homemaker temporarily, and (4) reapply for SSI.

The long-term goals were to (1) decrease isolation by helping the patient to get a telephone and securing a friendly visitor and (2) consider a change of housing.

Often, as in the case of Miss B., immediate action is required in order to ensure her safety at home. There may be a discrepancy between what the team thinks the patient needs and the degree to which the patient will accept help. However, suggestions which seem intolerable at first are accepted later. Obviously, assessment is continuous. People change; their situations and their needs alter.

Coordination With Outside Agencies

Often the assistance of several agencies is required to form a comprehensive network of care for out patients. Coordination by the social worker is imperative. This requires the establishment of good working relationships.[16-21]

We attempt to make our requests to other agencies reasonable, and we try to comply with their rules. We respond as positively and as quickly as possible to their needs and try to be understanding when ours cannot be met. We invite agency representatives to patient care conferences when appropriate and make ourselves available for meetings called by them. We strive to keep lines open at all times. Without cooperation with community agencies, the goals of the Chelsea–Village Program cannot be achieved. The following case report is illustrative.

Mr. D. is a 78-year-old single man with diabetes, glaucoma, and cataracts. His poor ability to walk keeps him homebound. Recently he fell at home and fractured his arm. This was deeply upsetting to him and left him feeling that he could do nothing for himself.

Mr. D.'s income falls in that fateful gap between too much for Medicaid and too little to pay for private help. Through the Federation of the Handicapped, and the Comprehensive Employment and Training Act (CETA), we were able to obtain a home health aide free of charge for a period of four months. This assistance was sufficient to give Mr. D. a chance to get back on his feet. Without this resource, he would have required nursing home placement, although he was adamantly opposed to the idea.

ESTABLISHING A RELATIONSHIP WITH THE PATIENT

The following step-by-step outline shows how the social worker–patient relationship develops.

The Referral

A referral is made to the program. The coordinator takes the basic information and reviews the case at a regular morning meeting with the nurse and social worker. A joint decision is made as to whether the program is appropriate for the patient.

First Visit

After a patient has been brought into the program, the coordinator schedules an appointment. The social worker, doctor, and nurse go together. The doctor and nurse concentrate upon making a medical evaluation. The social worker waits to obtain information from the patient directly and also talks with any relative, friend, neighbor, or agency contact who may be present. The worker listens to the patient's perception of existing problems and obtains data about finances, housing, and social contacts.

Follow-up

Social work procedures usually involve telephone contacts with relatives, if any, and the source of referral. Forms are completed, letters written, in order to obtain concrete services for the patient. Often bureaucratic knots must be unsnarled. These may include, for instance, erroneous termination of Medicaid or SSI.

Often the social worker will make return visits for further assessment. As the acquaintanceship deepens, less obvious but more significant problems may become apparent. Opportunity for counseling develops.

WAYS OF EFFECTING CHANGE

The social worker comes into the life of our elderly patients when their deviation from normal medical, social, or psychologic standards has reached the point that independence is threatened.[22]

In order to help the individual arrive at a stable state of well-being, the social worker must use creatively the body of knowledge and techniques she has acquired.[14]

In a program such as ours, the social worker performs a variety of functions as the needs of the case require.

Interpretation

To help our patients form contacts with the society around them, we work with neighbors, homemakers, doctors, policemen, nurses, family members, apartment managers, elevator operators, mailmen, and doormen. Skill in interpersonal relations counts.

Mrs. V. lives in a housing project. She is fearful and suspicious and won't leave her apartment to go to the ground floor for the mail, but her correspondence with a faraway sister is her only means of communication with the world. With her permission, I spoke with the mailman, who agreed to make an exception to his routine and deliver the mail to her door.

Mrs. N. is confused and can be extremely demanding. Homemakers tend to quit quickly. By interpreting the patient's behavior to the employee as a manifestation of illness and by explaining how to set limits on it, the social worker relieved the tension for the next homemaker. She has managed to stay on the job.

Using Community Resources Creatively

The social worker must make an imaginative assessment of the client's needs and have ingenuity and a thorough knowledge of the community, in order to ferret out resources in unexpected places.

Mr. T. is a blind, diabetic, 80-year-old retired lawyer, a double amputee. His request: "If only I could have someone read law books so that I wouldn't get rusty. Then I'd never notice my legs." The worker contacted a local college and was able to obtain the services of a student, who planned to enter law school. He visits Mr. T. weekly and not only reads but also discusses interesting cases with the gentleman.

Acting Aggressively

It is sometimes necessary for the worker to be aggressive with other agencies, neighbors, and landlords—to argue forcefully for the client. When necessary, she may insist upon reaching supervisors and executives. This technique must be used judiciously and only after normal procedures have failed, or it can be counterproductive.

Forceful intervention in our program is used most often in handling passive-aggressive behavior of bureaucrats in government agencies. Interceding for housing, foodstamps, and the continued services of homemakers are common examples. This kind of intervention demands legwork, patience, willpower, and control over one's emotions.

Developing Motivation through Counseling

Older people may need special efforts at stimulation and motivation because they have become passive, cannot remember recent events clearly, or are confused. These symptoms are common results of the desocialization, withdrawal, and inability to perform the activities of daily living which come from isolation, physical failure, and homeboundedness.[23-26]

Encouraging the older person to reminisce is a useful counseling technique.[27, 28] The social worker should become acquainted with the social and cultural factors which have shaped the life of her patient. Then she can ask insightful questions which encourage the patient to tell the story of his life. Reminiscence is a substitute for active experience. The use of memory provides a sense of continuity. Reminiscence may enhance the patient's sense of personal significance because it is selective and may screen out unpleasant memories. As the social worker listens, a relationship is created with the patient. Confidence develops, and trust grows.

Mrs. B had become more and more isolated because of her fierce need for independence, which caused her to refuse help of any kind. She began to hallucinate and developed severe paranoid symptoms. Repeated visits to her apartment and continued efforts to engage her in telling stories of early childhood in her beloved England offered more and more extended intervals during which she allowed the worker to bathe her and to pay her bills. Finally, Mrs. B. permitted the employment of a homemaker. The physical care of the patient was secured. She felt safe, and her psychiatric symptoms became less prominent.

Helping Patients Accept Disability

Preventing the sabotage of rehabilitation after a stroke or surgery is critically important. The older person's reaction to disability from serious illness can be devastating. It presents yet another in a series of many losses that elderly people experience.

Mr. S. had been depressed prior to his hospitalization. His severe arthritis caused a progressive loss of mobility and isolated him from his wife, who was

117

impatient and fault-finding. After having a pacemaker implanted and returning home, Mr. S.'s depression was worse. He wouldn't leave his bed.

The worker visited regularly and spent time with husband and wife separately. Mr. S. was allowed to express his anger. Mrs. S. was reassured as realistically as possible. Their relationship is happier, and the patient is less depressed, even though his physical state remains bad.

Mr. P., an 85-year-old asthmatic, lost his wife two years ago. His dependency increased, and he became more and more demanding of his homemaker. He made frequent visits to the emergency room by ambulance and called the program office two or three times a day.

The worker developed a consistent relationship with Mr. P. She now makes a weekly visit to his home and a phone call toward the end of the week. Encouragement to take medications as prescribed and the consistency of visits have served to reassure the patient. He has stopped calling the ambulance and appears to be at ease.

Overcoming Patient Resistance

Resistance of the patient to accepting needed services is often based on fear of losing independence or self-esteem, and it can be harmful to those very interests of the patient. Even wise, experienced, and sensitive workers have trouble getting patients to accept help, but it must be attempted, despite rebuffs.

Mr. L., a 77-year-old disabled man, was referred to the program by his daughter. He had developed hematuria. During the team visit, he submitted to the physical examination but said hardly a word except "NO!" to the doctor's suggestion that he be admitted to the hospital.

The worker had an opportunity during the visit to interview Mr. L.'s daughter. She described her father as a headstrong, frightened man. After consulting with the doctor and nurse about the symptoms and their possible meaning for Mr. L., the worker returned the following day and, with conviction, explained the potential good to be gained by prompt hospitalization.

Mr. L. agreed, but expressed a wish to go to the hospital without fanfare. No ambulance was to be called. The Program's vehicle went to pick up Mr. L. The worker and his daughter went along. Mr. L. had carcinoma of the prostate. It was treated. He has returned home and welcomes team visits.

Dealing With Disturbed Patients

We occasionally see in our program homebound, aged people who become deeply psychotic, act out their feelings, and yet cannot be hospitalized for legal reasons.[29-33] Neighbors worry about them and are upset by their presence in the building, police show up at the hospital to tell us about the latest episodes, and the patients are made to suffer not only from their own disorders but also from the distress they cause to other people.

Mrs. P., a 90-year-old woman alienated from her only son, lives in a project apartment. During a visit several months ago, the worker found Mrs. P. covered with insect bites. Her bed was full of bedbugs. The apartment was heavily infested with roaches. Mrs. P. sat like a queen in her bed, dressed in the remnants of what was once a fine wardrobe, all handsewn. The blanket was cluttered with leftover dinners. Mrs. P. both denied that she had bedbugs and roaches and yet cried that she had to live this way. She responded like a child to the bath that the nurse and the worker gave her in the tub but refused to allow any cleaning or transfer.

Mrs. P. had already been through 12 homemakers. The present homemaker was supervised, supported, and advised by the worker with great care. Arrangements were made for psychiatric consultation in the apartment. The patient was considered legally competent. She continued to refuse transfer to the hospital, but medication was given at home, supervised by the team and the homemaker. The acute psychiatric situation has improved, and the patient is clean and safe at home.

Working with Family Members and Friends

One-third of our patients live with a relative or friend. These personal contacts are of intense value to the patient, and to us, in achieving the goals of the program. The tasks of the relative are not easy, and we make strenuous efforts to provide counseling and other assistance in order to make the relationship viable and long-lasting.[34, 35]

We use two approaches: the family group, described in the next section, and individual contact.

Mr. B. has suffered memory loss and had recently become incontinent. His wife had no understanding of the cause, and tended to blame the patient, feeling that he should be able to control himself. Since this was impossible, Mrs. B. had become frustrated and angry, and so had he.

The social worker visited the couple weekly, and arranged additional telephone contact. She pressed ahead steadily with Mrs. B., cautiously but firmly stressing the irreversible physical nature of her husband's problem. She succeeded in working through Mrs. B's resistance to the employment of a home health aide. With better understanding and some practical assistance in the home, Mrs. B's attitude changed dramatically, toward kindness mixed with sadness.

119

The social worker can act as an intermediary, or neutral third party, in difficult family confrontations.

Mrs. T. maintained her own apartment and resisted vigorously her sister's advice to go to a nursing home. The patient was isolated from neighbors and family because of physical disability, confusion, and a long history of difficult interpersonal relationships.

The social worker engaged the sister in a series of discussions designed to help create a situation favorable to the patient's wishes. At length, the sister abandoned the idea of institutionalization for Mrs. T. and helped pay for a homemaker.

We encourage relatives to achieve a realistic appraisal of the home situation. Some are frightened and overwhelmed by their responsibilities, and overreact; others ignore the real and severe physical difficulties of the patient, hoping that the problem will simply disappear. Patients may be overdemanding and place an unbearable degree of stress upon the relative; or, in turn, are sometimes the victims of cruel behavior or are ignored. The social worker can often resolve these difficulties by providing advice in a persistent, calm, and understanding manner.

THE FAMILY GROUP PROCESS

The demands made by patients on their relatives can be grueling. The amount of time we spend in providing practical and emotional support to family members suggested to us the idea of forming a group among people who lived in the homes of our elderly, homebound patients. The group consists of spouses, adult children, and close friends.

A group develops an identity of its own. It has values and norms. It stimulates bonds of loyalty and affection. Members of the group provide mutual support and also help each other to fulfill the goals of the program for the benefit of the patient.[36]

The following material from a Chelsea–Village Program group conference is pertinent.

SOCIAL WORKER: The reason for bringing you together, the whole goal, was to try to keep people out of institutions and in their own homes, and I think the three of you are a very vital part of the program because you are doing that. You are keeping people that you love very much out of institutions, and you have a lot of experience in doing it. We can talk about how you've been helped to do it and how you can help each other to continue to do it. That's really the goal for this meeting. We're starting out with three people now, that's the core of the group, and we'll see how it expands.

120

H.W. (60-year-old man, a friend of 80-year-old male patient):   Well, may I say this about the necessity for keeping people out of an institution. I just want to say that my particular charge was in a very good institution, with wonderful people. That I could see, a very costly place, and after being there for a few weeks, I came to find that he was tied down to the bed. They were worried that he would fall out of the bed, but it seemed to me that they could have put a railing up, or some kind of a safeguard. Instead he was tied down with a sheet. I guess in order that he not be too much trouble in bodily functions. Various pipes were all connected to him. And he kept complaining of the pain that that gave him. He didn't know who I was or where he was. And I started to beg, ''Please, release him.'' ''Oh, no, you don't know what you're up against.'' ''Well, let me try. Please release him from those pipes.'' So he came home; and I can bear witness that in a matter of weeks, being in his own surroundings, with a sympathetic person at his side, the telephone ringing, and things of that sort . . .

E.M. (45-year-old woman caring for her 75-year-old mother):   In other words, he was back in life again.

H.W.:   Yeah, he got all his memory back. He knew what was happening. You have a bunch of people in an institution that are just degenerating into vegetables when they could be leading some kind of normal life in a family group.

SOCIAL WORKER: Okay, do you want to tell us a little bit about your situation?

J.L. (40-year-old woman caring for her 81-year-old father):   Well, for one thing, I'm Italian and Catholic. I have a father, and in the tradition of Italians, I have always catered to my parents. ''Honor thy father and thy mother.'' All the way. I mean, there was no such thing as entertaining the idea of putting them in a nursing home. Family members assisted as they were able. This was simply expected of the child. And so it's part tradition, part the fear that we have of institutions, of stories that we've heard about them on TV and such. And yet, you know, my father will sit back many a time and say, ''Why doesn't Christ take me so that I do not burden you?'' and I realize that he *truly* doesn't want to burden anyone. But he's helpless . . .

Through the weekly group experience, members are given an opportunity to talk about their feelings, discuss the possibility of the patient's death and their attitudes toward it, exchange ideas about ways to handle difficult situations with other family members, nurses, homemakers.[37-39] Useful insights are shared.

E.M.:   I don't think it's conscious on her part, I think it's completely unconscious, but I catch my mother doing and saying little things. It took me a little while to catch on to what's going on, but now I'm beginning to understand that she holds on to me more, is much more clinging . . .

121

SOCIAL WORKER: She didn't have very many radiotherapy sessions, but they anticipate people getting very upset with those treatments.

E.M.: She had some nights when she was dreaming. She had some very bad dreams.

SOCIAL WORKER: Is she talking about death? Her own death?

E.M.: No. She controls what she says to other people quite well. But the nurse told me one morning when I came to the hospital that she found mother crying. Mother denies it, which I thought was interesting. The nurse said to me she found her crying, and she was saying, "I want to die."

SOCIAL WORKER: I don't know that I've ever seen your mother cry.

E.M.: She cries with me. She won't cry with you.

SOCIAL WORKER: You're better off.

E.M.: I think what we are dealing with is a responsibility syndrome: you either got it or you don't got it. There are people who walk away from their parents, whether they are ill or well and whether they are financially stable or not. They take their wives, they say, "Okay, Mom, Dad, Bye. I've got a life of my own, and that's it." Off they go to the other end of the country to break the umbilical cord. But there are some people who, no matter what, will even take over comparative strangers because toward that particular person, it could be a relative or not, they feel a very special relationship, and they are that kind of person.

Individuals in the group can gradually become open to personal relationships. They can learn to help each other through the working out of feelings and emotions about their aged parents.

J.L.: I think E. was just a little bit too emotionally caught up last week.

E.M.: I was going to be very quiet this week. I felt I dumped my load last week.

SOCIAL WORKER: I'm interested in what you're saying. You think she was too emotionally caught up?

J.L.: More so than previous times. Normally, she isn't like that.

E.M.: I know. I had a trying week. I thought, "Oh, marvelous. I'll go cry on somebody's shoulder." Three shoulders yet. And be comforted. And everybody can say, "There, there," and go away feeling better. There's a lot to be said for that. Even if you're wrong—I think I said last week—even if you are totally wrong in feeling put upon. Let's say you're feeling sorry for yourself and you are wrong, you should exercise a little more self-control.

What I was trying to say last week is that I wasn't feeling guilty because I was upset. I felt I had a right to be upset. The thing that was so frustrating was there was no way out of it. There's no changing mother. I'm trying to diet, and my only solace, up to these meetings, for getting any gratification to combat the feeling of "the whole world is against me" has been eating.

Anxiety, weakness, and conflict may be revealed, and criticism of the program staff expressed:

J.L.: I don't want to leave him to live on his own. I'm afraid of what may or may not happen the time when I'm out of the house. You feel, not exactly guilty, but you're always assuming something may happen. Just when I'm taking time off to maybe enjoy myself, I think, "Oh,"—it isn't a guilt. Maybe it is—I don't know. See, I don't even go out because if I were to go out, in my mind . . .

E.M.: It would take away from *your* enjoyment to a degree.

SOCIAL WORKER: I think it's helpful for everybody in the group to know the added pressure that you have in your situation so that when we come back, week after week, we'll know.

J.L.: Why? When other people get involved, when too many people get involved, this can cause me personal pressure. Even social workers, meaningful as they are, sometimes don't understand. I was talking to one of the staff yesterday. He said, "What movies have you been to lately?" You know? What movies! He doesn't see that my social life is cut off. There are so many reasons that I just can't afford to socialize and get involved. I mean, I cannot cope with it. Taking care of an elderly person and having a social life! I would have to be obligated or compelled in some way. I got this request—to come to this meeting—this simple request—and I came. I have the free time, practically, and I came. This is the only time I will allow.

H.W.: Before we lose these points, you touched on two things so far: the guilt feeling of going out, even when you can, and the second thing, these so-called do-gooders who do more harm than good.

J.L.: Oh, I'm not saying, "do harm."

H.W.: Rub you the wrong way.

J.L.: No, but I feel as though I'm living in a vacuum. I have to be available to the social workers, I have to wait for them, be at home when they're coming. I mean, I have a life too—I want them to understand me.

The group process, therefore, offers potential benefits not only to the relatives but to staff members as well. It reveals to us aspects of our behavior which are insensitive and gives us the opportunity to achieve that valuable lesson, humility.

THE SOCIAL WORKER AS TEAM MEMBER

Relationship to Co-workers

The functions of the social worker go beyond the important but limited matter of making phone calls and filling out forms. Social workers help set

123

the tone for the entire program, for the thinking and conduct of associates, because the profession has as its primary concern respect for the worth and dignity of every human being. Social workers are attuned to the idea, perhaps more than are doctors and nurses, that each individual must have the opportunity to realize his or her maximum potential.[40] Social workers are advocates for the patient rather than for the system.

In the Chelsea–Village Program a consistent effort is made to create a harmonious meshing of social work, nursing, and medical functions. The benefits and difficulties of team formation are discussed fully in Chapter 8. Let us note here that because all team members in the program share the same goals, equal status for each professional person obtains fairly well. And yet, of course, there are difficulties.

From the social worker's viewpoint the major conflict concerns the patient's right to self-determination. This position sometimes conflicts with the doctor's attitude that physical well-being takes first priority.[41] The nurse stands somewhere in the middle. The following Chelsea–Village Program case report is pertinent.

The patient was a 79-year-old man with terminal carcinoma of the lung, living alone. Prior to our arrival, he had refused offers of help. Our first visit was on a Friday. It was apparent that the man was near death and might die over the weekend. The doctor said, "Let's call the ambulance." The nurse told the patient, "We're calling the ambulance now." The social worker moved to his bedside and said, "We'd like to call the ambulance. Is that alright with you?"

The man responded weakly, "I'm not in the mood. Have it come Monday." She said: "The doctor feels you may not make it to Monday." The patient: "I'll stay here this weekend and maybe take some rest." The doctor felt we should move him to the hospital anyway. The social worker thought that he knew he was dying and wanted to die at home. The nurse acknowledged the impossibility of the situation. When the ambulance arrived on Monday the man was dead.

Value of Teamwork to the Patient

Through teamwork, comprehensive care can be provided to patients. It is possible, by professional collaboration, to organize the treatment of highly complex social-medical problems. Older people who are feeble, confused, and alone are often incapable of acting as their own contractor of services. The team gives to the patient the major advantage of being a single source for all benefits.

In addition, in the Chelsea–Village Program, many people know the patient, and are available. We provide both accessibility and continuity.

124

SUMMARY

Home health care programs depend upon the skill of the social worker for community organization, group and casework, within the team structure. Equally important, social workers use their knowledge and experience to review continuously the goals and achievements of the program, maintain an active influence on policy, and are responsible for guiding the efforts of all staff members toward the basic purpose of helping older people remain safe and independent in their own homes.

REFERENCES

1. Forman LH: The physician and the social worker. Am Fam Physician 13:90, 1976
2. Weber RE, Blenkner M: The social service perspective. In Sherwood S (ed): Long-term Care: A Handbook for Researchers, Planners, and Providers. New York, Spectrum Publications, 1975, pp 253–313
3. Sharkey HB: Sustaining the aged in the community. Soc Work 7:18, 1962
4. Brody EM, Brody SJ: Decade of decision foɪ the elderly. Soc Work 19:544, 1974
5. Berl F: Growing up to old age. Soc Work 8:85, 1973
6. Cohen RG: Outreach and advocacy in the treatment of the aged. Soc Casework 55:271, 1974
7. Meyer CH: Social Work Practice. New York, Free Press, 1970
8. Hamilton G: Theory and Practice of Social Casework. New York, Columbia University Press, 1951, p 24
9. Lowy L: The group in social work with the aged. Soc Work 7:43, 1962
10. Brager G, Specht H: Community Organizing. New York, Columbia University Press, 1973, p 27
11. Perlman HH: Social work methods: a review of the past decade. In Trends in Social Work Practice and Knowledge. Anniversary Symposium. New York, National Association of Social Workers, 1966, Vol 10, pp 94–95
12. Dunham A: The New Community Organization. New York, Thomas Y. Cromwell, 1970, p 6
13. Perlman HH: The problem-solving model in social casework. In Roberts RW, Nee RH (eds): Theories of Social Casework. Chicago, University of Chicago Press, 1970, p 137
14. Hollis F: Casework, A Psychosocial Therapy. New York, Random House, 1972, p 261
15. Hollis F: The psychosocial approach to casework. In Roberts RW, Nee RH (eds): Theories of Social Casework. Chicago, University of Chicago Press, 1970
16. Rawlinson HL: Planning home care services. Hospitals 49:66, 1975
17. Trager B: Home care, providing the right to stay home. Hospitals 49:93, 1975
18. Wilson EH: The integration of hospital and local authority services in the discharge of patients from hospitals. Hospitals 48:113, 1974
19. Sillen J, Parker B, Mitchik E, Feldshuh B, Frosch W: A Multi-disciplinary Geriatric Unit for the Psychiatrically Impaired in Bellevue Hospital Center. New York,

Bellevue Geriatric Evaluation and Service Unit, Psychiatric Division, Bellevue Hospital Center, 1972

20. Quinn JL: Triage: coordinated home care for the elderly. Nurs Outlook 23:570, 1975
21. Austin MJ: A network of help for England's elderly. Soc Work 2:114, 1976
22. Freed AO: The family agency and the kinship system of the elderly. Soc Casework 56:579, 1975
23. Denes Z: Old age emotions. J Am Geriatr Soc 24:465, 1976
24. Bennett R: Social isolation and isolation-reducing programs. Bull NY Acad Med 49:1143, 1973
25. Strauss AL: Social isolation. In Strauss, AL (ed): Chronic Illness and the Quality of Life. St. Louis, Mosby, 1975
26. Carlson S: Communication and social interaction in the aged. Nurs Clin North Am 7:269, 1972
27. Pincus A: Reminiscence in aging and its implications for social work practice. Soc Work 15:47, 1970
28. Liton J, Olstein S: Therapeutic aspects of reminiscing. Soc Casework 50:263, 1969
29. Raskind MA, Alvarez C, Pietrzyk M, Westerlund K, Herlin S: Helping the elderly psychiatric patient in crisis. Geriatrics 31:51, 1976
30. Epstein LF, Simon A: Alternatives to state hospitalization for the geriatric mentally ill. Am J Psychiatry 124:955, 1968
31. Lipscomb CF: The care of the psychiatrically disturbed elderly patient in the community. Am J Psychiatry 127:8, 1971
32. Windle C, Scully D: Community mental health centers and the decreasing use of state mental hospitals. Community Ment Health J 12:239, 1976
33. Kirk SA: Effectiveness of community services for discharged mental hospital patients. Am J Orthopsychiatry 46:646, 1976
34. Silverman AG, Kahn FH, Anderson G: A model for working with multigenerational families. Soc Casework 58:131, 1977
35. Simos BG: Adult children and their aging parents. Soc Work 18:78, 1973
36. Social Work Practice. National Conference on Social Welfare. New York, Columbia University Press, 1962, p 177
37. Spoor JM: Terminal illness, some facts and feelings. Soc Work Today 5:702, 1975
38. Weisberg LM: Casework with the terminally ill. Soc Casework 55:337, 1974
39. Lebow GH: Facilitating adaptation in anticipatory mourning. Soc Casework 57:458, 1976
40. Pincus A: Toward a developmental view of aging for social work. Soc Work 12:31, 1967
41. Halliburton P: Doctors and social workers. Lancet 2:1320, 1974

CHAPTER 8

HOW TO MAKE HEALTH TEAMS WORK

Health care for homebound, aged people is complex. The multifaceted problems presented by these patients—medical, psychological, financial—are ordinarily beyond the capacity of a single health worker to handle. The combined skills of physicians, social workers, and nurses, working together, are necessary for effective service to patients.[1-4]

This chapter defines teamwork and discusses methods of team formation. It considers the benefits of teams to patient care and the advantages to staff members of the personal and professional interrelationships produced.

The creation of teams, both through a planned didactic process and through the learning-by-doing approach, is reviewed, and the characteristics of good team members are clarified. How to maintain effectiveness over a long time span is considered.

DEFINITION

The home health care team is a group of individuals working together, pooling skills and techniques, with the ultimate purpose of helping patients achieve complex goals. Through teamwork, separate and distinct professional functions are coordinated.

Through the coordinating process, the different professions come together, focusing on the individual as a whole in terms of his total environment and his total problem. The full force of the contributions of the disciplines can be brought to bear only in relation to each other.[5]

127

The use of health teams for this group of lost patients is a recent development, but the team concept in medicine is not. The team approach is a phrase used so commonly, in fact, that it has become a cliché. "We have unconsciously accepted not only the validity of the approach but also the premise that bringing together a group of different disciplines results in teamwork. It has become a platitude almost without meaning."[6]

Distinct goals must be established. The measure of team effectiveness is the success with which these goals are met. Success does not mean simply that there is a high level of camaraderie and good spirit among team members, although this is one of several vital factors. Teamwork, the product of this kind of intercommunication, must result in a practical application to the needs of the patient before it can be considered effective.

The possibility of poor teamwork exists, of course, and is easy to recognize: "Unnecessary duplication of effort; incomplete or forgotten tasks; team members pulling in different directions; team decisions not being followed up; grumbling behind the scenes; team meetings—less than satisfactory; sloppy verbal communication; and incomplete charts."[7]

Teams are made up of individuals. By working together, the combined skills of the group can produce a quality of service to patients which is greater than the sum of its parts.[8, 9]

THE BENEFITS OF TEAMWORK:
PERSONAL AND PROFESSIONAL GROWTH

For professional skills to be combined effectively there must be respect and harmony among staff members. It is wise to realize that there may exist destructive forces which can ruin the team. Only by recognizing such universal problems as the history of antagonistic relationships between professions, [10-13] the natural human tendency to resist giving up power, [14] the painfulness of sharing personal feelings with others,[15] and the complexities of partnership[16-19] can they be resolved. Then, through teamwork, grave difficulties in the care of patients can be overcome.

An important aspect of maturity is the ability to recognize one's own limitations. The bravado and insolence of youth commonly mask insecurity. Rigidity of professional behavior and the drawing of arbitrary distinctions between what nurses, doctors, and social workers are permitted to do are no different. Participation in a home health care program for aged people provides a grand opportunity for learning humility, the limitations of medicine, the childishness lying behind restrictive departmental rules, and the value of teamwork. In the same sense that mankind can

128

thrive only when the benefits of interdependence are recognized, so can these programs function only when people are willing to join their strengths.

Numerous slogans and aphorisms make the same point:

E pluribus unum
Gentlemen, if we don't hang together we shall all
   certainly hang separately.[20]
In union there is strength.

Work in home health care tests these truisms, measures them against the realities of daily work.

The defenses we each create to protect ourselves as individuals: our bodies, our privacy, our personal secrets, our petty shames and embarrassments, are often less necessary as we get older. We begin to recognize that our own problems in these areas are very much like those of others, that feelings of guilt we may be harboring are foolish and unnecessary, that it is safe to confide in people we have learned to trust, and that we can be more effective as human beings if we free ourselves from these restraints. This is what makes a good marriage. The same set of factors holds true in professional interrelationships. Our growth as health workers relates not only to our ability to understand the practical, factual aspects of our professions. We also grow as we learn to measure the value of the arbitrary guidelines established between the various disciplines and to cross these lines, with all necessary courtesy, when it is in the interests of our patients.

This major point—that the interests of the patient come first—is often forgotten as we proceed through our lives. If we are fortunate, we develop insights into our own professional behavior, in the same manner as we do in our personal lives, which permit growth. The tight bind of the guild mentality—that the rules of the profession take precedence over the needs of society—can be relaxed to an appropriate degree as we gain confidence. When this time of maturity arrives, it is possible to become an effective team member. The joining together of skilled people, when they are ready, makes a good professional marriage.

FORMING THE TEAM

People working in the health field inevitably enter into a team relationship carrying with them a feeling of partisanship about their own discipline and preconceived, stereotyped ideas about other professionals, as for example: *Doctors are arrogant. Nurses are servile. Social workers are hidden away, pushing papers.*

Furthermore, we cannot ignore the fact that at present most physicians are men, and most nurses and social workers women. For a group of people to become a team, sexual attitudes of dominance and subservience and the anger and competitiveness they produce must be faced and then put aside.[10]

The establishment of a new health delivery system, like any other new social undertaking, requires a period of trial, adaptation, education, and retrial which produces considerable turmoil before the system can be expected to function smoothly.[1]

People with experience have suggested two models to guide the formation of effective teams. The didactic approach includes a substantial amount of theoretical teaching of group dynamics and group sessions in which team members can face potential problems together. In this system, theory precedes practice. The alternative method—learning by doing—requires that the program organizers employ people who have particular personal and professional qualities and put them directly in contact with patients. The individuals are molded into a team by the pressure of work.

Didactic Team Formation

Training is indispensible to effective team formation, according to this viewpoint.[7, 21-23]

The classic example of didactic team formation is seen at the Martin Luther King Health Center in New York and the associated Institute for Health Team Development.[24]

Experiences at the King Center show the evolution of teams from the original disease-oriented medical concept to the patient-directed model. The former consisted of physicians and his/her assistants. The latter makes use of an interdisciplinary group, with medical, nursing, psychological, and other skills.

The rationale for extensive preliminary training and team practice is as follows:

It is naive to bring together a highly diverse group of people and expect that, by calling them a team, they will in fact behave as a team. It is ironic indeed to realize that a football team spends 40 hours a week practicing teamwork for the two hours on Sunday afternoon when their teamwork really counts. Teams in organizations seldom spend two hours per year practicing when their ability to function as a team counts 40 hours per week.[25]

This view emphasizes that there are specific team membership and team leadership skills which must be learned. The training of team members requires understanding of organizational psychology, organizational development, and group dynamics. Team development at the King Center included employment of outside consultants, experts in these fields, to train staff members.

Subject matters for this kind of training include:

Understanding the team's purpose
Understanding the community in which it works
Cultural background of team members
Relationship between the institutions and the community
Role expectation
Leadership
Methods of communication
Norm structure (the unwritten rules which govern the group)
Managing conflict

The King Clinic has been successful in producing effective teams, and, in addition, the Institute for Health Team Development has been a fruitful resource for institutions elsewhere who wish advice about this kind of training.

Learning by Doing

It is also possible to develop good teamwork by on-the-job training.[2, 26-28] Experienced professional staff members must be employed—people known to be intelligent, compassionate, and easy to work with through past association.

If teams are created in this way, the time and energy which would otherwise be spent in training and confrontation can be placed instead into direct patient care. Problems that develop can be reviewed in staff meetings. This process has the attractive advantage of emphasizing the needs of patients, rather than those of staff members, and, further, it concentrates upon the real functions of the team. "There is . . . no stimulus like the hint of a coming practical application."[29]

The proper choice of personnel is the preeminent need for success in forming effective home health care teams.

A standard level of professional competence is assumed. Substantial experience taking care of sick people is equally important, and particular aspects of personality and character are essential, as shown in this excerpt from a Chelsea–Village Program staff conference.

ATTENDING DOCTOR: There's something different about this group of people, and if we're different than the average group of health workers, how did we happen to get together in this way?

ELIZABETH HEALY (Social Worker): There is an overriding philosophy in the program that is well communicated when you're first introduced to it. People are either turned on by that philosophy or not.

IRMA STAHL (Social Worker):   Motivation. We all came with a specific interest in this work. We *want* to be here.

JAMES JANESKI (Social Worker):   My feeling is that we have looked at what works. We have always sought out staff members with very strong human values, people who are not autocratic or rigid. We're not always right, but. . . .

ATTENDING DOCTOR: We rarely have had an error in recruitment. Of the two nurses who left—and they were wonderful people—I recognize now that they were too immature to stand the emotional agony of seeing all those patients in distress. They were just out of nursing school.

By and large, we have been successful in attracting to us people who are humanistic. This was partly deliberate, partly intuitive. Once the core of the program was formed, newer people have coalesced around it, the way a crystal is formed.

To summarize, the personal and professional qualities that appear important in selecting people to work in home health care teams are the following:

Self-assurance

Willingness to accept criticism (insecure people make poor team members)

Personal warmth, flexibility, tolerance, and a sense of humor (all needed for the required give-and-take of team work)

Professional experience and skill (the patients and co-workers must be able to depend upon the judgment of each team member)

A humanistic outlook (the needs of the individual patient come first, before those of the staff, of the institution, and of the bureaucracies)

IS THERE TRUE TEAMWORK?
THE PROBLEM OF LEADERSHIP

Teamwork carries the implication that people are working together and communicating effectively with each other. The concept of health teams with which we started the Chelsea–Village Program in 1973 may well no longer be valid in the fifth year of the program; or so we wonder.

It is right to question the original goals, and modification may be required. Human beings and the societies they form are dynamic, constantly changing. Unless the program changes to meet newly recognized needs of patients and staff, it will become anachronistic, outdated, ineffectual, and then fail.

Some form of leadership is necessary. Without a guiding force, organization of care for patients cannot succeed. The questions: Who is the leader? Shall leadership be hierarchic (imposed from above) or egalitarian (equally available from any team member)?

Our work in the Chelsea–Village Program is based on the egalitarian model of leadership because this best meets the requirements of our patients. We recognize that the differing skills of our staff members may be called into use at varying times. Therefore leadership must be correlated with the actual condition of the patient and the needs that are paramount at the moment.[30]

We ask of our staff members that they be equally ready to wield or to yield authority.

The original ideal was to create teams of professional people with different skills who would function coequally. They would work toward cohesive, rankless decision making. But we understood from the start that no ideal is ever reached and that we could not provide a Garden of Eden for our staff to work in. The ideal would have required that we not function as normal human beings but instead be some kind of ethereal creatures who had no personal ambition, no neurotic qualities, no professional or personal sense of rivalry.

The following transcripts of conferences, held in the fourth year of the Chelsea–Village Program, concern our attempt to evaluate our success or failure in forming teams.

ATTENDING DOCTOR: How closely have we approached the ideal that our three professions and ourselves as individuals can be melded? Can we function without getting into a superior and inferior position in relationship to each other? Can we exert our own skills fairly well, without having the nurse, for instance, in the clichéd situation of traveling along behind the doctor doing the scut work? And how effectively have the social workers had their own ideas

133

considered honestly and fairly by other members of the team, rather than have the doctor end up being the boss?

SISTER TERESITA (Nurse):   I think I feel on an equal footing. Obviously, the disciplines are different, the knowledge is different, but my experience has been that the doctors generally respect what I say, and I certainly listen to what they say, and the social workers also.

ELLEN QUIRKE (Social Worker):   I have real conflict with doctors only if our patients are hospitalized. I've had two examples of physicians on the hospital wards saying to me, very arbitrarily, that one of our patients should be sent to a nursing home on discharge from the hospital. It's not easy for me to tell the doctors that I disagree with them, that this program can take care of the patient.

On the program my reaction to the doctors is a little different. Here medical matters are not the central issue, the way they seem to be within the hospital. With our patients, social, medical, and nursing needs are considered in combination. The way the doctor sees the nurse and social worker is different also. With our doctors there's a certain feeling; it comes from having been through tough experiences. There's a feeling of mutual respect because we've been there together.

ATTENDING DOCTOR: I understand that you feel relatively at ease in relating professionally to other people. It's really a different question about whether we function as a team. Do you think we fulfill the team's criteria of intercommunication, with practical application to direct care of patients?

IRMA STAHL: I feel that communication between team members could be improved. Some of the problems are within the team: too busy to have conferences, the logistics, the location. Considering the obstacles, though, I think we do famously. Patient care continues on very well despite the problems, because I think there are a lot of sharp people who see to it that things get worked out.

ATTENDING DOCTOR: All right. You've given a practical example of a problem. It hasn't been possible to carry out the idea of having the three team members of each day meet to discuss the cases afterward. Everyone's too busy.

SISTER TERESITA: I may be coming in with blood that I have to run up to the lab. The social worker may not have gone on the visit at all because she knows the patient and is working on other matters. The doctor probably has to rush back to a sick patient in the hospital.

STAHL: There are certain cases that present real challenges to coordination.

The difficulties of getting team members together for case conferences needed to be worked out. The fact that this problem exists indicates in part a maturing process taking place within the program. Originally we

134

insisted that all three professionals come on every visit, and it was easy to discuss cases informally enroute back to the hospital. Later, it was clear that many visits by the social worker were redundant. We had enough self-confidence and flexibility to change.

By freeing the social worker of wasted visits, however, we created the new problem: difficulty in getting together for case review. This was solved by establishing a regular but informal early morning conference each day. The plan works but has created yet another issue: too many meetings take time away from patient care. And so it goes . . .

A program which relies upon team work, to be durable, must be dynamic. As new problems appear and as perceptions alter team members must be ready to change. Flexibility is essential.

MAINTAINING THE TEAM APPROACH

Once the team has been formed, it must sustain itself over an indefinite span of time. An initial burst of enthusiasm is not sufficient for this purpose. New problems may appear and, in fact, should be expected. Proper growth of the team requires that a sense of personal and professional support be developed among the staff, the feeling that every person on the team can be relied on.

Teams can fail, cease to function. Programs can stop, patients be abandoned. The common causes for failure are clear: power struggles between individuals, disagreement over professional duties and divisions of functions, losing sight of the original goals of the program.[31] Anticipation of problems may prevent failure.

Support of Associates

Each member of the health care team has particular qualities to contribute.[32] Doctors, for instance, provide obvious diagnostic and therapeutic resources, and these skills are essential not only for the benefit of the sick patient but also for the doctor's associates. The nurse and social worker have the right to count upon the physician for guidance in medical matters, for understanding of how physical factors contribute to the complicated network of difficulties which the usual patient faces. In addition, the doctor must supply a fair share of psychological strength to the team. Without mutual support, the ability to be effective disintegrates.

It is easy to become overwhelmed by the challenges of this kind of patient, to become callous, supercilious, or to quit.

If the team members work together, however, and can rely safely upon

135

each other, complex problems in patient care can be resolved, even in the most deplorable of circumstances, as shown in this Chelsea–Village Program staff conference transcript.

ATTENDING DOCTOR: One of our first cases, Mrs. M.V., an aged woman with severe chronic lung disease, made me ask, "What the hell are we doing here, anyway?" We satisfied ourselves that her living situation was just too awful to let her stay. She seemed to feel that way also. But she wouldn't leave for the hospital.

SISTER TERESITA (Nurse): The first two times we went there she was covered with urine and feces. Zora (program homemaker) went to clean her and Mrs. V. let her help. That was unusual. She was more likely to say something like, "Leave me alone. Who called you? I don't need you people. GO!" And we always did, but we kept coming back. The three of us practically had to hold each other by the hand. Nobody else would see her anymore. She managed to get the visiting nurses out, and they never came back. The neighbors tried once, and they never came back either.

About the fifth time we went, she broke into tears and said, "Besides being nasty, how can I say thank you?" After that she was very sweet.

ATTENDING DOCTOR: She was willing to listen to a rational discussion of her illness and seemed to trust us. Now she was willing to enter the hospital. It seems, looking back, that because Sister and I believed that together we could help Mrs. V., she finally believed it too.

Making Communication Easy

Making it easy for staff members to talk with each other is clearly essential to good health of the team. Communication methods can be formal—witness regular staff conferences—but must extend as well into every aspect of the daily professional life of the staff. Willingness to talk, to listen, to understand, to react are vital.

The merit of easy communication is, of course, improved quality of patient care through use of the combined skill and experience of team members. An example of the decision-making process is seen in this staff conference transcript (the patient under discussion is an 85-year-old woman, living alone, who has begun to display psychotic behavior):

BARBARA RUETHER (Coordinator): I got a call yesterday from a neighbor. Miss Q. manages to get herself out into the hallway and screams that she wants to murder somebody.

ATTENDING DOCTOR: Obviously we need an immediate psychiatric evaluation.

136

ELLEN QUIRKE (Social Worker):   What's the point of having the psychiatrist go up there? If he wanted to give her medication, she wouldn't take it, and she absolutely will refuse to come out of the apartment to be hospitalized, although I think she should be.

ATTENDING DOCTOR: Do you believe that hospitalizing this woman would do anything except make her worse?

QUIRKE: Well, what can be done for her in her home? She will not trust anyone.

ATTENDING DOCTOR: What do you mean?

SISTER TERESITA (Nurse):   She is really paranoid. According to her, the roaches got into her apartment because the superintendent brought in two big bottles of them and dumped them. Also, it's Ellen's fault (social worker) that there are bedbugs, and that Irma (social worker) stole $2,000 from her. I really do believe she needs to be hospitalized.

QUIRKE: But how can we get her in? We'd almost have to have a straightjacket.

SISTER TERESITA: The ambulance drivers cannot take a patient against her will. One way of arranging this would be for a doctor to request the police to help. The police can force the patient to be taken if a doctor says it is necessary for the patient's interest.

ATTENDING DOCTOR: Now, wait a minute. Let's not leap to conclusions here. What really makes you think the problem is that urgent?

QUIRKE: She keeps a scissors by her bed, and she keeps a knife by her bed. She came after Alice (homemaker) with an icepick the other day. Alice really has a bad time, between the roaches, the screaming, and the icepick.

ATTENDING DOCTOR: Well, obviously, the ideal homemaker for somebody like this is a blind, deaf woman with a bulletproof vest.

SISTER TERESITA: Come on now, Doctor, let's concentrate on doing something practical for this patient.

ATTENDING DOCTOR: It seems to me, on balance, that her situation at home is untenable. Suppose I ask one of the hospital psychiatrists to go with you, Ellen. As quickly as possible. Let's see what he thinks. If we finally decide that she should be hospitalized, it can be done through the police, as Sister suggested. She could be placed on medication and maybe improve enough so we could help her come back home.

By means of open communication between staff members, the rigidities and misunderstandings that exist between the professional disciplines can in part be counteracted. This staff conference transcript is pertinent.

ATTENDING DOCTOR: We've been doing this work for over four years. We

137

tried to establish the program without any formal attempt at educating our-selves as teams and going through a course in psychodynamics, and so forth, but there are certain obvious areas where the potential for conflict between staff members exists. I guess the major such area is between the doctor and the nurse, who do not normally work in teams. The nurse is trained in school and on the floor to be subservient; the doctor is trained to be the boss. The social worker, the poor thing, is usually thought of as being off in a corner, writing a letter or on the telephone. She certainly is not thought of as a member of the team either, and she's not a source of conflict because nobody ever sees her except maybe over a coffee once a week in the dining room. So the situation in which we find ourselves is unusual. How effectively are you able to work as a member of this kind of team?

JEFFREY STALL (Medical Resident): Well, I see myself as the number three person in the hierarchy.

F. RUSSELL KELLOGG (Fellow in Community Medicine): Well, that solves *that* problem!

STALL: I see my role as subservient to nursing and social service. In this age group, given the problems of being old and living in New York City, social workers have the most to give. Probably because of the limits on medical therapy for the aged . . .

MARC SHERMAN (Fellow in Community Medicine): So you consider yourself third by definition of what you provide, but in another way I think the doctor's first. The doctor organizes and keeps everything together.

MICHAEL GARVEY (Medical Resident): That's not necessarily true. Often the nurse or the social worker has more insight into the patient's total needs than I do. Any one of us may be the person to put it all together. It depends on the particular case.

ATTENDING DOCTOR: Chris, do you see any difference in your relationship with doctors and social workers in this program, compared to your previous work?

CHRISTINE VITARELLA (Nurse): Remember, I was a nurse on the ward. A patient might come to my desk and say "I need my check," and I would say, "I'll get hold of the social worker." That was my idea of her work, get a check, arrange for a nursing home bed, and that was the end of it. Here it's all different. First, I watched in the morning, and now I sit in on the informal meetings. I've watched how Sister Teresita puts in a little medical informa-tion, and Irma or Ellen some social feedback, and together they'll find a solution. That's the team approach.

WORKING TOGETHER—WORKING SEPARATELY

The program and the patients will thrive if staff members work together and will shrivel and die without cooperation and team feeling.

A man we know was given the unusual opportunity to take a guided tour of heaven and hell. In hell he found masses of pitiful creatures, starved and emaciated. Tables of delicious food were just within reach, but they were prohibited from eating because their outstretched arms were held rigid by long metal forks. They could not bend their elbows to feed themselves. In heaven, the setup was the same, but the people were happy, cheerful, healthy, and well-nourished. Our friend asked his guide to explain the difference. "Simple," he said. "In heaven they feed each other."

REFERENCES

1. Beloff JS, Korper M: The health team model and medical care utilization. JAMA 219:359, 17, 1972
2. McHugh JG, Chughtai MA: The importance of team work in geriatric care. Nurs Times 71:140, 1975
3. Bakst HJ, Marra EF: Experience with home care for cardiac patients. Am J Public Health 45:444, 1955
4. Katz S, Vignos PJ, Moskowitz RJ, Thompson HM, Suec KH: Comprehensive outpatient care in rheumatoid arthritis. JAMA 206:1249, 1968
5. Katz S, Halstead L, Wierenga M: A medical perspective of team care. In Sherwood S (ed): Long-term Care: A Handbook for Researchers, Planners, and Providers. New York, Spectrum Publications, 1975, Chap 5, p 222
6. Garrett JF: Social psychology of teamwork. In Harrower MR (ed): Medical and Psychological Teamwork in the Care of the Chronically Ill. Springfield, Thomas, 1955
7. Rubin IM, Fry R, Plovnick M: Improving the Coordination of Care: A Program for Health Team Development. Cambridge, Mass, Ballinger, 1975
8. Reader GC: Organization and development of a comprehensive care program. Am J Public Health 44:760, 1954
9. Bartlett H: Social Work Practice in the Health Field. New York, National Association of Social Workers, 1961, p 226
10. Record JC, Greenlick MR: New health professional and the physician role: an hypothesis from Kaiser experience. Public Health Rep 90:241, 1975
11. Mullaney JW, Fox RA, Liston MF: Clinical nurse specialist and social worker —clarifying the roles. Nurs Outlook 22:712, 1974
12. Bates B: Physician and nurse practitioner: conflict and reward. Ann Intern Med 82:702, 1975
13. Somers AR: Redefinition of professional roles to assure personalized care. In Health Care in Transition: Directions for the Future. Chicago, Hospital Research and Educational Trust, 1971
14. Shakespeare W: Julius Caesar
15. Salinger JD: Catcher in the Rye. New York, Modern Library, 1958
16. Glass MM: Potash and Perlmutter: Their Copartnership Ventures and Adventures. New York, Grosset & Dunlap, 1911
17. Scullard HH: From the Gracchi to Nero; A History of Rome from 133 BC to AD 68. London, Methuen, 1959, pp 109–173

18. Clough AH (ed): Plutarch's Lives, Life of Pompey and Life of Caesar. Boston, Little, Brown, 1882, Vol 4, pp 50–152, pp 256–329
19. Plaut TF: Portrait of a health care team. In Wise H (ed): Making Health Teams Work. Cambridge, Mass, Ballinger, 1974
20. Parton J: Life and Times of Benjamin Franklin. Boston and New York, Houghton, Mifflin, Cambridge, Mass, Riverside Press, 1864, Vol 2
21. Silver GA: Foreword. In Wise H (ed): Making Health Teams Work. Cambridge, Mass, Ballinger, 1974
22. Rubin IM, Beckhard R: Factors influencing the effectiveness of health teams. Milbank Mem Fund Q 50:317, 1972
23. Friedlander F: The impact of organizational training laboratories upon the effectiveness and interaction of ongoing work groups. Personnel Psychiatry 20:289, 1967
24. Martin Luther King Health Center, 3674 Third Ave, Bronx NY 10456. Institute for Health Team Development, 3329 Rochambeau Ave, Bronx, NY 10467
25. Rubin I: Introduction. In Wise H (ed): Making Health Teams Work. Cambridge, Mass, Ballinger, 1974
26. Simson SP, Bleiweiss LJ, Hertz CG, Storey PB: The development of a primary health care team, a case study from the Penn Urban Health Services Center. Primary Care 1:530, 1974
27. Roth ME, Tarnopoll I: Organization of a coordinated home care program in Erie County, New York. Public Health Rep 82:639, 1967
28. Marsh GN: Primary medical care: the cooperative solution to the volume problem. JAMA 235:45, 1976
29. Flexner A: Medical Education in the United States and Canada. New York, Carnegie Foundation, 1910, p 59
30. Siller J: A summary: delineation of boundaries of professional practice in education. Arch Phys Med Rehabil 52:411, 1971
31 Rothberg JS, Anderson N, Fordyce WE, et al: Interdisciplinary forum. Arch Phys Med Rehabil 52:397, 1971
32. Loeb PM, Robison BJ: Experience of a physician-nurse practitioner team in care of patients in skilled nursing facilities. J Fam Pract 4:727, 1977

CHAPTER 9

THE CHART

A medical chart must be created for each patient receiving home health services. Proper patient care requires first-rate documentation; and this holds as true for community-based programs as for standard hospital inpatient services.

PURPOSES OF THE CHART

The ultimate purpose of the chart is to serve as a tool in the delivery of care. This function is carried out by its use as a device for communication between personnel, repository of data, legal documentation, safekeeping of information, and case review and conferences.

Communication between Personnel

In home health care programs for the aged, complex medical-social issues are commonplace. The professional staff members who know the patients, even if they remain intact as a team throughout the course, are regularly supplemented by other workers. In order for the disparate pieces of data to be usable, they must be written in the chart. An observation not recorded is an observation not made.

Members of the team may understand their mutual tasks initially, but after time passes, aspects of a particular case may be forgotten unless the facts are recorded. Easy retrieval of patient data occurs only if recording is proper, comprehensive, readable, and well organized in the first place.

Furthermore, organization of a network of care for the patient, a necessary task for many aged, homebound people, requires stable and reliable contact between program staff and a number of outside organizations. Flow of information back and forth is constant, and the chart contains it all in a useful, available format, if the staff has done its recording promptly and accurately. The preparation of a request for a homemaker to be supplied by an agency, the service of a visiting nurse, entrance into a Meals-on-Wheels program, change of housing, eligibility for Medicaid—all depend upon financial and other data available in a proper chart.

The chart contains a permanent collection of documents about the patient and his or her problems with the world at large. These must be so filed within the chart that they are physically secure and easily retrievable. The following kinds of documents find their way regularly into our records:

> Letters to and from patients in the program
>
> Copies of our correspondence with outside agencies, such as the Housing Authority, Department of Social Services (home attendants), and with landlords
>
> Documents from government agencies addressed to us or copies of those sent to the patient
>
> Visiting Nurse Service forms, requests for service, and home health service reports
>
> Copies of hospital records; correspondence from previous physicians and other health workers
>
> Copies of diet lists and other medical instructions

These documents, and the contents of the entire chart, must be available as needed. The safekeeping of information is primarily a staff requirement, needed for proper long-term care, in compiling information, preparing reports, and organizing grant requests. In addition, the data may be demanded by auditing agencies, particularly if government funds have been supplied.

A request for a review of a chart can come from unexpected sources as well. One of our records is involved in the case of a disputed will, in which the mental state of the testator at the time the document was drawn is in question.

Legal Documentation

The chart is a legal instrument and can be subpoenaed in case of suit. The best defense to a claim of medical malpractice is denial of liability, and a first-rate chart is an essential tool. Proper documentation can prove that "due care in diagnosis and treatment"[1] was followed.

A chart can sin by omission as well as commission. Completeness of record-keeping is as important as the quality of the notes. As Angela Roddey Holder, JD, puts it[1]:

While proper completion of all records on each patient is obviously time-consuming and probably an active nuisance, a physician who is sued by a patient some considerable time after treatment is terminated will be in a much more favorable position when his records indicate clearly to the court that proper treatment has been given. On the other hand, records which disclose negligent treatment will materially benefit the patient's case. Records which have been altered for any reason, even the most innocent, should always include notations of the date and reason for change. If a negligence suit is filed subsequent to alteration of a record, and that alteration is apparent, it will undoubtedly be construed as a dishonest attempt to avoid liability.

At this writing the Chelsea–Village Program has not been threatened with legal action, but we feel prepared to defend ourselves effectively, in part because we insist on full documentation of all we do.

Case Review and Conferences

The chart is essential for proper case review. Frequently, it is at the time of the conference that the disparate sections of a complex clinical puzzle are pieced together, with the help of the chart as a source of basic information. In a meeting, the chart serves as a physical representation of the patient. The following material from Chelsea–Village Program conferences is pertinent:

DOCTOR: We don't seem to be getting anywhere with Mrs. M. Every time we solve one problem, she comes up with another. We don't seem to be able to satisfy her.

ELLEN QUIRKE (Social Worker): I notice that a year ago, in my first note, I recorded that Mrs. M. said, "Do you really want to know what's wrong with me? I'll start at the top of my head and go all the way down to my toes." That remark indicates how she's carried on throughout, and we could have anticipated our present difficulties from Day 1.

Another case:

ATTENDING DOCTOR: To show the importance of taking a good medical history, one of Mr. T.'s complaints on a visit yesterday was "a burning pain in my abdomen every time I have a bowel movement." I couldn't figure out what this was about. But as I review the chart now, I see that somebody prescribed prune juice three times a day a month ago. I'm sure his colon is irritated.

Raw data from the record may produce insight into patient behavior.

F. RUSSELL KELLOGG (Fellow in Community Medicine): This patient is a relatively young man, in his 60s, whose history dates back several years, when he had a CVA with a residual left hemiplegia. He was in a nursing home for an extended stay and finally signed himself out of the nursing home and managed to get back to his original apartment. He lives in the Trollope Hotel, which is a dive.

ATTENDING DOCTOR: According to the chart his income is $300 a month and the rent is $230.

LAURA STARITA (Coordinator): It's an awful place to pay that much money for. But his chart shows that he thinks living in a dump that takes all his money is preferable to a nursing home.

CHARTING TECHNIQUES

The marks of a first-rate chart are accuracy, brevity without sacrifice of thoroughness, and readability.

Information should be complete and up-to-date. The comments of all members of the professional team should be included, in a continuous manner. They should not be broken up into separate areas for doctor, nurse, and social worker. A continuous charting system permits an easy understanding of the course of events in each case, whereas compartmentalization impedes the flow of data. In addition, allowing all the professional health workers to write comments in the same section enhances teamwork.

All notes should be signed and dated by day, month, and year; and written either on the spot, in the home of the patient, or immediately upon return to the hospital. Prompt reporting imparts all the freshness and immediacy of the information.

THE PHYSICAL STRUCTURE OF THE CHART

The physical material which makes up the chart, portability, proper labeling, and division into useful sections with proper tabulation, are important. While not of much intellectual interest, attention to these points can make significant practical difference to the daily effectiveness of the program.

A home health care program places unusual physical demands upon the chart. Records must be carried along to the patient by the team, rather than allowed to remain behind in the hospital. Therefore, the chart must be unusually sturdy and yet not excessively bulky or heavy.

Our records are enclosed in flexible plastic binders, which serve the purpose adequately. On the outside of the binder is a label with the patient's name and chart number and our program's name, address, and phone number, in case a chart is lost. This potential event has yet to take

144

place because we carry the records for each day in a highly visible bright red case, hard to forget.

The chart is divided into appropriate sections, by tabbed interleaves of heavy paper, as follows:

Medication sheet
Basic data sheet
Comments of coordinator
Professional record—initial history and physical examination form, continuation sheets
Social service work sheets
Laboratory, x-ray, EKG reports ⎫
Correspondence ⎬ These are self-explanatory and not discussed further in this chapter.
Hospital records (copies) ⎭
Computerized printout

Medication Sheet

A flow sheet to record the patient's medications, and to keep up to date, is essential to proper patient care (Fig. 9-1). The hazards of confusion about which drugs have been prescribed, proper dosage, and frequency of use are all controlled by this technique.

Basic Data Sheet

This information is available at the front of the chart in order to facilitate on-the-spot preparation of documents that require basic data, such as prescription blanks, renewal of homemaker service forms, and Visiting Nurse Service requests (Fig. 9-2). The sheet is filled out at the first visit by any of the professional staff members present, or beforehand by the coordinator to the extent possible.

Comments of Coordinator

These comments serve as the introduction of the patient to the professional team. Included is information about the source of referral, degree of urgency, impediments to entering the apartment (key at barber shop downstairs, rotten stairwell, vicious dog), attitude of the patient, and whether special equipment is needed.

145

M. M.

39 - 93 - 30

NAME OF DRUG	DOSAGE	DATE STARTED / STOPPED	NAME—M.D. / NAME—M.D.	NAME—CLINIC / NAME—CLINIC	ADVERSE REACTIONS
Digoxin	.25 mgm T qd	8/10/74	PaB	C.V.P.	
X Hydrodiuril X	50 mgm T qd	8/10/74 / 10/2/75	PaB. / PaB		
X Aldomet X	250 mgm T id	8/10/74 / 1/18/76	PaB / PaB		
X E.T.A X	T tbsp 8 id T HS	1/18/76 / 1/28/76	PaB / PaB		
X Lasix X	40 mgm O.D.	1975 / 11/16/76	PaB / PaB		
KCl 25% Sol	1 tbsp Bid	8/10/74	Aub / Madeira		
X Lasix X	80 mg od	11.16.76 / 2.2.77	Amb / Madeira		
Banana	T od	1975	Amb		
Lasix	40 mg alt 80 mg	2.2.77	Madeira		

FIG. 9-1.   Medication record.

Name__M_____ Program Chart #__0455__
      Last   First   Middle   Hospital Chart#__39-93-30__
Address_____HORATIO St. NYC 10014_Apt#_5L_Telephone#__929-0000__

Date of Birth _7__8__1898__ Sex: (M)_ F__

Referral: Source_HOME CARE, NORA Tolchin_

              Reason for Referral_Homebound_

              Date of Referral_7/30/76_Date of Initial Visit_9/8/76_
              Re-ReFERRAL- 8/27/76 UPON DISCHARGE
Marital Status: S__ M__ W__ D__ Separated_____

Others in Household_____(FRIEND of 42 yRS).

Interpreter needed: Yes__ (No)_

Language Spoken: (English)_ Spanish__ Italian__ Other_____
                                          (write in)

Income - Amount and Source

DSS_____Social Security_$288/mo_other_250_pension_
                                        (Amount) (Source)

Social Security#__000-00-0000__

Medicare#__000-00-0000-A__

Medicaid#__NoT eligible__

DSS Center_____

Previous Medical Care: When_6/20/76 - 8/28/76_

Where_SVH_

For What Problem_BPH / s/p CVA(L)_

Interested Individuals or Agencies

Name(Person or Agency)	Address	Tel. No.	Relationship(Service)
Nora Tolchin		x 1354	Home CARE SVH
Miss HORAN		924-1717	VISITING NURSE

Visiting Team: M.D._Madeira_ R.N._Duque_
            Social Worker_Quirk_

FIG. 9-2. Basic data sheet, SRO Hotel—Chelsea–Village Program.

10/16/75   Patient aged 88 fell September 30 and hurt head. Refuses to come to clinic. Has no regular medical supervision. Neighbor says woman needs assistance but refuses to cooperate. Volunteer from Village Visiting Neighbors will be there when we arrive.

Another case:

4/4/76   75-year-old Danish man with terminal CA of prostate and bony metastases referred by Visiting Nurse Service (VNS) after discharge from (other) hospital. Patient had refused to go to nursing home or to Calvary Hospital. Wanted to die at home.

Patient does not have Medicaid and has no means of transportation to get back to hospital for follow-up care. Was discharged on stilbestrol, and aspirin for pain.

Mrs. B., landlady, has agreed to patient's wish to die at home. She checks patient up to 4 PM, when she goes to work. Her husband also helps out. A VNS aide has been placed five days a week, 11 AM to 1 PM

VNS reports that recently there have been conflicts between landlady, aide, and patient—landlady may have alcohol problem. Patient has been very depressed, refusing to take medications or eat, forbidding aide to shop or cook.

—B.J. Ruether, Coordinator

Professional Record

The initial history and physical examination are recorded on standardized forms which permit considerable freedom of space to the physician. These forms (Figs. 9-3 and 9-4.) are not simplistic check-off devices which stifle insight, and yet they have the benefit of presenting an organized framework in which to write.

In our follow-up records we utilize a problem list and problem-oriented notes, taking advantage of the substantial advances in technique advocated by Dr. Lawrence Weed and others.[2-11] The concept of a problem-oriented medical record (POMR) is particularly applicable and useful in a home health care program for the aged because the problems, in both medical and social areas, are so numerous and challenging. As J. Willis Hurst points out[12].

By enumerating the problems by *numbers* it becomes possible to develop plans that are clearly displayed by use of the same numbers. It becomes possible to write orders that are identified by the same numbers. It also makes it possible to number the items in the progress notes and in the discharge summary in the same way.

In our better records, problems are listed, usually identified by number, and easily followed page-by-page, through the chart. Each note analyzes the problem under discussion by recording subjective (S) and objective (O) information, the staff member's assessment (A) and interpretation of the data, and a plan (P). The SOAP note style, if carried out consistently, creates a structure which promotes ease of communication. In practice, this system is more effective and easier to follow, than is one that uses the

148

**ST. VINCENT'S HOSPITAL
AND MEDICAL CENTER
OF NEW YORK**

**INITIAL HISTORY
AND PHYSICAL EXAMINATION**

DATE	
NAME	
ADDRESS	
AGE	
SEX	
CHART NO.	REG. NO.

Chief Complaint:

Personal History:

Social History:

Family History:

Past History & Illness:
Surgical Procedures, Trauma:

Allergies:

System Review:
Head:

Respiratory:

Cardiac:

Gastrointestinal:

Genitourinary:

Neuromuscular:

Emotional:

FIG. 9-3.   Form for initial history and physical examination.

149

**ST. VINCENT'S HOSPITAL
AND MEDICAL CENTER
OF NEW YORK**

PHYSICAL EXAMINATION FORM

P.   BP.   HT.   WT.   TEMP.

DATE	
NAME	
ADDRESS	
AGE	
SEX	
CHART NO.	REG. NO.

General Appearance:

Skin

Hair:

HEENT:

Neck:

Nodes:

Spine:

Breasts:

Lungs:

Heart:

Abdomen:

Genitalia:

Rectal:

Extremities:

Neurological:

FIG. 9-4.   Physical examination form.

150

traditional essay written out conscientiously by a typically compulsive health worker, and, of course, it is far superior to the illegible scrawl we sometimes see, a product of laziness and lack of consideration.

The following material from Chelsea–Village Program charts may provide useful examples:

Problem List–90-year-old woman–10/25/75 [follows initial history and physical exam]
1. Hypertension
   A — poorly controlled high blood pressure
   P — will start reserpine 0.25 mg bid, Hydrodiuril 50 mg po qd
       Obtain electrolytes, creatinine, urinalysis
       Orange juice 6 ounces daily
2. Arthritis
   A — not severe, apparently worse in past
   P — ASA 0/5 qid prn
       Obtain ANA, rheumatoid factor on next visit
3. Homebound
   A — not strong, cannot get out
   P — obtain homemaker

Return Visit–11/7/75
1. Hypertension
   S — no symptoms
   O — 160/95 right arm sitting
   A — doing well
   P — reserpine 0.25 mg bid
       Hydrodiuril 0.5 q day
       Orange juice, bananas
       Return in six weeks

Return Visit–2/6/76
1. Hypertension
   S — no headache, syncope, chest pain
   O — BP 150/80, P-80, regular
      — Patient alert and oriented. Color good.
      — Heart-rhythm regular, S_1 and S_2 normal, no murmur
   A — good control BP
   P — Rx same

The problem-oriented medical record is a technique, not a substitute for persistent, thoughtful, intelligent medical, nursing, and social service

151

work. As emphasized by Dr. Jefferson Vorzimer,[13] "Finally, a word of caution: the POMR is only a tool—its use does not guarantee high quality care. Placing a paintbrush in someone's hand does not mean he will become a fine artist."

The professional record contains a continuous flow of comments from all the professional staff members who see the patient. Nurse's and social worker's notes are included, although they usually do not follow the problem list format of the physician's comments. We have not as yet succeeded in training all of our staff to use this technique.

It should be noted that we have not required in our charts a standardized method of recording the basic data that are subsequently used for creation of the problem list. A preprinted data base for our kind of patient would be so bulky it would be impractical, and also a heavy psychological burden. "Do you really mean I have to fill out all those papers on every patient? Forget it!" would be a reasonable response.

We collect our data as best we can, often in bad surroundings, from individuals who communicate poorly, without assistance of friends or relatives. With patience, and in due time, we learn what we need to know.

Social Service Work Sheets

Substantial quantities of information are often obtained by our social workers, through counseling sessions and contact with relatives or other agencies. This material may be too lengthy to fit conveniently into the continuation sheet format. It may be several pages in length. Therefore, separate work sheets are utilized and provide our social workers opportunity, without undue restraint, to record data that are critically important to an understanding of the patient.

Computerized Printout

The quantity of information we have available about each patient can become unwieldy and may get lost. We solved this problem by having the material computerized. A simple data form is filled out on each visit, a process that takes no more than 15 to 30 seconds, and a printout results, which is placed in the record. While this technique is, of course, not essential to the conduct of the program, we have found the computer to be a helpful tool.[14] Figure 9-5 is an example.

```
CHELSEA-VILLAGE PROGRAM PATIENT RECORD AS OF    3/18/1977                    PAGE 1

GENERAL INFORMATION

SMITH, JANE                              DOC    BRICKNER
170 8 AVE                                NURSE DUQUE
NEW YORK NY                              SOC W QUIRKE
TELEPHONE NUMBER  999-9999
MEDICARE NUMBER 999 -99 - 9999-A    MEDICAID NUMBER PAOAA- 99999 99- 9- 999
HOSPITAL CHART NUMBER  99- 99- 99        C-V PROGRAM NUMBER 236
PATIENT-S SEX FEMALE
DATE OF BIRTH    7/25/ 1893     DATE OF FIRST VISIT IN PROGRAM   9/16/1974
MARITAL STATUS   WIDOWED             NUMBER OF CHILDREN 4
NUMBER OF BROTHERS  3           NUMBER OF SISTERS 0
FOREIGN BORN
MAJOR NATIONAL ORIGIN      IRISH
SECOND NATIONAL ORIGIN     IRISH
ETHNIC GROUP               IRISH
PRIMARY LANGUAGE   ENGLISH
SECOND LANGUAGE    NONE


HOUSING                          ON ENTRANCE
                                 TO PROGRAM


LOCATION OF UNIT                 CHELSEA
TYPE OF UNIT                     APARTMENT
FITNESS FOR HUMAN HABITATION     BORDERLINE
FITNESS FOR PATIENT              BORDERLINE
NUMBER OF ROOMS IN UNIT          4
TELEPHONE                        NOT IN UNIT
BATHROOM                         IN UNIT
COOKING FACILITIES               NOT IN UNIT
ELEVATOR                         NONE 6 FLIGHTS
ENTERED CURRENT UNIT IN          1937
ENTERED CURRENT NEIGHBORHOOD IN  1937
                                 MOVE NEEDED--PATIENT REFUSES


ROOMMATES
NUMBER OF PEOPLE IN UNIT 1
ROOMMATE TYPE 1          NONE
ROOMMATE TYPE 2          NONE
ROOMMATE TYPE 3          NONE


MEDICAL
CAUSE OF HOMEBOUNDEDNESS  CARDIAC DISEASE
PREVIOUS SOURCE OF MEDICAL CARE    SVH
REASON FOR LACK OF CONTACT    PATIENT BECAME HOMEBOUND
PATIENT IS NOT AN ALCOHOLIC
PATIENT IS NOT A DRUG ADDICT
PATIENT IS SEMI-AMBULATORY


APPLIANCES USED CURRENTLY
CANE
APPLIANCES USED BEFORE C-V PROGRAM BUT NOT CURRENTLY
NONE
NUMBER OF PRE C-V PROGRAM HOSPITALIZATIONS IS    1
```

FIG. 9-5.   Computer printout of patient data. (Continued)

PROBLEMS IN CHARTING

The difficulties we face in achieving the perfect chart are in part due to the nature of our program, in part the natural consequence of human frailty.

1. Because the records of the Chelsea–Village Program are kept separate from the standard St. Vincent's Hospital charts, information that

```
CAUSE 1   UNCLASSIFIED NEUROLOGICAL
CAUSE 2   NONE
`AUSE 3   NONE
NUMBER OF HOSPITALIZATIONS IN C-V PROGRAM IS       0
CAUSE 1   NONE
CAUSE 2   NONE
C JSE 3   NONE

FINANCIAL
INCOME PER MONTH FROM WELFARE IS $     0
                 SOCIAL SECURITY IS $  193
                        FAMILY IS $     0
                      PENSIONS IS $    50
       SAVINGS AND INVESTMENTS IS $     0
                 OTHER SOURCES IS $     0
         TOTAL INCOME PER MONTH IS $  243
COST PER MONTH OF HOUSING AND UTILITIES IS       $  75
COST PER MONTH OF FOOD IS                        $  60
COST PER MONTH OF TELEPHONE IS                   $  13
COST PER MONTH OF DRUGS AND MEDICAL SUPPLIES IS  $  10
OTHER COST PER MONTH IS                          $   0
TOTAL EXPENSE PER MONTH IS                       $ 158
C-V PROGRAM PLACED PATIENT ON MEDICAID
PATIENT ON MEDICARE BEFORE C-V PROGRAM

COMPLEMENTARY SERVICES
VISITING NURSE
HOME HEALTH  AID
NONE USED FORMERLY
HOMEMAKER OBTAINED FOR PATIENT BY C-V PROGRAM
COMMUNITY WORKERS OBTAINED FOR PATIENT BY C-V PROGRAM
ADDITIONAL SOCIAL SERVICE COUNSELING OBTAINED FOR PATIENT BY C-V PROGRAM

OUTSIDE CONTACTS
RELATIVES
NUMBER OF LIVING CLOSE RELATIVES (PARENTS,SIBLINGS,CHILDREN,SPOUSE)   1
NUMBER OF VISITS PER 28 DAYS BEFORE C-V PROGRAM                       4
NUMBER OF OTHER RELATIVES WHO HAVE EVER VISITED                       0
NUMBER OF VISITS PER 28 DAYS BEFORE C-V PROGRAM                       0
NUMBER OF FRIENDS AND NEIGHBORS WHO VISIT                             0
NUMBER OF VISITS PER 28 DAYS BEFORE C-V PROGRAM                       0
NUMBER OF VISITS PER 28 DAYS FROM COMMUNITY AGENCIES                  0
INCREASE IN HUMAN CONTACTS CAUSED BY C-V PROGRAM IS          24 PER MO
TIMES OUT OF HOME PER 28 DAYS
              0         TO NUTRITION CENTER
              0         TO SENIOR CITIZEN CENTER
              0         TO STORE
              0         FOR OTHER

CARE IN CHELSEA-VILLAGE PROGRAM
SOURCE OF REFERRAL  UNCLASSIFIED SVH REFERRAL
QUALITY OF REFERRAL SATISFACTORY
PATIENT-S ATTITUDE TOWARDS C-V PROGRAM WAS ACCEPTING
PRESENT STATUS OF PATIENT IS ACTIVE--IN CARE AT HOME
39 VISITS MADE      DATE OF LAST VISIT  2/28/1977
DOCTOR VISITS 28  NURSE VISITS 27  SOCIAL WORKER VISITS 25
```

FIG. 9-5, continued.

should be written in both places is sometimes missing. We attempt to photocopy material for this purpose but are not always up to date.

2. As previously noted, the difficult surroundings in patients' homes —crowded, dirty, poorly lit—tend to inhibit the writing of careful, comprehensive notes.

3. Preparation of a problem list and maintaining it through the body of the record takes training and effort. This technique does not come

naturally to health workers accustomed to a different system. Most of the younger physicians in the program have adapted but the older doctors favor their own routine. Nurses and social workers tend to lag because their schooling has usually not encouraged the use of this method.

4. Sloth (forgetting to write a note), gluttony (sprawling sloppily over an entire page), covetousness (failing to return the chart to the office), and pride (excessive erudition) are typical human sins. We are subject to all of them, but at least up to the present our charts have avoided expressing anger, lust, and envy.

REFERENCES

1. Holder AR: Medical Malpractice Law. New York, Wiley, 1975
2. Weed LL: Medical Records, Medical Evaluation, and Patient Care. Chicago, Press of Case-Western Reserve University, 1971
3. Weed LL: Medical records that guide and teach. N Engl J Med 178:593, 1968
4. Weed LL: Quality control and the medical record. Arch Intern Med 127:101, 1971
5. Bjorn JC, Cross HD: The Problem-oriented Private Practice of Medicine, A System for Comprehensive Health Care. Chicago, Modern Hospitals Press, 1972
6. Phillips DF: The problem-oriented system. Hospitals 46:84, 1972
7. Case Records of the Massachusetts General Hospital (Case 27-1971). N Engl J Med 285:103, 1971
8. Kane RA: Look to the record. Soc Work 19:412, 1974
9. Schnell PL, Campbell AT: POMR—not just another way to chart. Nurs Outlook 20:514, 1972
10. Goldfinger SE: The problem-oriented record: a critique from a believer. N Engl J Med 288:606, 1973
11. Birk P, Farth E: Manual for the Problem-oriented Medical Record. Problem-oriented Medical Record Subcommittee, Medical Records Committee, Albany Medical Center Hospital, February, 1971
12. Hurst JW: Ten reasons why Lawrence Weed is right. In Hurst JW, Walker HK (eds): The Problem-oriented System. New York, Medcom Press, 1972
13. Vorzimer JJ: Coordinated Ambulatory Care: The POMR. New York, Appleton-Century-Crofts, 1976, p 43
14. Schmidt EC, Schall DW, Morrison CC: Computerized problem-oriented medical record for ambulatory practice. Med Care 12:316, 1974

SECTION THREE
Life Support Services

CHAPTER 10
FOOD AND NUTRITION

Nutrition cannot be defined narrowly. . . . Human nutrition, as opposed, perhaps, to nutrition as a laboratory science, encompasses the production, distribution, cost, availability, accessibility, and acceptability of food, and, as such, interfaces with poverty, education, and a variety of circumstances in which the elderly are entrapped. . . . [The] elderly do have special nutrition problems, because they have special health, educational, economic, transportation, and sociological problems.[1]

Aged, homebound people commonly face difficulty in organizing for themselves a proper nutritional program. The problem of sustaining the motivation to prepare and to eat meal after meal alone is considerable. Even worse, the practical aspects of obtaining any food at all are a major daily issue for people who are isolated and disabled.

Attempts to solve this problem center around the home delivery of meals, to those people who cannot leave home; and the formation of group meal programs to serve individuals who are less handicapped. No food program is worth its salt, however, unless it offers a nutritionally sound, properly prepared attractive product.

NUTRITION

Special consideration must be given to the creation of adequate nutritional standards for people who are both old and disabled. Caloric requirements tend to decrease with advancing age, but protein, vitamin, and mineral needs are essentially the same for old and young.[2-5]

The differences between the nutritional requirements . . . are not due to any differences in principle. They are due to different demands imposed by the physiology of aging, to changes in bodily constitution, to reduction in energy requirements, and by . . . failures in the absorption of nutrients from food.[6]

159

The need for a standard level of nutrients, combined with a decreased requirement for calories in older people, means that the margin for error in their diets is slim. Since they eat less than their younger counterparts, the food must be qualitatively superior if a satisfactory state of health is to be maintained.[3]

Good health is a reasonable goal. Inadequate food, to emphasize the obvious, leads to illness, occasionally to malnutrition, starvation, death. Remarkable recoveries from what appeared to be serious physical or mental disease can occur when individuals improve their level of nutrition. A program which provides wholesome, palatable meals to aged people is, therefore, both a therapeutic and a preventive health service.[7,8]

In the Chelsea–Village Program we have worked with patients whose illness and disability proved to be primarily caused by inadequate nourishment, who have ceased to be homebound when this was corrected and they were provided with a reliable source of food. For examples see the case study in Chapter 6, as well as the following Chelsea–Village Program case report.

Patient A.K., a 66-year-old woman, was discharged from a state mental institution after 30 years of hospitalization and, at length, settled into an abandoned building for housing. She foraged in garbage for food. We were called to see her by a block association member who found her lying in the doorway of the building begging for something to eat. She had become weak due to lack of food, and collapsed. Her tenuous hold on a system of life, a food chain connected to local garbage, was inadequate.

We succeeded in moving her on an emergency basis to a senior citizen's housing unit which contained a common dining area. With adequate nourishment she became mobile and is able to function.

PROBLEMS IN ACCESS TO FOOD

Poverty

Almost one-third of the people over age 65 in the United States live on an income of less than $4,000 yearly.[9] In some parts of the country the figures are even lower.[10]

Many aged individuals who survive on public assistance and social security find that they have no money left at the end of the month to purchase food, and from reasons of pride or ignorance they will not publicly acknowledge their poverty to social workers or others who might help them.[11]

The older person attempting to live on a reduced income gradually gives up all the "unnecessary" things in his life. When an income that allows for only the barest necessities . . . shrinks still further, he is forced to decrease his expenditure on food, which results in a reduction in the quantity or nutrient value, or both, of the food he purchases.[9]

Since it is obvious to everyone that food is required for life, we may wonder why older people do not guarantee for themselves adequate nourishment and forego other expenditures. In fact, many elements other than money enter into determining the place of food on the priority list; and numerous factors beyond lack of money interfere with the ability to obtain food. In short, poverty among older people cannot by itself account for widespread malnourishment of the aged in this society. Many older people who can afford adequate food are not well enough, knowledgeable enough, or motivated enough to make the effort to obtain wholesome meals. More money is not in itself the answer to the problem of malnutrition among the elderly.

Physical Disability

As we have discussed earlier (Chapter 1), people of advanced age often suffer from physical disability. While this loss of function may be relatively trivial when compared with the problems posed by acute illness, it can be quite sufficient to interfere with an older person's ability to obtain or prepare food.

Arthritis, failing vision, hemiplegia, or mental confusion can make shopping seem too much of an effort, and even such simple procedures as opening cans, taking off cellophane wrappers, opening screwtop bottles, peeling potatoes, and slicing bread can present real problems to the frail, older person.[4, 12]

Lack of Knowledge and Skill

Inadequate information about nutritional values and inexperience with cooking techniques are common difficulties which interfere with the creation of a proper diet for older people. It is easier—less threatening—to settle for tea and toast than to prepare a meal. This often holds true for those who are in relatively good health and with adequate money—even these individuals may be tempted to select foods which require little preparation and are of low nutritive value.[13-15]

In another respect older people are no different from the population at large: they often are simply ignorant about what consitutes a good diet. What little is known may be outdated, a set of memories from a childhood 60 years or more earlier.[13, 16]

Lack of Motivation

Human nutrition cannot be studied in a vacuum. It is more than a laboratory science. Social and psychological factors are involved. We are raised to regard mealtimes as occasions to be with other people. Our eating patterns are established in a social context. Companionship at a meal may be almost as important as the food itself.

Therefore, elderly people living alone, and especially those who are recently bereaved, are particularly at risk to the threat of malnutrition. The lonely and grieving widow may feel no desire to cook, now that there is no one but herself to cook for and eat with.[9] The widower may find himself for the first time in his life responsible for shopping and cooking, and his uncertainty about how to perform these tasks may stop him from trying.[4]

The result is a downward cycle of bereavement, loneliness, depression, apathy about life in general and food in particular, lack of self-care, loss of self-respect—all leading to illness or death.[9]

OBTAINING FOOD
THROUGH A MEALS-ON-WHEELS PROGRAM

The Need

The delivery of food to the person in need is a key factor in the success of a home health care project for the aged. Our own experience in the Chelsea–Village Program shows that two-thirds of our homebound patients live alone. The services of a part-time homemaker for shopping and cooking are a great advantage, but even in these circumstances the provision of one hot meal a day from another source is crucial to long-term survival.

Meals-on-Wheels programs are widespread throughout the country, their popularity based on a perception of the need and made possible by the passage of the Older Americans Act in 1965. Various titles within this legislation, and other laws as well,[17, 18] are designed to provide funds for food and nutrition services to older people. These programs are sponsored by a wide variety of voluntary and civic associations (women's clubs, community councils, and family service organizations) and professional nonprofit agencies, like Visiting Nurse Services and hospital auxiliaries.

Finding the Patients

The first step and the greatest challenge in any successful effort to deliver meals is to identify the people in need. It is a waste of resources, and not in the best interests of the elderly population itself, to provide Meals-on-Wheels to those who are capable of leaving their homes to dine in restaurants, shop for and prepare their own meals, or have a family member or neighbor who can help them in obtaining food.[19] The problem, however, is that the dependent elderly most at risk and with the highest priority for access to the program are also the most difficult to reach and the hardest to help.

Those most in need include the recently bereaved, those living alone, individuals with mental disorders, and extremely aged people, especially if they are out of contact with the health care system.[19] Often these people are so disconnected from the social network through which most services are delivered that they are ignored or passed over by traditional programs.[11, 20, 21]

All sources of community contact must be used in order to locate the people in need. The level of interest in the community at large can be raised by publicity campaigns, newspaper articles, speeches before public groups, comments at meetings—all with the intention of using local people as case finders and sources of referral. Particular emphasis should be placed on contacts with senior citizens' centers and agencies which commonly deal with people in trouble: the Visiting Nurse Association, hospital social service departments, the police. Unorthodox resources should be sought as well: mailmen, neighborhood shopkeepers, superintendents of buildings. Other useful referral sources are discussed in Chapter 3.

We must seek further. Many older, helpless people living in dense urban areas occupy apartments or rooms which are below minimum standards. This is illegal housing, and their addresses may not exist or be unlisted. The post office, for instance, may be unaware of their presence. Because these people are homebound and dependent on others for aid, shopping patterns may be unknown to local merchants.[11] In an official sense, these people do not live at all, and yet they need to eat. The ultimate case-finding resource must be used for this group: door-to-door search.

Frequency, Number, and Nature of Meals Served

Generally the number of people served a hot portable meal by any one program ranges from about 20 to 40. Most programs operate Monday through Friday and deliver either one or two meals each day per person. Usually provision is made for special meals, such as those required by diabetics or people on low-salt diets.

The most advanced Meals-on-Wheels programs—those that provide

163

two meals a day—deliver the noon and evening dinners at the same time. Efforts are made, through the use of insulating and packaging techniques, to control the temperature of the food until it is delivered. The evening meal is brought cold. The recipient is expected to heat it at the right time, or it may be designed to be eaten uncooked.[19]

It is wise to consider the physical and psychologic factors that enter into acceptability of food for individual clients. These considerations range from the need for soft foods for people with dental problems; to racial, geographic, and religious habits and requirements.[22, 23]

A typical menu, according to one hospital-based Meals-on-Wheels program,[2] is as follows:

Hot Noon Meal
One serving tender meat, or alternate food high in protein
Two servings vegetable (one may be a potato)
One serving salad (vegetable, fruit, or high protein food, such as cottage cheese and egg)
One serving dessert (cake, pudding, fruit)
One slice bread and one serving butter
Beverage (coffee or tea)

Most meals are simple, without sauces and gravies. Each meal should contain at least one-third of the daily nutritional needs for each patient.

An incident in our own program shows that the benefits of home delivered meals can surpass the mere matter of nutrition.

A.B. is an 82-year-old man living alone in a single room of a brownstone building. The patient has severe arthritis of both legs, and his walking ability is limited to a slow sideways shuffle. The bathroom is in the hall, impractical for him to reach. Prior to our first visit the patient had already been placed on a Meals-on-Wheels program. We found his room lined with containers from the program, occupying every horizontal surface, each neatly packed with urine and feces.

The Site

A central location for preparation, packaging, and distribution of food is essential. Some programs[2, 24, 25] rent or are given the kitchen of a church, senior citizens' center, or other local agency. Others[26] purchase food prepared and ready for distribution from a restaurant or catering source. Institutional kitchens of hospitals or nursing homes, often underutilized for parts of the day, can function as headquarters.

It is worthwhile to emphasize the advantages of a hospital relationship to a Meals-on-Wheels program. Hospitals are a natural. They produce meals economically, the institution and its staff are accustomed to preparing large quantities of food designed for people in borderline health, and in particular they have the experience to produce special diets. Hospitals have access to volunteer services which these programs need.[19] For a hospital, the additional burden can be compared to that required for an additional floor of patients: a challenge but not an impossibility.[19, 24, 26]

The purchase of commercially prepared meals relieves program staff of some problems and responsibilities. The concomitant loss of control, however, carries with it the possibility, perhaps the probability, that quality will suffer. Caterers usually demand a minimum number of clients to be served[26] and may insist on other requirements that run counter to the best interests of the patients.

Another alternative, a kitchen operated by the sponsors of the Meals-on-Wheels program, even with all its potential problems, is the most likely to meet its goals. The staff has full control over operations: quality of food, timetable of delivery, attitude and ability of staff members. Through its own kitchen the program has the maximum opportunity to develop a service sensitive to the needs of its clients.

Staffing

Staffing patterns depend on organizational structure. If the portable meals program is part of a larger institution, such as a hospital, the only personnel needed may be a kitchen coordinator and volunteer driver. The coordinator spends about four hours each day packaging meals and preparing labels and production sheets for the next day.[24]

If a multipurpose community organization, such as a Visiting Nurse Service or a senior citizens' center, is the program sponsor, personnel must include a nutritionist to direct food purchasing and preparation, a part-time cook, and volunteers for delivery.[27]

The problems are more complex if the program starts from scratch. Policies and procedures must be developed, arrangements made for the use of cooking facilities, a complete staff obtained, and a network of community contacts created. A new program usually is the product of a preexisting lay organization, such as a religious community, fraternal body, or other charitable or civic-minded group.

The governing board should appoint a director of the food program to head the staff and implement established policy. The director will make policy recommendations based upon his or her experience in administering the program and act as liaison between staff and board.

165

Important assets of a director, to be considered in the appointment, are[11] (1) experience in working with older people, (2) administrative background and proven ability, and (3) knowledge of the local community and the capacity to establish and maintain links with its people, agencies, and resources. For a typical job description see Figure 10-1.

Past professional work in nutrition is a plus but not as important as organizational ability because the job is primarily administrative. Consultation can be obtained in the fields of dietetics, nursing, medicine, and social work as needed.[11]

A cook with particular skills is a vital asset. He/she should be experienced in planning raw bulk purchases and in the economical use of food. The cook should know how to plan an attractive, nutritional menu and be sensitive to the textual, taste, and dietary requirements of older people.

Salary: $10,700 + liberal fringe benefits

Minimum Qualifications:

1. Minimum of three years' experience in supervisory or administrative position in nutrition, social work, education, public health, recreation, or related field, preferably with the aged in a community setting.
2. An academic degree in nutrition, social work, or a related field,

OR

A Baccalaureate Degree with a minimum of seven years experience, three years in a supervisory or administrative position, in nutrition, social work, or related field,

OR

A high school diploma with a minimum of ten years experience, five years in a supervisory or administrative position in nutrition, social work, or related field.

Duties:

1. Responsible for planning, implementing, and overall adminstration, supervision, and coordination of the service operation of the program.
2. Organizes the advisory committee.
3. Overall responsibility for reports.
4. Attends community meetings.
5. Maintains liaison with other agencies and programs.
6. Hires and fires staff.
7. Oversees work, functioning, and upkeep of physical plant.
8. Works with appropriate community groups.
9. Interprets agency programs and policies through public relations.
10. Responsible for formulating philosophy, objectives, guidelines, and administrative procedures.
11. Alert to new ideas and community needs.
12. Initiates plans for appropriate program changes based upon the results of actual field services and reports.
13. Maintains all records, fiscal, and reporting systems.

FIG. 10-1.   Job description for program director of Meals-on-Wheels.

Furthermore, he/she must learn quickly about packaging techniques and feel the importance of timing, so that food arrives in the patient's home while still hot.

The final link is an individual or group of people who deliver the food. These can be paid employees, but more often volunteers are available. Even for a position which appears to be as simple as food deliverer, screening is necessary. No program wants to be faced with the problems produced by an inconsiderate representative, an unreliable person, or worse, a thief. In these circumstances, even at no salary, the cost is too high.

Packaging and Delivering the Goods

Meals-on-Wheels programs face a common problem in the proper packaging and safe transport of the food prepared under their auspices. There is an obvious disadvantage to preparing a meal three or four hours before it is to reach the client's home. It will be unattractive, and some of its nutritional value will be lost.[13] Aluminum foil, plastic, paper, styrofoam, other disposable packaging materials, and a variety of appliances and devices for heating and cooling in the vehicle are in use, all designed to keep hot meals hot and cold meals cold.[11] Keeping food hot is the greater problem, especially if the local board of health has particularly stringent requirements about the temperature of conveyed foods in its health code, and the delivery route is long. These problems have been solved in at least one instance by the use of microwave ovens.[24] An Ohio program[26] has fitted a van with modified airline equipment, containing both refrigerating and heating components. Meal Packs, a vacuum-type metal container designed to carry hot food, have been effective for some programs.[27]

Most Meals-on-Wheels programs rely on volunteers who use their own cars or public transportation to deliver meals, but there are other potential resources.

Volunteers can, for example, drive school buses, station wagons used for transporting handicapped children, and even taxicabs. Taxi services can be donated by the private enterprise sector as a public service. Asking automobile dealers and manufacturers to supply vehicles for the program should be considered. There is a precedent in cars donated to the driver instruction programs in local schools.

It is not unreasonable to look into the route delivery systems already existing in communities (e.g., milk, utility, or bread and pastry companies, etc.) to explore their participation in a delivery system. Many large urban areas, too, have several private enterprise lunch wagon businesses which already have provisions to carry hot food and who already traverse all sections of the city. Although it has seemed to be very difficult to gain support from commercial companies for social ventures with negligible profit margins, no system should be dismissed without realistic approaches and evaluation. It may be that one in an area would be quite appropriate and willing to participate but has never been viewed in this light and, as a result, has never been approached. The need exists and some innovative approach could make program expansion or continuation feasible.[19]

FINANCES

Cost

In truth, no reasonable universal estimate can be given regarding what it will cost per meal, or per individual, for application to a specific program.[11]

The cost of a Meals-on-Wheels program includes salaries, food, packaging, housing, equipment, maintenance, and insurance. Since most programs lack sophisticated accounting procedures, it is difficult to make cost measurements for each meal prepared or each person served.

As a rough estimate, the range of cost per meal cited by a variety of programs ranges from $0.50 to $2.00. The variation is not related to program size or geographic location, nor to the nature or variety of services offered.[11] Among the elements which serve to confuse cost estimates are (1) the use of volunteer staff members, (2) the receipt of donated food, and (3) free provision of delivery services, space, equipment.

For a typical program budget, vintage 1977, see Figure 10-2.

Where Does The Money Come From

For support, look first to government. Most Meals-on-Wheels programs grow out of Titles III, IV, and VII funding within the Older Americans Act.[19, 21, 24, 28, 29] Government funding at any level tends to be restrictive, however, and to require arbitrary elimination from the program rolls of some people in need. Therefore, it is wise to seek additional support elsewhere.

Look for contributions from auxiliary groups within the community, fraternal organizations, money-raising events, trade union special funds, professional groups, religious and charitable bodies, local philanthropies, businesses, and interested individuals. In-kind contributions of food, supplies, and equipment should be sought as well.[7, 11]

Project Name *Community Luncheon Clubs of Greenwich Village* CAMFR ID No. _____

Address Sixth Avenue, N.Y., N.Y. 10014

Budget Period *10/1/76* to *9/30/77* _____

(Effective Date)
(Leave Blank—For Office Use Only)

Explanation of Change		Present Budget	Revision (+ or −)	Revised Budget
Personnel Services				
Director	*35 hr*	$ 12,720.00	$ —	$ 12,720.00
Bookkeeper	*15 hr*	8,000.00	− 4,885.00	3,115.00
Program Asst.–Driver	*35 hr*	6,000.00	+ 1,200.00	7,200.00
Program Asst.–Rec/Cler.	*20 hr*	4,000.00	−	4,000.00
Social Worker	*17½ hr*	0	+ 6,000.00	6,000.00
Total Salaries	(3100-5)	30,720.00	+ 2,315.00	33,035.00
Employer's Share of FICA Taxes	(3601-2)	2,292.00	+ 136.00	2,428.00
Unemployment Insurance	(3602-0)	1,028.00	+ 127.00	1,155.00
Fringe Benefits	(3700-2)	−	−	−
Total Personnel Services	(3000):			
(3100) + (3601)	(3700)	34,040.00	+ 2,578.00	36,618.00
Other Than Personnel Services (OTPS)				
Participant Cost	(7101-9)	7,410.00	−	7,410.00
Consultants and Substitute Pay	(4000-6)	3,050.00	−	3,050.00
Renovations	(5300-9)	−	−	−.
Utilities	(5500-4)	9,000.00	−	9,000.00
Maintenance	(5200-1)	500.00	−	500.00
Recreational and Educational Supplies	(6101-0)	500.00	−	500.00
Office and Household Supplies	(6102-8)	2,400.00	−	2,400.00
Equipment	(6200-0)	0	+ 4,290.00	4,290.00
Staff Travel	(6300-8)	100.00	−	100.00
Participant Transportation	(7200-9)	100.00	−	100.00
Communications	(6950-0)	1,800.00	−	1,800.00
Printing and Duplication	(6960-9)	360.00	−	360.00
Food	(7300-7)	103,026.00	−	103,026.00
Other Costs—Specify	(6990-6)			
Van Insurance, Van Maintenance, Gas and Oil		2,180.00	−	2,180.00
Total OTPS		130,426.00	+ 4,290.00	134,716.00
Total Budget Available to Contractor				
(Total Personnel Services + Total OTPS)		164,446.00	+ 6,868.00	171,334.00
Direct Central Payments: HRA Fringe Benefits		−	−	−
Agency Insurance		−	−	−
Total Direct Central Payments		5,097.00	+ 978.00	6,075.00
Total Budget (Total Budget Available to Contractor and of Total Direct Central Payments)		169,563.00	+ 7,846.00	177,409.00
In-Kind Contributions		35,944.00	+ 41,338.00	77,282.00
Estimated Participant Contributions		7,200.00	−	7,200.00
Total Budget Plus In-Kind and Estimated Participant Contributions		212,707.00	+ 49,184.00	261,891.00

Contractor's Signature _____ Date _____

Department for the Aging Approval _____ Date _____

FIG. 10-2. Budget revision form, Title VII Nutrition Luncheon Clubs.

Fee Policy

It is common for participants to pay some portion of the cost of their meals, often a token amount. This policy meets the wishes of most clients to maintain a degree of pride and a sense of dignity. If the fees are based on a sliding scale dependent on income, no individual is likely to suffer. One sliding scale devised for a Chicago pilot program had a minimum fee of $1.00 and a maximum fee of $4.00 for two weeks of service.[26] If there is truly no money available, programs provide service free.

Writing a Title VII Proposal

If you are going to seek federal funds to start a Meals-on-Wheels program, Title VII of the Older Americans Act of 1965 is a possible source. Preparation of a grant request is a tedious and lengthy process. The quantity of paperwork required is extensive, and the completed document may well pass 50 pages in length. The following material may be useful.

Title VII (P.L. 89–73), as amended (P.L. 92–258, P.L. 93–26, P.L. 93–351, and P.L. 94–135), authorizes and provides funds for the National Nutrition Program for Older Americans (NPOA), conducted by the Administration on Aging. The National Nutrition Program is designed to provide inexpensive, nutritionally sound meals to older Americans and their spouses, particularly those with low incomes or otherwise in greatest need. It is also designed to help reduce the isolation of the elderly in society. Funds are allocated to states on the basis of their population aged 60 and over. In each state the nutrition program is administered by that state's agency on aging, unless another agency is designated by the governor and approved by the commissioner on aging. The administering agency makes grants, contracting with public and nonprofit institutions and organizations for the actual provision and delivery of meals.

The state agency is responsible for insuring that awards are made to initiate projects which serve minority, native American, and limited-English speaking individuals, at least in proportion to their numbers within the state. Meal sites are required to be located in urban areas that have heavy concentrations of target-group older Americans and in rural areas that have high proportions of eligible older persons. The state agencies are also responsible for providing advisory assistance in the form of panels composed of the consumers of the service, members of minority groups, and persons knowledgeable about the provision of health, nutrition, and other supportive services. No one may be turned away from the program for inability to pay, and there is no means test. However, all participants are given an opportunity to pay all or part of the cost of a meal.

Once a community group, preferably a coalition of nonprofit and public organizations, such as churches, synagogues, and senior citizen centers, has met to begin planning a meals program and arranged for the use of a physical site with the appropriate equipment, the group should complete the formal application for Title VII funds on the "Title VII Older

170

Americans Act Application'' form. A project officer will be assigned from the administering government agency. This person will be a valuable resource throughout the operation of the meals program for technical assistance and referral to services offered by the agency of which he/she is a part. The project officer may, for example, be able to put program staff in touch with specialists in counseling, interior maintenance and repair services, group activities, and outreach, who will be useful in program development.[29]

As a guide in planning, we suggest that you be prepared to answer the following questions in detail if you are going to submit a proposal.

A. General description
    1. How do you plan to allocate your space for the activities and services of your program?
    2. How do you plan to set up and implement your fiscal and management information system?
    3. How many persons do you plan to serve?
B. General description of your hot meals program
    1. How do you plan to set up your meals program?
    2. How many meals per day _____ per week _____ will be provided?
    3. How will you implement your meals service?
    4. How will you develop your menu (and assure any type of specialized meals if needed)?
C. Supportive services. What are your plans for
    1. Information and referral
    2. Publicity and outreach
    3. Recreational activities
    4. Nutrition education
    5. Shopping assistance
    6. Transportation and escort services
    7. Health and welfare counseling
D. In regard to funding sources
    1. Who was involved in the development of the proposed schedule of contributions?
    2. How was the proposed schedule adopted?
    3. How will the schedule of contributions be presented to participants in your project?
    4. What method will be used to collect contributions?
    5. How will the money be used?
E. How do you plan to utilize USDA (United States Department of Agriculture) programs?
    1. Food Stamps
    2. Donated foods

171

If there are no Meals-on-Wheels available in a community, federal food stamps or commodity distribution may be useful. These two programs are widely available in the United States, and of the nearly 15 million beneficiaries, approximately 2.5 million are age 65 and older.[20]

Food Stamps

The food stamp program, now the predominant form of food assistance available in the United States, was begun in 1964. Its purpose is to supplement the purchasing power of low-income groups, including the elderly, by subsidizing the amount of money they spend for food. Depending on income, participants exchange money for food stamps which are worth more than what they have paid. People with little or no income get the stamps free.[20] The stamps can be used to purchase a wide variety of foods at local grocery stores and supermarkets. Constituents of special medical diets are included.

[Eligibility for] food stamps depends on . . . income, savings, and other assets. . . . Income standards are the same for all ages. [An individual living alone] can have a yearly income of $2,100 and still be eligible for food stamps; a couple may have a yearly income of $2,700. People with incomes above these limits may also be eligible if they have unusual expenses, such as big medical bills or high rent payments.[20]

Commodities or Direct Food Distribution

Commodities, or direct food distribution, programs operate for the benefit of the poor, including the elderly, in areas not served by the Food Stamp Program. Food is free to eligible groups, donated by the Department of Agriculture and distributed through local governments, public and nonprofit charitable institutions, schools, and other local centers. Eligibility for the program is determined by social service or welfare agencies according to income standards established by each state and approved by the Department of Agriculture.[20] The department pays for the processing and packaging of the foods and for transporting them in carload lots to receiving points chosen by the participating states. State and local governments pay all costs of intrastate transportation, storage, distribution, and the certification processes of those who are to receive the food. If a county or city cannot finance the donation program for its low-income people, the Office of Economic Opportunity will consider applications for assistance under the Community Action Program.[19]

Food is of standard quality and includes such staples as canned meat, fruit juices, vegetables, cheese, peanut butter, and nonfat dry milk. Theoretically, each person receives enough food to supply a nutritionally adequate diet.[20]

Problems exist in this program which make participation by the homebound, aged difficult:[19]

1. The pick-up location may be inaccessible
2. Dates for pick-up of food, perhaps once per week or month, may be inconvenient
3. The commodities offered may be unfamiliar to the potential receiver, or their use in food preparation alien or disliked
4. Packaging may be outsized and difficult to carry or store

GROUP MEALS

Many aged individuals share to a degree the problems of poverty, physical disability, lack of knowledge and skill about buying and preparing food, and live alone, and yet they can manage to reach a nearby central location once daily.

A noon meal provided in a social context for a group of people small enough to provide intimacy helps to solve a number of interrelated problems at once. Nutrition is improved, participants develop a greater interest in life and the world about them, social intercourse is increased.[13, 21, 30]

Providing food for a group in a central location is superior in terms of cost and human relationships to the delivery of single meals eaten in isolation. For the people with whom we are primarily concerned, group meals are by definition out of reach because our patients are homebound.

We note here the significance of group meal programs, however, because

1. Our patients may improve and be able to leave their homes, and yet require partial assistance in obtaining food. In the Chelsea–Village Program, for instance, 72 out of 466 patients are no longer homebound and are able to move around the community despite advanced age. Group meal programs are ideal for these people.
2. Funding sources for Meals-on-Wheels apply, in most cases, equally to

173

group meal programs. Often, one project supplies both kinds of food service. Various titles under the Older Americans Act apply.[17]

CONCLUSION

Any plan designed to help older people remain independent in their own homes depends on a series of linkages. Every part of the process must be thought out and followed through, or failures will take place. This fact applies particularly to our group of patients, a set of individuals who face many obstacles in obtaining, preparing, and eating food, and in many other aspects of life as well. This Chelsea–Village Program case report makes the point.

A.G., a 77-year-old woman living alone, had her cooking and shopping done by a homemaker five days a week. On Saturdays and Sundays she prepared food for herself but had recently not been able to carry this out. She was placed on a local Meals-on-Wheels program for the weekend, but when the homemaker returned on Monday the patient was too weak to stand up. The meals had been delivered but were sitting on the kitchen table uneaten. She had to be hospitalized. Her explanation: "The food didn't look appetizing." The fact: she had become ill and couldn't eat, a point which the Meals-on-Wheels staff member missed.

In citing this case we emphasize the continuity of care and the sharing of responsibility which must take place if homebound, aged people are to be helped. No single component of service, including the provision of food, can stand alone.

REFERENCES

1. Watkin DM: Nutritional needs of elderly intertwined with other factors and attitudes affecting health. Geriatrics 29:40, 1974
2. Braley I: Hospital-prepared meals for homebound aged persons. Hospitals 37:82, 1963
3. Mayer J: Aging and nutrition. Geriatrics 29:57, 1974
4. Latchford W: Nutritional problems of the elderly. Community Health 16:145, 1974
5. Young VR, Perera WD, Winterer JC, Scrimshaw NS: Protein and amino acid requirements of the elderly. Curr Concepts Nutr 4:77, 1976
6. Eddy TP: Nutritional needs of the old. Nurs Times 70:1499, 1974
7. Williams IF, Smith CE: Home delivered meals for the aged and handicapped. J Am Diet Assoc 35:146, 1959
8. Carmody D: Lunch programs feed mind and body of elderly. New York Times, Monday, Nov 25, 1974, p. 33

9. Garetz FK: Breaking the dangerous cycle of depression and faulty nutrition. Geriatrics 31:73, 1976

10. Butler RN: No place to live. In Why Survive? Being Old in America. New York, Harper, 1975, Chap. 5

11. Holmes D, Howell S, Lewis L, Schwartz J: Guideline for Nutrition Programs. Prepared for the Administration on Aging, Social and Rehabilitation Service, Department of Health, Education, and Welfare, Washington DC, 1972

12. Caird FI, Judge TG, Macleod C: Pointers to possible malnutrition in the elderly at home. Gerontol Clin (Basel) 17:47, 1975

13. Exton-Smith AN: Health and nutrition of the elderly. R Soc Health J 88:7220, 1968

14. Rockstein M, Sussman ML: Introduction, food for thought. In Rockstein M, Sussman ML (eds): Nutrition, Longevity, and Aging. New York, Academic, 1976

15. Grills NJ: Nutritional needs of elderly women. Clin Obstet Gynecol 20:137, 1977

16. Woods D: Nutrition for all. Medical interest seems to be awakening. Can Med Assoc J 116:531, 1977

17. Older Americans Act of 1965, as amended, Title VII (42 USC 3051)

18. Food Stamp Act of 1974, as amended (7 USC 2016-2025)

19. Howell SC, Loeb MB: Food service programs for the older adult. Gerontologist 9:75, 1969

20. Luhrs CE: Feeding the elderly. Am J of Clin Nutr 26:1150, 1973

21. Pelcovits J: Nutrition for older Americans. J Am Diet Assoc 58:17, 1971

22. Trager J: Foodbook. New York, Grossman, 1970, p 315

23. Kalson L: Kosher Meals-on-Wheels. Gerontologist 14:33, 1974

24. McAllister W: Implementing a portable meals program. J Am Diet Assoc 66:375, 1975

25. Ossofsky J, Anderson A: A Nutrition Program for the Elderly. A Model Community Action Program to Provide Low-cost Meals to the Elderly. National Council on the Aging, Inc., 1828 L St. NW, Washington DC, April 1972

26. Rosbach CC: A Report of Home Delivered Meals Programs. Visiting Nurse Association, 1540 N. Jefferson St., Milwaukee, Wisconsin 53202, March 31, 1969

27. Henry CE: Feeding elderly people in their homes. J Am Diet Assoc. 35:149, 1959

28. Baltimore's new geriatric nutrition program. Md State Med J 23:33, 1974

29. Guidelines for Local Planning, Project Development, and Proposal Submission for a Nutrition Program for the Elderly under Title VII, Older Americans Act. New York City Mayor's Office for the Aging, 250 Broadway, New York, NY 10007

30. Todhunter EN: Life style and nutrient intake in the elderly. Curr Concepts Nutr 4:119, 1976

CHAPTER 11

HOUSING

THE PROBLEM

Of all the problems which homebound, aged people face, the most difficult to solve is the need for adequate housing. The building stock of inner cities is deteriorating,[1-4] and many units are substandard by any definition. New private housing is too expensive for most aged people.[5,6] Space in government-sponsored projects is in great demand, and there are significant waiting periods.[5,7-8] Many older people do not survive long enough to make the move. Some are forced to enter institutions because their homes become unsafe.[9,10]

Most older, disabled people who live in cities occupy rented apartments.[5] Rents rise, and incomes fall behind. Despite the fact that most individuals reserve money to pay for housing, even to the extent that they suffer from inadequate diets,[15] the costs often become impossible to meet.

There is a national shortage of adequate housing. In competition with the rest of the population, older people and poor people have a handicap: less money. With limited buying power, they get the residue of a limited stock. According to national estimates, at least 30 percent of older Americans—six million people —live in substandard housing.[7]

In New York City, for instance, half of the households headed by persons over age 65 have a yearly income of $3,000 or less.[5] These people must pay or be evicted, and finding another place to live is difficult. They compete with younger apartment seekers in an extremely tight market.

A report of the Community Council of Greater New York in 1970 noted:[12]

. . . almost 45% of old New Yorkers occupied unsuitable quarters in deteriorated areas of the city. About half of these housing units were in hazardous condition. A similar number of apartments were of standard quality but unsuited to the physical status of the aged occupant. Many others lived in apartments too expensive to maintain, but no cheaper alternative was available.

In the Chelsea–Village Program we work with aged people who in high

176

proportion have low incomes and severe housing problems. A study of our first 466 patients[13] showed that "361 lived in housing considered generally fit for human habitation; 105 in unsafe condition." When the physical status of the individual was considered, "278 people had living quarters fit for their needs; 188 (40%) did not."

In this category, typical examples included individuals with amputations living in walk-up buildings, wheelchair-bound patients who could not get into the bathroom, people with generalized weakness whose plumbing and kitchen fixtures were deteriorated, of poor utility, and hard to use.

It is particularly important to note the following: "Of the people whose housing was considered altogether unsafe, or inappropriate to their needs, 46 refused to consider a move."

This Chelsea–Village Program case report is pertinent:

D.A., a 65-year-old woman, was referred by the St. Vincent's Hospital Social Service Department. At our first visit she was found in bed, disabled by arthritis.

8/7/73   Doctor's Note: Patient is living in intolerable conditions. "Bedroom" is 15 feet long—6 feet wide. Bathroom in hall. Well-fed roaches and many cats.

9/21/73   Social Service Note: Called housing authority for emergency placement. Told to call back in 10 days.

10/3/73   Social Service Note: Housing authority has placed patient on priority list. Minimum estimate for move is three to six months.

1/5/74   Coordinator's Note: Arrangements had been made to carry patient to appointment with housing authority, but she refused to go. She insists that she doesn't want to live in a housing project. She prefers "a cripple home."

1/8/74   Social Service Note: Patient is interested in entering a nursing home but can't go because she has "no clean clothing." We will get her some clothes.

The patient ultimately refused to go to a nursing home.

9/17/74   Student Nurse's Observation Note: D.A. was seen today complaining of pain in her leg which she feels keeps her from going out. The apartment must be detrimental to her health due to the cluttered, poorly lit, roach-infested bedroom, dirty sink, lack of bathroom (a commode is used), no telephone. Safety features are absent. She does not appear to be anxious to leave these conditions if given the choice.

We continued to urge a move; the patient refused. On 5/31/77 she was found dead in her bed.

People's perceptions of their homes, and their own wishes, are far more important than our outsider's view in formulating decisions about moving. We have learned that there is a difference between offering help and inflicting it.

SEEKING SOLUTIONS

Efforts to solve problems in housing focus on money, maintaining or improving the home, and finding new living space.

Money

When income is inadequate to meet the costs of housing, and a move is vetoed, the obvious possibilities are limited to increasing the money supply or lowering the rent.

It is not necessary to look for a villain to explain the financial crunch that afflicts aged tenants. Most landlords are presumably honest, decent people who strive to conduct a proper business life. Some are unscrupulous. Most tenants pay the rent, maintain their apartments decently, and keep the public areas of their building clean. Some do not.

Landlords must ask progressively higher rents in order to provide proper services. The cost of fuel for heating has been a particular problem.[14] But many aged people cannot pay higher rents. Even those fortunate enough to live in a rent-controlled building, who have obtained a senior citizen rent increase exemption (discussed below), are not safe, because the building management may go bankrupt and all tenants be evicted.[14]

Following are potential solutions to the problem of rising rents.

TENANT ORGANIZATIONS. Older people should join with fellow tenants to negotiate with landlords fair rules for rent increases and conditions of tenancy. They must use the court system, particularly the housing court (discussed below), and other legal avenues to defend their rights. Old, isolated people are likely victims of intimidating landlords, and they should be protected by tenant advocates and staff members of government agencies.

RENT CONTROL. Whether or not to restrain artificially, by law, the rent of apartments or to permit these rents to rise as the free economy dictates is a question of social policy. There is no question, however, that the need of many aged people to remain in their own apartments is fulfilled by rent control laws. When there are no such laws, older people suffer.

This is a matter that spans the country. A correspondent in Seattle, a lawyer, comments[15]:

Your example [the Chelsea–Village Program] inspired me to try to help the elderly myself. There are a disproportionate number of them living in old apartment houses in the inner city. Their rents were fairly reasonable and they made out until entrepreneurs residing in the Vancouver, B.C., area began buying up those apartment houses and jacking up rents unmercifully. They had heard about HUD subsidies. There is no rent control here so they were able to do it. For more than a year I worked trying to get a rent freeze because those landlords had raised rents to the point where some old people had less than $20 left out of their social security after they paid rent and utilities. I drafted the ordinance myself—it would not have required the city to spend one penny for enforcement; it was modelled on the State's Consumer Protection Act and Residential Landlord-Tenant Act and I used New York's preamble to invoke the police power of the state which exists for emergencies. I thought it would be adopted, because there are more tenants than landlords. However, landlords are better organized so every member of the City Council voted it down, the Mayor and the Hearst paper came out against it. While I was working on this, I came to the conclusion that the elderly are the most exploited group in our society. A lot of people on government salaries are making their living off them; but they do not want to do anything for them for which they will not get paid.

In New York, the state rent control law has been of significant value. Many aged people in New York City both occupy relatively inexpensive housing units and have been in the same places for years,[16, 17] thereby fulfilling necessary eligibility requirements of the rent control law.

Data from the Chelsea–Village Program confirm these points:

Average monthly apartment rent of 167 consecutive patients from whom the information is available is $129, the median $85. Rents range from zero (occupants of illegal housing, squatters) to $550. The average Chelsea–Village Program patient has lived in the same apartment 12 years (data from 163 cases) with a range of zero to 60, and a median of 13 years.

Rent-controlled apartments are those built before February 1, 1947, containing six or more units. Their rents prior to 1971 were below levels of the free market economy. Rent control is necessitated by the extremely low rate of vacancy in New York City, especially in Manhattan.

In June of 1971 legislation was signed that allowed decontrol of apartments voluntarily vacated.[18] At that time there were about 1.3 million rent-controlled units in the city. Rents for vacated apartments immediately rose sharply, in some cases doubling.[19] An interesting phenomenon then took place. Promptly after the law went into effect, the Office of Rent Control began receiving complaints by older people of harassment and denial of building services from landlords who wanted them to move.[5]

179

Recent attempts to modify the law focus upon controlled rents only for people in genuine financial need.[20]

MAXIMUM BASE RENT.   A 1972 revision of the New York Rent Control law created a maximum base rent (MBR). This legislation was designed to preserve older housing stock in the city by permitting measured rent increases to landlords who maintained their buildings adequately.

The MBR is a figure computed by the Rent Guidelines Board that represents a fair rent for a rent-controlled apartment. The sum is determined through a complex formula based on statistics from the Bureau of Labor and on the rent base, the monthly rent paid for the apartment on December 31, 1971. The MBR is supposed to be the maximum amount a landlord can charge, but since the formula can be reviewed and changed every two years, the MBR cannot be regarded as a stable figure. Since the MBR is thought of as the fair rent for a particular apartment, the provisions for rent-controlled units allow the landlord to charge 7½ percent more each year, until the rent reaches the MBR. The figure the rent-controlled tenants pays is called the maximum collectible rent. The maximum collectible rent includes the 7½ percent yearly increase until it reaches the figure of the maximum base rent.

SENIOR CITIZEN RENT INCREASE EXEMPTIONS.   If you have made an attempt to understand the foregoing information you will recognize the difficulties faced by tenants in maintaining their rights. The problems of older people, who may be frightened, uncertain, or confused, are obviously worse.

Aged individuals in the city have been given partial financial relief, at the risk of further confusion, by the Senior Citizen Rent Increase Exemption Program.[21, 22] By its provisions, their rents are frozen and exempted from increases under the maximum base rent formula if:

1. The apartment is rent controlled
2. The occupants are age 62 or more, and
3. Are not receiving public assistance (Supplementary Security Income recipients are eligible)
4. The occupant is head of the household, and
5. The total disposable income of the household is not more than $5,000 per year. The District Rent Office has a formula for computing total disposable income.

A flaw in the program is pointed out in this excerpt from a Chelsea–Village Program staff conference.

180

IRMA STAHL (Social Worker): We tried to get a rent-increase exemption for Mr. F. [89-year-old Yugoslavian man disabled by metastatic cancer] As you know, he has deplorable living conditions—broken windows, no heat—but he is vehemently against moving to a project. He's terrified at the prospect—the idea that he'll get mugged in the elevator. He feels so vulnerable. Also, he has friends downstairs in the coffee shop who visit him daily, bring him food. He'd lose those contacts. When I point out the broken window to him, he says, "Oh, but the sun shines in." So we got an inspector there to review that room for rent-increase exemption. Mr. F. is technically eligible for subsidy, but the inspection report said the buidling was in such bad shape that they wouldn't subsidize it.

ATTENDING DOCTOR: This poor man falls below the law.

RENT SUBSIDY. Various subsidy devises exist.[22] A particularly useful example is the Section 8 Housing Assistance Program, created by the Housing and Community Development Act of 1974[23] and sponsored in New York City by the City Housing Authority.

In New York City under the Section 8 program, the Housing Authority makes monthly payments to the landlord on behalf of eligibile tenants. These payments close the gap between the amount the tenant can afford to pay and the full rent. The eligibility regulations for maximum income and rent, while obviously necessary, can create bizarre results. This Chelsea–Village Program case report is apposite:

R.R. is a 74-year-old ex-United States Congressman living in a privately sponsored, middle-income building, paying $267 monthly for rent of a one-bedroom apartment. He has diabetes, is totally blind, with a below-knee amputation on the right, and partial loss of the left foot. He lives a bed–wheelchair existence.

His assets gradually dwindled, because total income was $312 and expenses $377 per month. When he had less than $1,000 left in the bank, we applied for rent relief under Section 8 but were stymied by the regulation that the maximum limit for Section 8 assistance on a one-bedroom unit is $225.

The patient, with confidence that he could deal with the bureaucracy by telephone himself, because of his political savvy and background, decided to challenge the ruling. A doctor's note in the chart records that: R. told me yesterday that he had a conversation with somebody at the housing office. The man on the phone said the rent was too high. R. said to him: "You tell me how I can find an apartment for $225 a month or less which includes utilities, in Manhattan, considering that I'm blind and have a double amputation." The answer was: "That's *your* problem."

Some local housing authorities sponsor programs of housing rehabilitation, often combined with a system through which the Housing Authority itself leases property from the private owner and then offers it to eligible low-income individuals and households. The Authority makes up the difference between the actual cost of the apartment and the special rates of public housing tenants. This permits aged people to remain in their own community and in their own apartment, which in some cases can be rehabilitated under the provisions of the program.[24]

Programs such as Section 8 are ultimately funded by the United States Department of Housing and Urban Development's Housing Assistance Program. The purpose of the funds released through this program is to provide rent supplements for families and individuals whose incomes are 80 percent or less of the median area income and who meet the other eligibility requirements contained in the federal guidelines.

Recipients of supplements may live in new, rehabilitated, or existing housing, and generally pay 25% of adjusted monthly income for rent. In some cases, an income of 50% or less of the median area income can qualify a recipient for rental at 15% of adjusted monthly income.[25]

Under another federal program Old Age Assistance recipients in several states may qualify for a plan under which their monthly government check is increased to help repay a loan taken out for minor home repairs.[8] This permits older people with limited incomes to improve and rehabilitate their own homes and go on living independently in the neighborhoods they know.

TAX REDUCTIONS FOR ELDERLY HOME OWNERS.   It may be assumed that ownership of a home provides housing at costs low in relation to income, that homeowners always have the option of selling and the freedom and financial means to move elsewhere. Unfortunately, this is not true. As Dr. Robert Butler points out, 48 percent of aged homeowners have a net equity of less than $25,000, and that although they can live rent-free, "they are at a disadvantage if they wish to sell and move elsewhere. Many older people find themselves trapped in their homes, unable to find available or alternative living arrangements at reasonable prices in a suitable locale."[5]

The elderly are often unable to pay their property taxes, much less the expense of utilities and maintenance. Some older people have been paying taxes they cannot afford on homes that have doubled or tripled in assessed value. The result is a forced sale and a move into less desirable quarters.[26]

The typical urban household spends approximately 3.4% of its income for property taxes, but elderly homeowners frequently find the burden much more substantial. Their taxes average 8.1% of their retirement income, but can go as high as 20 to 40%. Property taxes averaging $1,500 annually on modest homes are not uncommon, and one can quickly see what this does to a modest retirement budget. In major American cities the vast majority of aged property owners can expect to pay $300 at the very least for property taxes.[5]

Legislative relief of overly burdensome property taxes for aged homeowners is in order. The social cost of the status quo is too severe. To date, 24 states* and the District of Columbia have created methods through which these taxes are reduced or partially rebated when they are above the amount the state considers reasonable for the individual taxpayer. In some cases renters are given financial relief through the same legislation. Most programs are administered by the state income tax department, others through separate offices, either at the state or county level.[27]

In many instances, the tax reduction plan is worked out by the establishment of an income percentage as the maximum property tax burden any household should have to bear. If taxes exceed this level, the excess is refunded. In Wisconsin, for instance, where the tax relief plan originated, homeowners and renters with incomes between $3,500 and $7,000 got back from the state in 1974 80 percent of local property taxes that exceeded 14 percent of their income. Some 190,000 residents saved an average of about $185.00 each.[27]

Other relief plans become effective when the homeowner's income falls below a stated figure. In New York City, for example, where realty tax exemption is 50 percent of the assessed property value, the following conditions apply[22]:

1. The owner must be 65 years of age or over. If there is more than one owner, each must be 65 years or over
2. Combined annual income must be less than $6,000 for the preceding year
3. The property must be used exclusively for residential purposes

An alternative method creates a sliding scale, which grants an automatic rebate or credit to taxpayers in the various income classes regardless of

*Arizona, Arkansas, California, Colorado, Connecticut, Idaho, Illinois, Indiana, Iowa, Kansas, Maine, Maryland, Michigan, Minnesota, Missouri, Nevada, North Dakota, Ohio, Oklahoma, Oregon, Pennsylvania, Vermont, West Virginia, Wisconsin.

the amount of property tax they are required to pay. As income rises, rebate size falls.

Maintaining and/or Improving the Home

. . . [For] too many older people whose homes are their only tangible asset, there is barely enough income to meet even the day-to-day personal necessities. . . . Faced with no other alternative, too many older people have to give home and property maintenance the lowest priority in their list of expenditures. . . . To repair them costs money, at least for materials and usually for labor as well.[8]

As house or apartment deteriorates, the ability of people to live safely declines. Older people are particularly likely to occupy housing of poor quality and to meet these challenges at a time of life when they are least able to cope. As age advances, people are physically less mobile, less able to change housing, less able to make small repairs, less able to find help or to pay for it. Often, then, an older person cannot go to a better location, cannot maintain the present one, and simply sits helplessly inside the decaying shell of a home.

Physical hazard is the prime consideration, but beyond this, poor quality of the environment has a notable effect on the development of illness. The stresses placed upon people who live in deteriorated, dangerous surroundings produce disease.[3,6] This correlation is supported, for example, by a special study of the 1960 Housing Census conducted in 1963. It revealed that those older people in the poorest health occupied the worst of the substandard and dilapidated housing units.[8]

An obvious answer to the problem of deteriorating housing is the development of programs to maintain the physical environment for disabled older people.[3,6] In the development of a home repair program, consideration should be given to the following checklist of items, all of which must be in proper order for safe, healthy housing.

Cooking facilities (hot and cold running water, stove and refrigerator)

Bathroom facilities (tub or shower, sink, toilet, portable commode, and, if needed, safety railings)

Laundry facilities (in unit or nearby)

Stairs

Elevator

Locks

Windows (unbroken glass, clean and functional)

Fire protection (clear exit; electrical wiring and appliances in good repair)

Organizing of a repair squad may involve the use of skilled volunteers, participation by local business and unions as a gesture of good will, or the employment of handymen.[8]

An excellent example of original thinking in this area is a program created by the Department of Community Medicine at Mt. Sinai Hospital, New York City.[3]

In 1971 the hospital, the New York City Board of Education, and the New York City Health Department began a program known as the East Harlem Environmental Extension Service. This was organized as a nonprofit corporation by community and professional people, building owners, and health workers. The organizers realized that the local housing problem was not a lack of apartments but rather an inability on the part of the tenants to maintain them. The program provided direct maintenance services to area residents under contractual agreements with building owners. The ultimate purpose was to improve the quality of neighborhood housing and provide jobs for some of the unemployed in the community, at the same time training them in marketable skills. The program was publicly subsidized. Its trainees worked at boiler maintenance, plastering and painting, electrical repairs, simple plumbing, carpentry, replacement of broken or empty windowpanes and of screens, rodent and pest control, correction of faulty wiring, repair of heating systems and cooking facilities.

The program ended in 1973 because of inadequate funding, but during its tenure at least 10 buildings were saved from abandonment, housing maintained for a number of aged people, and the concept proven viable.

To implement a repair program and sustain it, money is needed. Volunteers wear out. Funding should be sought from federal and state government and the local community. Sources may include grants, Federal Housing Authority-insured loans from banks, and low-interest borrowing through the local Housing Authority for home improvements.[8]

The sponsoring agency must supply proper working conditions, safeguards for employees, supervision, and insurance. Repair work must be inspected and approved by government agencies. The program must adhere to building and safety codes.

Finding New Living Space

In the housing market, the aged poor are at a disadvantage. Space is in short supply and is likely to be found first by people who are young and vigorous. In addition, the quality of available housing is questionable. Finally, the cost of uncontrolled housing is beyond the ability of most aged people to pay. A recent study by the Community Council of Greater New York,[28] for instance, states that a retired couple requires an income of $641.25 monthly for a moderate living style. Of this, $155.80, or 25 percent, is allotted for rent.

These figures compare interestingly to data from the Chelsea–Village Program. Here, income of patients, based on information from 145 individuals, averages $246 per month. The median is $220 and the range from $56 to $910. The average Chelsea–Village Program patient pays almost 50 percent of total income for rent.

PUBLIC HOUSING.   Local housing authorities are responsible for administering the public housing projects of a region and various other programs which assist low-income individuals and families to obtain decent housing. Some public housing projects are especially designed for the elderly, and the management will make a particular effort to provide needed services.[25] In New York City the Housing Authority currently provides 4,604 apartments in 23 developments exclusively for the use of older people. Despite fairly onerous eligibility requirements, there is a substantial[22] waiting list.

Rents in public housing are relatively modest. In New York City, for instance, the overall average is $93 per month.[22] The poor maintenance of project buildings is a health and safety problem, however, in large part related to the low rent levels. In public housing, rent covers only about 60 percent of operating routine maintenance cost. In 1972, the Department of Housing and Urban Development altered the regulations and required that rent for tenants of new projects be set at a level which covers 85 percent of costs. As a consequence, the poorest families are excluded, since rents are based on a figure of 25 percent of income. The greatest impact is upon the poor aged, who have little hope of increasing their incomes.[5]

Local housing authority personnel are permitted to respond to requests for urgent attention. Waiting lists can be passed over occasionally in truly horrendous situations. In our Chelsea–Village Program experience, of three patients who moved from deteriorated private housing into projects, two succeeded only by urgent prodding on our part. One outlasted the waiting list.

For each such case it is necessary to attract the sympathy and understanding of a responsible individual at the Housing Authority, to develop an informal line of clout. A sense of personal involvement has a remarkably beneficial effect. It eases the bypassing of bureaucratic obstacles, but it may produce a degree of cynicism, as indicated in these notes from a Chelsea–Village Program staff conference.

IRMA STAHL: As far as I know, everybody comes up against the same thing —the Housing Authority is an obstacle. Unless the case is really drastic, and you spend a lot of time pushing it, we're all told, "Too bad—the waiting list is too long."

LAURA STARITA (Coordinator): Let's face it! It all depends on who you know. The priority lists aren't used at all. They're just pieces of paper. We all know that; it's just that no one ever comes out and says the truth. It's who you know in the Housing Authority that counts, if you want to move.

This is not always true. We have succeeded in arranging a move by going through channels, but a high tolerance for frustration is a necessity.

The following notes from a Chelsea–Village Program chart are pertinent.

7/17/73   R.B. is a 69-year-old woman with advanced chronic lung disease, living on the fourth floor of a walk-up apartment house. Plumbing and heating services are absent. The stairwell and walls are collapsing. There is garbage in the halls and in the public bathroom. The patient's physical disability makes it impossible for her to get out of the house, and yet the conditions under which she lives threaten her ability to survive.

She agreed to our suggestion that we try to arrange transfer to a housing project.

8/15/73   Patient is very upset and desperate about housing conditions. "I don't want promises, I want something concrete." We sent in the forms two weeks ago.

10/1/73   We have written letters to the Housing Authority, gotten the City Office for the Aging and Hudson Guild to apply pressure also. We have been told she is on the waiting list.

10/4/73   Letter received from the Housing Authority. "After your phone call we checked our files but could find no record of an application for Miss B. We enclose forms." The forms were filed again.

1/8/74   Miss B. was interviewed by employee of the Housing Authority.

3/12/74   No action since January. A Chelsea–Village Program physician called a Housing Authority social worker, explained the urgency of the move based on medical reasons. She agreed to recommend the move.

5/12/74   Miss B. was interviewed again by an employee of the Housing Authority.

8/19/74   Approval for move has come through.

187

Public housing offers a satisfactory solution to the problem for relatively few people, because the amount of government-sponsored construction falls far below the need.[5, 7, 8]

As of December 31, 1975, there were only 139,531 units of public housing in New York State,[29] a miniscule amount in comparison to the volume of housing in the private sector. Since older people generally cannot afford the latter and do not live long enough to reach the end of the waiting lists of the former, the problem is nearly intractable.

LIMITED PROFIT HOUSING.   Section 202 of the Housing Act of 1959 permits government loans to nonpublic sponsors of new housing. The Administration released $375 million for Section 202 housing in 1976, enough to finance approximately 25,000 housing units.[30] The present administration plans to release an additional $375 million for Section 202 loans in fiscal 1977 for another 20,000 units. The money is used to assist private, nonprofit corporations, consumer cooperatives, limited profit sponsors, and public bodies or agencies to build housing for the elderly or handicapped families. The Department of Housing and Urban Development provides direct loans of up to 100 percent of project cost to these sponsors, to be repaid at not more than 3 percent interest per year for a maximum of 50 years. The sponsor undertakes either to construct new housing or to rehabilitate previously existing structures so that they are suitable for the elderly and the handicapped. The program is intended to assist people whose incomes are too high for public housing and too low for the private market. Therefore the rents for Section 202 Housing are above what can be reasonably asked of the most impoverished aged. For these people, rent assistance or supplementation program funds can be called in to enable them to afford Section 202 Housing.[24]

Semi-independent Housing

For elderly people who can no longer live alone safely, prefer to avoid the burdens of housekeeping, or have been evicted, senior residential facilities are available.[24] This form of housing has an institutional flavor, but a degree of freedom can be preserved.

These units are similar to hotels, with private or multiple bedrooms, communal dining area, a health-oriented staff. They are a midpoint between independent living and a nursing home or health-related facility. In New York, the State Board of Social Welfare is responsible for setting of standards, licensing, and general oversight.

People who are bedbound or need continuous medical/nursing care are not eligible for entrance into this type of housing, but some assistance with bathing, dressing, and moving about is available. Housekeeping services and meals are provided.

By state regulation, to be called a senior residential facility the unit must house more than four people. Most are larger. There are 587 such homes in New York State, with a capacity of about 34,000 people.[31] Sponsorship is provided by government agencies (usually at the county level), nonprofit organizations such as church groups, lodges, or unions, or, as is often the case, privately owned corporations run for profit, called ''proprietary homes for adults.''

People living in senior residential facilities may be eligible for support under the federal Supplementary Security Income (SSI) or Social Service Programs. In 1977 SSI pays a maximum of $386.70 monthly for this kind of housing. Medicare and Medicaid do not pay for these facilities, but some medical costs are covered.

There is a natural tendency to believe that residences sponsored by nonprofit social agencies are in some manner more wholesome and attractive than are government or proprietary institutions, and more responsive to individual and community sensitivities. Certainly, control of the home by a broad-based civic organization means that management may call upon a wide membership for financial and political support.[25]

There are, however, some difficulties connected with sole reliance on nonprofit agencies. Housing facilities operated by private groups tend to be member-oriented and therefore limited in their ability to solve the general housing problems of older people;[16] or money may be in short supply after a time and the agency need to fall back upon government for support. Loss of policy control results.

Most senior residential homes run by nonprofit agencies—particularly church-related facilities—have stood up to the threat of future insolvency by establishing founder's fees or life-lease contracts as an important part of their financial structure.

A founder's fee is paid by the first occupants of a facility and entitles the resident to lifetime use of an apartment or nonhousekeeping unit. The resident is secure and makes, at the same time, a contribution to a church or other nonprofit agency by helping to finance capital investment in the facility and pay off the mortgage. The first residents must also pay a monthly charge for maintenance and other services based on operating costs. People who move in later are sometimes required to pay a life-lease fee or make a life-contract arrangement which calls for a sum based on the new resident's life expectancy. This is usually less than the founder's fee. The life-lease also guarantees an older person lifetime occupancy of a dwelling unit and is supplemented by a monthly charge. Both founder's fees and life-lease contracts guarantee living quarters for the balance of a life, but ongoing operating services, health care, and other programs must be paid for separately. After the resident's death the apartment reverts to the sponsor organization, not to the person's estate.[25] In some cases provision is made by sponsors for people who cannot afford the full cost of a facility.

Foster Homes

Foster homes follow the same principles as senior residential facilities, serve the same purposes and clients, but are smaller. In New York State, they can house a maximum of four persons. They are commonly the actual home of a family, particularly valuable, then, for aged people who will fit well in an intimate setting.

In the foster home program, a family, which may consist of one mature adult who does not work outside the home, agrees to shelter, protect, and supervise an elderly person with physical or emotional problems which make independent living not wise. The attitude of the foster family is crucial because it must provide more than shelter, food, and personal services. The owner is expected, in addition, to show friendly concern and a real interest in the patient's welfare. Some voluntary agencies maintain private foster homes for adults, but most homes used by voluntary agencies are certified by the State Board of Social Welfare in New York City and by the New York City Department of Social Services.[32] Foster homes must comply with fire protection, health, and sanitation ordinances.

The rate of reimbursement to foster home proprietors for the room and board they provide to residents on public assistance is negotiated with the local social services department.

In New York City this rate is currently $270.00 or $275.00 per month for a single room, depending on the elderly person's private sources of income (such as Social Security or Supplemental Security Income), and $265.00 for shared accommodations. In addition, an allowance is paid to the elderly resident on Supplemental Security Income or in the public assistance category for personal needs such as clothing. Medical care support is provided by Medicare and Medicaid.

A variant of foster care, called "day care," is designed to provide temporary relief to a spouse or other relative who ordinarily has the full responsibility for an elderly person. In this program the patient is left for a short time, perhaps several days, in the care of a foster home family.[6]

Hotels can provide freedom from the responsibilities of home upkeep and meal preparation, while still allowing an elderly person to remain part of a larger community composed of all age groups. There is a wide range of quality in hotel facilities. Some offer two or three meals daily, good linen service, a doctor or nurse in residence, a clinic or infirmary, a social worker, and a range of activities, all included in the monthly charges. Some hotels, usually older and in convenient downtown locations, cater especially to retired people and are redesigned appropriately.[25] These hotels, in part because they are older, are often well constructed.

At the other end of the scale is the single-room occupancy (SRO) hotel, which houses aged people who cannot afford to live elsewhere.[33] The rent is relatively low, in the range of $35 per week, but the rooms are small and poorly maintained, the walls are thin, and the building often is not fireproof. The rooms may all be double occupancy, and bathroom facilities often are shared by an entire hall.[34] There is usually no maid service, and the residents may have to accept responsibility for duties ordinarily provided by management.[25] SRO hotels tend to deteriorate as supervision becomes lax, maintenance haphazard, and buildings older.[33]

Unless hotel room rates are covered by rent control, the possibility of sudden, marked increase in room price always exists. Payment plans for commercial hotel quarters vary. Advance of the first or the last month's rent or a yearly payment to guarantee the resident's stay is a common requirement.[25] In any case, potential customers should know in advance exactly what is offered and what is required before signing up.

Some hotels offer a life-care plan.[25] This may mean no more than the promise of food and shelter, inadequate for an aged, disabled person removed from his or her own community and friends. Some hotels advertise low rates and favorable conditions, which they do not fulfill. Hotels have been known, for instance, to offer reduced costs to older people on condition that they perform work which is found to be beyond their ability or strength.[25]

Housing Emergencies

Situations occasionally occur in which the need for housing is so extreme that the only alternative is to have an aged person sleep on the sidewalk. Eviction, fire, flood, building collapse are persistent sources of trouble in major metropolitan areas.

Public policy[35] permits local agencies of Housing or Relocation and

191

Management Service to provide emergency quarters.[22] The use of hotel space is the first choice for immediate placement. Because the city government usually pays the bill, and because hotels are expensive, the next step is often transfer to public housing, if it is available, or to low-rent housing in the private sector. In New York City, victims of fires are entitled to priority and bypass the long waiting lists for public housing.

Aged people who suffer from a housing disaster that endangers health, safety, and financial security, and who are eligible for Supplemental Security Income benefits, may receive an emergency cash fund which can be used for rent or security deposits.[21]

HOUSING VIOLATIONS AND LEGAL ASSISTANCE

Older people whose own homes have building code violations and who lack the money or strength to make repairs can obtain assistance from the local Housing Authority under the provisions of federal legislation.[36] Loans and grants for home maintenance are available to elderly homeowners living in urban renewal areas or code-enforcement areas.[8, 24]

People living in rented quarters face a different set of problems. It is increasingly common[33] to find the court system becoming the principal local office for resolution of housing complaints of poor, aged people and a forum for negotiations among tenants, community groups, landlords, and government agencies. Legal Aid Societies should be contacted for people who need legal counsel and lack money to pay for service.

In New York City the Housing Section of the Civil Court handles all housing cases. Under the supervision of judges or hearing officers, the court may:

Impose civil penalties for housing code violations
Enforce liens on real property and rents
Issue orders to correct violations and collect costs for these corrections or for demolition, contracted by the city
Handle eviction procedures, deal with rent strikes
Appoint receivers
Remove violations of record
Compel compliance with the housing maintenance code and multiple dwelling law[22]

Valuable as this kind of court may be, it represents a bureaucratic approach to the complex problem of housing. As such, it often misses the point, or is blind to the human situation behind the case.

192

Public health approaches to inner-city housing maintenance and repair services have tended to emphasize the role of code enforcement. . . . But, paradoxically, as urban housing codes have become ever more progressive, sophisticated, and enlightened, urban core-city housing conditions have worsened all over the United States. The slum housing economy is today too weak and disorganized to comply with campaigns to enforce these standards. . . . The "housing" problem is a housing maintenance and conservation problem. The owner "gives up" on trying to improve conditions—Why?—rent and housing codes, lack of money, bank mortgage policies, management problems, narcotics, crime and the social difficulties of the urban poor.[3]

Improvement of the situation depends more on availability of money and better organized efforts to rehabilitate buildings than on improved published standards in code enforcement guides.

SOURCES OF HOUSING INFORMATION

In order to find housing, arrange for repairs, obtain available funds, or seek legal redress, people must know the housing system. As the material in this chapter indicates, the system is complex, disorganized, and easily subject to abuse by insiders. In order to get help, one must find people or organizations that are both knowledgeable and motivated. Useful information and referral sources likely to be found in any metropolitan area or county are listed in the Appendix.

REFERENCES

1. Special Committee on Aging, United States Senate: Congregate Housing for Older Adults; Assisted Residential Living Combining Shelter and Services. Committee Print, Washington DC, US Government Printing Office, Nov 1975
2. Select Committee on Aging, United States House of Representatives: Hearing: Problems of the Elderly in Syracuse, NY. Washington DC, US Government Printing Office, 1977
3. Richter ED, Jackson S, Peeples S, Wood C, Volante R: Housing and health, a new approach. Am J Public Health 63:878, 1973
4. Bild BR, Havighurst RJ: Senior citizens in great cities: the case of Chicago. Gerontologist 16:39, 1976
5. Butler RN: No place to live. In Why Survive? Being Old in America. New York, Harper, 1975, Chap 5
6. Gelwicks LE, Newcomer RJ: Planning Housing Environments for the Elderly. The National Council on the Aging, Inc., 1828 L St NW, Suite 504, Washington DC 20036, 1974
7. Tivern MB: Older Americans; Special Handling Required. National Council on the Aging, Inc, 1828 L St NW, Suite 504, Washington DC 20036, June, 1971

8. Chandler S: Home Maintenance and Repair Program for the Older Poor. Community Action Program, OEO and National Council on the Aging, Inc., 1828 L Street NW, Suite 504, Washington DC 20036, March, 1972

9. Select Committee on Aging, United States House of Representatives: Elderly Crime Victims: Personal Accounts of Fears and Attacks. Hearings before the Subcommittee on Housing and Consumer Interests. Washington DC, US Government Printing Office, 1976

10. Select Committee on Aging, United States House of Representatives: Crime Against the Elderly. Hearing before the Subcommittee on Federal, State, and Community Services, Washington DC, US Government Printing Office, 1977

11. Garetz FK: Breaking the dangerous cycle of depression and faulty nutrition. Geriatrics 31:73, 1976

12. Citizen's Committee on Aging: Report of the Home Health and Housing Program. Community Council of Greater New York, 225 Park Ave South, New York, NY 10003, 1970

13. Brickner PW, Janeski JF: The Chelsea–Village Program—the four-year report. Department of Community Medicine, St. Vincent's Hospital, 153 West 11th St, New York, NY 10011

14. "Bankruptcy" forecast for many walk-ups. New York Times, Sunday, May 26, 1974, p 1

15. Donohoe M: Personal communication, 4/26/77

16. Andrews RB: Housing for the elderly: aspects of its central problem. Gerontologist 3:110, 1962

17. Birren JE: The abuse of the urban aged. Psychology Today 3:37, 1970

18. Farrell WE: Governor signs measure to decontrol empty flats. New York Times, Thursday, June 3, 1971, p 31

19. Farrell WE: Decontrolled apartments show sharp rise in rents. New York Times, Sunday, August 8, 1971, p 1

20. End rent control, New York City urged. New York Times, Sunday, June 12, 1977, p 29

21. Rights and Benefits for Older New Yorkers. The New York City Department for the Aging, 250 Broadway, New York, NY 10007, April 1977

22. Bartley E, Hill G, Godek C, Jaffe R: The Housing Advocate, A Handbook on Tenant's Rights in New York City Programs, Regulations and Laws. New York City Office for the Aging, 250 Broadway, New York, NY 10007, July 1974

23. Housing and Community Development Act of 1974, Title I (42 USC 4501 et seq)

24. Senior Opportunities and Services, Technical Assistance Monograph No. 7: Improving the Living Environment of the Elderly Poor. The National Council on the Aging, Inc, 1828 L St NW, Suite 504, Washington DC 20036, 1971

25. A Guide for the Selection of Retirement Housing. The National Council on the Aging, Inc, 1828 L St NW, Washington DC 20036, 1976

26. Life for the Elderly in 1975: Many are Hungry and Afraid. US News and World Report 78:48, Feb 10, 1975

27. "Circuit breakers" lighten the property tax load. Changing Times 29:37, 1975

28. Kihss P: Social Security checks fall short in budgets of New York's elderly. New York Times, Monday, June 13, 1977, p 25

29. Statistical Yearbook. Office of Public Affairs, Department of Housing and Urban Development, 451 7th St SW, Washington DC 20410

30. Special Committee on Aging, United States Senate: The Proposed Fiscal 1977

Budget; What it Means for Older Americans. Staff Report, Washington DC, US Government Printing Office, February 1976

31. Directory of Domiciliary Care Facilities for Adults in New York State. The New York State Board of Social Welfare. Two World Trade Center, New York, NY 10047, June 1, 1976

32. Neilan WJ, Seymour MJ: Manual, Housing for the Aged. Information Bureau, Community Council of Greater New York, 225 Park Ave South, New York, NY 10003, June 1972

33. Legislative Priorities: 1977, A Human Needs Agenda. Community Service Society of New York, Department of Public Affairs, 105 East 22nd St, New York, NY 10010, December 1976

34. Brickner PW, Greenbaum D, Kaufman A, O'Donnell F, O'Brian JT, Scalice R, Scandizzo J, Sullivan T: A Clinic for Male Derelicts, A Welfare Hotel Project. Ann Intern Med 77:565, 1972

35. 1160 of the Administrative Code of the City of New York

36. Home Rehabilitation Loans (Sect 312, Housing Act of 1964); Home Rehabilitation Grants (Sect 115, Housing and Urban Development Act of 1965); Homeownership Rehabilitation (Sect 235 (j), National Housing Act) (1968); Supplemental Loans (Sect 241, National Housing Act) (1968)

CHAPTER 12

SOCIAL CONTACT AND TRANSPORTATION

Six and a half million aged Americans live alone.[1] Efforts to create contact for these people with other human beings include programs that (1) increase their mobility and (2) bring visitors to the home. Transportation methods are a significant part of any system designed to provide social contact. They are discussed in the second portion of this chapter, following an analysis of the problem of social isolation and attempts at solutions.

SOCIAL ISOLATION

Six factors lead to isolation in older people:

1. The high frequency of widowhood. The life expectancy of women —76.1[2] years in the United States at present—is 8 years greater than that of men.[3] As a result, of the 6.5 million people over age 65 living alone or with nonrelatives, 5.0 million are women.[1]
2. Demographic patterns: the break up of the extended family, the move of younger people to the suburbs, and the abandonment of older people who are left behind in the central city.[4-6]
3. The physical consequences of aging, which make moving around difficult or hazardous.
4. Common attitudes in our society that make aged people feel unwanted, guilty for being alive, and more comfortable hiding themselves away.[7-10]

196

5. Enforced retirement, usually at age 65, with the result that there is less natural opportunity for human relationships and less money.[11]
6. Death of friends, relatives, and a falling apart of the social network.

Being over seventy is like being engaged in a war. All our friends are going or gone and we survive amongst the dead and the dying as on a battlefield.

—Muriel Spark, *Memento Mori*[12]

The feelings of older people about being alone vary from fear and depression[13-16] to acceptance. Occasionally, older people insist on being alone. In this regard, information about our patients in the Chelsea–Village Program is noteworthy.

Two-thirds live alone. 25.5 percent of the Chelsea–Village Program patients never married. Of female Chelsea–Village patients from age 65 to 74, for example, 35 percent never married, compared to 6.6 percent of the whole US female population from the age of 65 to 74 (see Table 1-5).

Clearly, in any group of isolated, older people, a considerable number have always been alone, a consequence of individual personality traits and behavior patterns. Efforts to provide social contact must be geared to the wishes of the patients. Let each individual make the choice. To inflict a gushing well-wisher on a person who values privacy is opprobrious do-goodism.

And yet, for most people, programs which relieve loneliness are a blessing. This is true despite an initial diffidence which an older person may express. Disengagement, a term used to describe the withdrawal of older people from the society around them, is often the result of a "progression of losses, diminutions of strengths, decreasing opportunities for meaningful and restorative personal and social experiences, and increased isolation."[17]

It may be assumed that disengagement is a normal and expected process, a natural phasing out of the feelings, activities, and social ties of aged people as they prepare to depart from life.[5, 17, 18] While this is a matter of debate for sociological theorists, we prefer to take our clue from Mrs. O'H., a Chelsea–Village Program patient, reacting to the presence of a homemaker: "Gracie is very good. I thought I'd go crazy being alone."

For some people, contact with others is of such critical importance that it outweighs all other considerations, as indicated in this Chelsea–Village Program case report.

E.L., a 72-year-old sculptor disabled by chronic left- and right-sided conges-

197

tive heart failure, lived on the third floor of a walk-up loft building. His studio and co-workers were on the second. Despite medical advice to the contrary he insisted on coming down daily "just for company" because he was too ill to work. He was able to make it one way but was too short of breath to climb back up. After being rescued several times, an alternative was worked out: his bed was moved into the studio.

Those who have always lived alone may be at an advantage in facing the social deprivations common to older people.[19] Although they, too, face increased isolation in old age, their lives have been relatively independent and so they are better equipped to deal with solitude, less likely to be lonely, than older people who have recently been deprived of a spouse or close friend.

The critical question, then, if we are preparing a program to relieve social isolation, must be: Does the person involved wish to withdraw from people and activities, or is he or she being forced to do so by conditions and processes beyond control?

Value of Social Contact

For those people who will accept a relationship with others, social contact serves two functions: (1) pleasure and the preservation of emotional and intellectual well-being and (2) observation by another of personal health and safety.

Long periods of unwanted isolation, with absence of stimuli from the outside world, can result in anxiety, depression, agitation, or apathy and ultimately in physical illness.[5,8,13,15,17,20,21] Because of an understandable sense of rejection that older people may have, a feeling of being unwanted, defensive reactions may take place.

> Or, as the snail, whose tender horns being hit,
> Shrinks backward in his shelly cave with pain,
> And there, all smothered up, in shade doth sit,
> Long after fearing to creep forth again. . . .
> —W. Shakespeare, *Venus and Adonis*[22]

Individuals may repel all efforts by others to establish contact, while desperately wishing to relate at the same time. This exquisite ambivalence, an effort to protect against further rebuffs, is exemplified by this comment from a Chelsea–Village Program patient: "Besides being nasty, how can I thank you people?"

A pleasurable interest in life can be reestablished in sad, confused, apathetic people through well-planned programs offered with kindness and attention to individual needs.

Visitor Programs

Friendly visitor programs can be established to fulfill specific needs of isolated older people: (1) human contact; (2) chore services, and (3) observation of the physical and emotional state.

People who participate in these programs fill in the gap and carry out functions which are not precisely health or social services, do not require professional knowledge or skill, and could be performed by a thoughtful neighbor, friend, or relative, if there were one. In times of crisis, the visitor is available as an advisor or go-between and, on a regular basis, can observe or monitor. The visitor is a companion and shopper, reader and writer, a sharer of hobbies and gossip and carries out any activity that benefits the older person, strengthens interest in life and human relationships.[21, 23, 24]

Of the numerous friendly visiting programs presently in existence,[23, 24] the Village Visiting Neighbors[25] is a prototype.

Village Visiting Neighbors*

This program was established in 1972 in Greenwich Village, Manhattan, by a consortium of local agencies and interested individuals, including churches, synagogues, and block associations and their members, settlement houses, the Visiting Nurse Service of New York, and St. Vincent's Hospital. The founding purpose was to organize a group of volunteers to visit homebound, aged people in the community in order to develop a personal relationship and to carry out simple tasks. In 1977, it has under care about 75 active clients. A board of directors is legally responsible for the conduct of the program, its coordinator, and the volunteer visitors. Board members are representatives of the original sponsoring organizations, volunteer visitors of experience, and aged people.

From the beginning Village Visiting Neighbors grasped its responsibility, as an organization, to screen volunteers, establish standards and exercise supervision, so that aged clients were not abused. The board has raised money for a paid coordinator and established bylaws, training programs, regular meetings, proper documentation of visits, and guidelines for conduct of the volunteer staff. These guidelines are widely applicable:

*Village Visiting Neighbors, Inc., 371 Avenue of the Americas, New York, NY 10014.

1. Be dependable. Do not promise more than you can fulfill.
2. Be cheerful, without undue exuberance.
3. Make appointments for visits ahead of time—and keep them.
4. Accept conditions in the home as you find them, barring matters of immediate safety.
5. Encourage the client's confidence in professional health workers involved in the case.
6. Engage the cooperation of other household members, if any.
7. Respect the confidence of the client.
8. Keep relations on a friendly, cheerful plane, but dignified.
9. Maintain your interest and enthusiasm; realize that you have an opportunity to bring freshness in from the outside world.
10. Remember that the client's span of interest may be short due to fatigue or illness. Plan the program of the visit accordingly.
11. Be flexible. Respond to the client's interests.
12. Encourage the revival of old hobbies as a source of continuing interest for future visits.
13. Plan ahead. Bring with you materials needed for craft work, games, reading, writing.
14. Be aware of and understand the client's handicaps.
15. Accept the client as he or she is.

Certain negatives are emphasized as well:

1. Do not give medication or offer medical advice.
2. Do not suggest treatments.
3. Do not consult with physicians or other health workers on behalf of the client.
4. Do not discuss other clients' problems.
5. Do not lift the client. This takes skill and training, as well as strength.
6. Do not undermine the client's confidence in others who help.
7. Do not criticize or give advice on housekeeping or other conditions in the home.
8. Do not give money to the client, and do not accept money or gifts of substance. Remember, you are a visitor.
9. Do not be discouraged or frustrated if your client is slow to develop interest in you.
10. Do not get emotionally involved. Try to be objective but not calloused or tough.

The training program for volunteers consists of discussion focused on the following topics, conducted by the coordinator, with questions and answers:

The process of getting old

Attitudes of the elderly (especially the homebound) and the volunteer's reaction

Relationship between the volunteer and the elderly client

Medical problems of the elderly

The nursing home

Understanding the end of life

Activities for senior citizens

The coordinator is the key to making the program work. She knows every volunteer, visitor and aged client, maintains records, conducts the training programs and regular meetings, and is responsible to the board of directors for the daily activities of the organization. Either alone or with a membership committee she interviews all volunteers and, with a coordinating committee, develops procedures designed to maintain order. A summary of these procedures follows:

VOLUNTEER VISITOR

1. Interview visitor and give him/her an application.
2. Have visitor return completed application to coordinator.
3. Get written or telephone reference and enter on visitor's application.
4. File application in Visitor's Available File.
5. Enter visitor's name, address, and telephone number in card file.
6. Send name and address to corresponding secretary.
7. Send name and address and phone number to head of membership committee.
8. Send visitor welcome letter and guidelines and first month report sheet.

ELDERLY CLIENTS

1. Interview elderly client (and the person who referred him/her whenever applicable) and enter all information on Elderly Application Form.
2. File application in Elderly Available File.
3. Enter name and address and phone number in card file.

MATCHING

1. Match elderly client and visitor, and file elderly client and visitor's application in Permanent File, elderly client application on top. Complete both sheets.

2. Complete both cards in card file, noting names and telephone numbers on each card.
3. Send to head of membership committee the name, address, and phone number of elderly client matched to visitor, whose name he/she already has.

VISITOR INACTIVATED

1. Inactivate visitor's index card and cross out name on his/her elderly client's card.
2. Put card into Inactive File and note reason for inactivity.
3. Send a note reporting inactivity to membership committee head.
4. Send a note reporting inactivity to corresponding secretary.

ELDERLY CLIENT INACTIVATED

1. Inactivate index card of elderly client and cross out name on his/her visitor's card.
2. Put record into Inactive File and note reason for inactivity.
3. Send a note reporting inactivity to head of membership committee.

(*Note:* Whenever visitor or client is inactivated, always put the counterpart back into the Available File and proceed as with new visitor or elderly client in matching with a new name.)

GENERAL SUPERVISION OF MATCH

1. After first visit get in touch with visitor and client to find out if match is all right.
2. Make sure that visitor will notify coordinator when he/she stops or interrupts visiting for any reason whatsoever (illness, vacation).
3. Make sure that visitor will call coordinator and tell him/her about problems of any kind that develop with elderly client.
4. Make sure visitor sends in monthly report sheets.

Financial Aspects

Titles I and XVI of the Social Security Act provide money for information and referral agencies, protection services, and self-support systems for the handicapped. These resources may be used to fund friendly visitor programs, depending upon decisions by individual state welfare agencies.

Other resources for grants include the various state commissions on aging, which operate with money from the Administration on Aging, the United States Department of Health, Education, and Welfare, and a wide variety of local agencies and private philanthropies.

Budgets for these programs are ordinarily modest, since the bulk of service is volunteered. A recent budget for the Village Visiting Neighbors is given in Figure 12-1.

The Telephone

People can be severely disabled and continue to use the phone. Telephone contact provides a variety of advantages for homebound aged people: relief of loneliness, information, protection and safety, and emergency assistance.

Organized systems in which the phone is a key resource are relatively

---

**Proposed Budget
to Cover the Period 7/76 to 6/77**

	Amount Requested
A. **Salaries**	
Program coordinator	$12,000
Secretarial services	1,000
Subtotal	13,000
Fringe benefits	1,300
B. **Occupancy**	
Building rent	2,400
Utilities	120
C. **Furniture and Equipment**	
1 Typewriter—purchased	350
2 Desks and chairs—purchased	100
D. **Operating Supplies and Office Expense**	
Consumable supplies	100
Reproduction	300
Postage	200
E. **Telephone**	
Installation and service	450
F. **Staff Travel**	100
Grand Total:	**$18,420**

FIG. 12-1.   Budget for Village Visiting Neighbors.

simple to conduct, inexpensive, practical, and in common use. Ordinarily, they are called Telephone Reassurance Programs, but all of the above benefits result.[26]

These programs are usually developed by religious or service organizations and use volunteers to call clients on a schedule, either from a central location or the volunteer's home. The call provides a daily check on physical condition and a source of human contact. If the older person fails to answer or if the number is persistently busy, the caller assumes that there is trouble, and immediate help is sent.

Clearly, an organized program requires advance preparation of a network of contacts, including police, fire, and ambulance services, personal physician, and the location of building superintendent and/or friend of the client. The name, address, and phone number of the next of kin are important, as is a list of medications and medical information. All this should be recorded clearly and systematically for each client and be available instantly to the caller. Further, each volunteer should understand ahead of time how to react in any contingency.

It is wise for the volunteer to visit first with each person he or she will be calling to explain the service, obtain the required basic information, establish a mutually convenient time for the call, and personalize the relationship. The client must be responsible for informing the volunteer in advance if he or she will not be present at the usual time to answer the daily call. False alarms and wasted effort will result otherwise.[27]

Local telephone companies may be persuaded to reduce costs if the expense of a phone is a burden to individual clients, and to waive the deposit or installation fee.[27] Special equipment is also available, including devices for hard-of-hearing patients and touchtone systems for people with poor use of arms or hands.

With imagination, additional uses of the telephone can be devised. Programs presently exist, for instance, which provide an older person with a number to call simply to talk to somebody.[28] Telephone hotlines have been formed to provide immediate medical advice or the services of a clergyman.[27]

Occasionally the telephone may be the only method of communication with the outside world that a person will permit. The following excerpts from a Chelsea–Village Program case conference are pertinent:

IRMA STAHL (Social Worker): T.T. is a woman in her 60s referred to us by a Meals-On-Wheels Program. The patient had insisted for months that the food be left outside her door. No one from the program ever saw her. Finally, almost by mistake, one of the deliverers was let in. The patient was blind. The apartment was filthy. Her clothing was rags. People from the program then

204

called us, figuring she needed medical help. She is happy to talk with me on the phone—for a good half-hour or more—very pleasant, mentally acute, rational, alert, but if I ask her any personal questions or invite myself over, she says, "I've got to hang up," and she does.

She finally agreed to let someone shop for her. I got a young high school girl interested. The process consists of T.T. slipping money under the door, and the groceries are brought and left there. No physical contact occurs.

ATTENDING DOCTOR: This situation reminds me strongly of the cases of Emilia Lucca and Eugenia Ronder.[29]

STAHL: For now I feel we have to settle for telephone contact. She's embarrassed or afraid. A visitor on the phone is not like someone coming through the door who's going to see her. She is willing to accept regular phone calls, and I feel we must—and should—be willing to adapt to her wishes.

TRANSPORTATION

For homebound, aged people, ability to move from place to place is markedly decreased or absent. Transportation methods must be created for these individuals in order to (1) move them to outside locations by appointment, (2) bring services and staff to the home, (3) carry equipment and supplies, perform errands, and (4) handle emergency situations.

Taking People Outside the Home

People who are homebound require assistance in order to go out.[30] There exist a variety of systems created to make movement around the community easier[31-33] or cheaper[34] for older people whose physical condition permits considerable independent activity. Efforts have been made, for instance, to improve the physical features of urban transit systems: signs made more easily readable, steps shallower, lighting brighter. According to Eckman and Furman,[35] the Massachusetts Bay Transportation Authority, on the advice of aged consumers, applied nonslip surfaces to steps, installed handrails and lightweight turnstiles. In San Francisco, the Bay Area Rapid Transit System is designed with elevators from street to train and doors, aisles, and bathrooms which accommodate wheelchairs. Various bus systems have made changes by lowering the steps and widening the aisles.

Programs designed to handle the transportation problems of the most deeply isolated aged—those living in rural areas—also exist across the country.[36] These projects have ordinarily started with funding provided in the form of grants that require a gradual takeover of costs by the local agency. Programs have often failed to survive this step because transportation services are expensive, especially in rural areas where distances are great.

And as valuable as these various approaches are for many people, they are not particularly useful for the disabled group under consideration here, the homebound aged.

The facts of life in our society require, however, that people reach out in order to receive legal benefits, fulfill their needs for recreation and social contact, carry out personal chores, and obtain particular kinds of health service.

For the homebound, community agencies can be successful in providing transport services through organizations like the Red Cross, or arrangements can be made to use school buses during much of the day. Taxi companies can be asked to provide service at reduced cost, and volunteers can be recruited who are willing to use their own cars. Obtaining a vehicle may be easy, compared to other problems. If patients must be carried, moved in a wheelchair, assisted with a walker, if stairs must be traversed, or substantial distances covered on level ground, one or two strong people may be needed. Not every volunteer is appropriate. Further, legal risks are involved in moving people. Both personal liability and vehicle insurance must be obtained.[32] A casual approach to these points invites disaster.

In the Chelsea–Village Program, we have had to arrange trips for our patients to welfare and housing offices, banks and lawyers, hospitals for tests which require fixed equipment that cannot be brought into the home, dentists, and public meetings or special events that they wished strongly to attend. The only organized transportation system which applies in New York City for these patients is the ambulance or ambulette to and from medical institutions, paid for by Medicaid. For the other purposes we use a vehicle and driver, with additional staff as necessary. Insurance coverage is arranged through St. Vincent's Hospital's policies for other vehicles and employees.

We use our best judgment about safety factors. When the patient's physical condition is particularly fragile we have occasionally had to find money to hire an ambulance or ambulette, with crew, or been successful in asking private ambulance companies to provide free service for individuals, by planning the trip for times of day when business is slow.

Bringing Services and Staff to the Home

For our aged patients to remain independently at home, a comprehensive network of services must be provided. In many obvious ways, transportation methods are involved in this network. If the older person cannot go out, food, medications, supplies, and professional health staff must be brought in. It is our experience in the Chelsea–Village Program—a program that takes doctors, nurses, and social workers to the home—that a driver and vehicle are an essential efficiency. Professional staff time is simply too expensive for the delays of public transportation.

Emergency Situations

In a true health emergency, an ambulance must be called. Programs that provide chronic care at home are unlikely to double successfully as emergency services. Attitudes, training, equipment, response time, numbers of staff people required, and nature of the vehicle are all different. In the Chelsea–Village program we have instructed our patients, and their relatives, if any, accordingly.

The Driver's Job

The needs of older, homebound people are diverse, and staff members who work with them must be supple, in order to serve them well. It is not possible to anticipate every contingency.[37] The job description of the Chelsea–Village Program driver reflects this viewpoint (Fig. 12-2).

The driver and vehicle provide a safety factor. Our ability to transport

---

Job Summary: Chauffers staff and patients, delivers supplies.

Responsibility: Under the coordinator's supervision:

1. Chauffers and escorts program personnel to patients' homes.
2. Chauffers patients from home to other locations, with assistance as necessary.
3. Performs general chore services for the program and for patients when a vehicle is required.
4. Delivers goods and supplies.
5. Performs related assigned duties and performs clearly unrelated assigned duties, as needed.

Skill: High school graduate or equivalent.
Must have ability to empathize with the needs of patients and serve these needs in a sensitive manner.
Must be bilingual in English/Spanish, English/Italian, or English/Hebrew.
Possess New York State driver's license, must have good safety record as driver.

Effort: Some strenuous physical effort required while transporting patients.

Working Conditions: Indoors and outdoors in all types of weather.

FIG. 12-2. Job description for driver for Chelsea–Village Program.

and escort staff members into deteriorated neighborhoods and buildings has made it possible to serve patients trapped in these areas with less anxiety about crime.

The driver provides a method of delivering needed material to the home without the need to rely on other people who may be unmotivated. He also performs errands for patients and generally acts to fulfill the variety of human needs that arise unexpectedly. As examples, we have placed 50 ornamental plants donated by a wholesale florist and a birthday cake for a centenarian, carried a hospital bed which was a gift to the program on condition that we supply the vehicle and muscle to move it, and removed various deceased pets.

MONEY FOR TRANSPORTATION SERVICES

Federal Funds

Federal money is available for transportation services under a wide variety of sponsorships and legislative statutes. These are summarized in a publication of the Department of Health, Education, and Welfare.[36] In order to start a local transportation program, advice should be sought from the United States Department of Transportation,* the United States Administration on Aging,† and the Offices of Aging of states and cities. Likely sources of federal money follow.

URBAN MASS TRANSPORTATION ACT OF 1964. Under this legislation (Section 16(b)(2), as amended), money is allocated each year for capital assistance grants and loans to private, nonprofit corporations and associations which provide transportation services to the elderly and handicapped. In 1976, $22 million was available. Money for the purchase of vehicles can be obtained under this act. The government will pay 80 percent of the cost; the local agency must provide the remainder. The United States Department of Transportation can supply information and application forms.

TITLE III: OLDER AMERICANS ACT. Under Title III the Federal Administration on Aging awards grants to the states to assist in the development of comprehensive and coordinated services to the aged. These include transportation methods. In fact, the regulations for Title III state that plans for local areas *must* include transportation assistance in order to

*United States Department of Transportation, Office of the Secretary, Washington, DC 20590.

†United States Department of Health, Education, and Welfare, Office of Human Development, Administration on Aging, Washington, DC 20201.

ensure that older persons can actually receive the other benefits that are created under this Title.

The major inhibiting factor in funds sought under Title III is that plans are approved and supported for a maximum of one year. Refunding is not automatic.[36]

TITLE VII: OLDER AMERICANS ACT. Up to 20 percent of a state's allotment under Title VII (the nutrition program for the elderly) may be used for supportive services, including transportation. Logically, for support under this Title, transportation funds should be used to bring patients to food or vice versa.

Tying transportation and food service programs together is rational planning for any group which is considering comprehensive services for the homebound aged.

TITLE VI: SOCIAL SECURITY ACT. Under this Title (the service program for aged, blind, and disabled people) a broad range of benefits is available, including transportation. Programs are administered by state social service departments and are permitted to serve only people who are applicants for or are actually receiving Supplemental Security Income (SSI) benefits. In order to apply for money the appropriate state agency should be contacted, with plans to stimulate the bureaucratic imagination by using Title VI money in an organized way, for a comprehensive transportation system, rather than the doling out of individual services.

TITLE XIX: MEDICAID. Individuals covered by Medicaid can have ambulance or ambulette trips to clinics, hospitals, and doctors' offices paid for under this program, as well as services of taxicabs, common carriers, and privately owned vehicles, depending on regulations adopted by the various states. The limiting factor here is the requirement that services be for medical purposes only. The legislation inhibits overall planning by its emphasis on individual trips.

Surplus Federal Property

Vehicles for the program can be purchased cheaply as surplus federal property. Information is available in the pamphlet *Buying Government Surplus Personal Property* available from the General Services Administration.*

*Office of Personal Property Disposal, Federal Supply Service, General Services Administration, Washington, DC 20405.

State Funds

The federal funds described above are largely allocated by the states. In addition, state-generated funding sources exist. These include direct allotments for transportation from the state budget and a variety of other specific allocations. State lotteries, and property, cigarette, motor vehicle, parking lot, gasoline, and other tax sources are expressly authorized to support special transportation services and have been tapped in recent years.[31, 36]

In order to penetrate the bureaucratic maze and learn how to apply for available transportation money, locally elected state legislators are a good source of information.

Philanthropic Agencies

A transportation program may thrive with little money and minimal external regulations if it can be organized at the local level. Philanthropic agencies with a background in transportation—the Red Cross, Muscular Dystrophy and Cerebral Palsy Associations, American Cancer Society—can band together to establish a comprehensive transportation service for the aged. The experience, the vehicles, the staff, and the volunteers are available. All it takes is an organizing group with motivation to put across the concept, to overcome the inevitable petty rivalries and disputes over power and authority which will arise.

REFERENCES

1. Facts About Older Americans. US Department of Health, Education, and Welfare. Office of Human Development, Administration on Aging. DHEW Publication No (OHD) 77-20006
2. Department of Commerce, Bureau of the Census: Statistical Abstracts of the United States, 96th ed. Washington DC, 1975
3. Department of Commerce, Bureau of the Census: Current Population Reports. Demographic aspects of aging and the older population in the United States. Washington DC, US Government Printing Office, May 1976, Series P-23, No 59
4. Bild BR, Havighurst RJ: Senior citizens in great cities; the case of Chicago, Chap 5, Housing. Gerontologist 16:8, 1976
5. Carlson S: Communication and social interaction in the aged. Nurs Clin North Am 7:269, 1972
6. Birren JE: The abuse of the urban aged. Psychology Today 3:37, 1970
7. Strauss AL: Social isolation. In Chronic Illness and the Quality of Life. St. Louis, Mosby, 1975, Chap 6, p 54

8. Hess BB: Stereotypes of the aged. J Commun 24:76, 1974
9. Comfort A: On gerontophobia. Med Opinion Rev 3:31, 1967
10. Busse EW: Viewpoint; prejudice and gerontology. Gerontologist 8:66, 1968
11. Butler R: The right to work. In Why Survive? Being Old in America. New York, Harper, 1975, Chap 4, p 64
12. Spark M: Memento Mori. New York, Meridian Books, 1960, p 37
13. Lynch JJ: The Broken Heart. New York, Basic Books, 1977
14. Walton M: An old person living alone in the community. Gerontol Clin (Basel) 10:358, 1968
15. Denes Q: Old-age emotions. J Am Geriatr Soc 24:465, 1976
16. Thompson MK: Adaptations to loneliness in old age. Proc R Soc Med 66:887, 1973
17. Gossett HM: Restoring Identity to Socially Deprived and Depersonalized Older People. Nursing Home Project: United Hospital Fund of New York, lecture delivered at the Fall Membership Meeting of the Community Council's Citizen's Committee on Aging, October 20, 1966
18. Steine R, Woolf LM: Synthesizing hospital care with a senior center program. Gerontologist 13:197, 1973
19. Gubrium JF: Being single in old age. Int J Aging Hum Dev 6:29, 1975
20. Bennett R: Social isolation and isolation-reducing programs. Bull N Y Acad Med 49:1143, 1973
21. Pidgeon H: Voluntary and public cooperation in the care of the elderly. R Soc Health J 2:93, 1975
22. Shakespeare W: Venus and Adonis. In The Complete Works of William Shakespeare. New York, Walter J. Black, 1937
23. Robinson W: Caring for the elderly in Camden. Nurs Times 69:439, 1973
24. Robison S: Home visits to the elderly. Am J Nurs 74:908, 1974
25. Sheppard N: Shut-ins find a link to outside. New York Times, April 30, 1976
26. Greene MS: Ring-a-Day: a telephone reassurance service. Health Social Work 1:177, 1977
27. Match SK: Establishing Telephone Reassurance Services. Office of Economic Opportunity. The National Council on the Aging, Inc., 1828 L St NW, Washington DC 20036, July, 1972
28. Let's End Isolation. Department of Health, Education and Welfare. DHEW Publication No (OHD) 75-20129, p 18
29. Doyle AC: The adventure of the red circle; and The adventure of the veiled lodger. In The Complete Sherlock Holmes. Garden City, NY, Garden City Publishing Co.
30. Carp FM: The mobility of older slum-dwellers. Gerontologist. 12:57, 1972
31. Fishbein G: Innovative transportation systems involve more than "tokenism". Geriatrics 30:140, 1975
32. Project Helping Wheels. United States Department of Health, Education, and Welfare, Administration on Aging. Publication No (OHD/AOA) 74-20102
33. Kaye I: Transportation problems of the older American. In Cull JC, Hardy RE (eds): The Neglected Older American, Social and Rehabilitation Services. Springfield, Ill, Thomas, 1973, Chap 6
34. Morlok EK, Kulash MW, Vandersypen HL: The Effect of Reduced Fares for the Elderly on Transit System Routes. US Department of Health, Education, and Welfare, Social and Rehabilitation Service, Administration on Aging

35. Eckman J, Furman W (eds): Handbook and Directory of Nursing Homes and Other Facilities for the Aged Within a Fifty Mile Radius of New York City. New York, Basic Books, 1975

36. Transportation for the Elderly, The State of the Art. Department of Health, Education, and Welfare, Office of Human Development, Administration on Aging. Publication No (OHD) 75-20081, Jan 1975

37. Kerr J: Please Don't Eat the Daisies. New York, Fawcett World, 1976

CHAPTER 13
THE HOMEMAKER

We have seen homemakers provide eyes and ears for the social worker, the psychiatrist, the physician and nurse with a kind of carefulness and continuity that can never be achieved through single home visits, office consultations, or even in the institutional setting.[1]

Help in the home is essential for many aged, homebound people if they are to survive and remain independent of institutions. The provision of adequate food and housing is not sufficient for older people whose physical mobility and strength are borderline. Assistance in cleaning, cooking, shopping, other domestic services, and minor medically related functions must also be made available if nursing home transfer is to be avoided.

Homemaker programs must be integrated with other health and social services in order to fulfill their mutual purposes. Homemakers by themselves cannot replace or generate basic medical and social welfare services,[2] but by their nature they emphasize the point that

. . . much more is involved in health than just health care, no matter how broadly the latter is defined. Environmental and behavioral threats to good health are inherent in many conditions of contemporary American society. . . . Obviously, homemaker services alone cannot stem this tide. They symbolize, however, the need for reintegrating health, welfare, and community services as they apply to the individual and to the family.[3]

Homemakers, housekeepers, and home health aides are defined separately through job descriptions, but it is wiser to stress the similarities rather than the differences among these positions. People employed in these categories are engaged in overlapping services related to the health, safety, and general welfare of their aged patients. The titles of the various jobs in this field tend to be confusing and to result in fragmentation of service.[4] Training should be designed to resist this tendency and to cover

213

a comprehensive array of duties. The philosophy must prevail that the patient's interests come first.

HISTORY

Organized homemaker services were originated early in this century with the goal of preventing the institutionalization of children who required special attention or whose mothers were incapacitated.[5,6] Until 1965 most programs remained child-oriented. With the passage of the Medicare and Medicaid laws, however, attitudes changed because there was a new flow of money. In the 1950s about half of the known agencies limited their services to families with children, but in 1974 only 6 percent were so restricted. Adults, particularly the frail elderly, are now the major beneficiaries.[6]

ORGANIZATION AND STANDARDS

A dominant pattern of organization for this growing form of service is not yet established. The trend is for homemakers to be added to the various programs offered by multiservice agencies, but about one-fourth of the known homemaker programs are independent.[6]

There is no national standard of quality, but an attempt at creating guidelines is being made by The National Council for Homemaker–Home Health Aide Services. The Council, established in 1962, working with national social welfare and health agencies, public and voluntary, at the local and the state levels, has produced a set of standards for all types of homemaker services. Included are statements on the purpose and function of homemakers, organization and administration, staffing and orientation, the education of homemakers, techniques of record-keeping, and community relations.[7,8]

In 1972 the Council began the process of evaluating and approving programs that comply with its standards.[6] Currently, 118 of the 1,700 programs across the nation are approved. The Council's standards serve as models for departments of social service, aging, health, mental health, and rehabilitation in a number of states.

Our experience indicates that the most effective arrangement for deploying homemakers is a system in which they are part of a large agency. In this way, the multiple forms of assistance needed by homebound, aged people can be integrated rationally. The Chelsea–Village Program utilizes homemakers for its patients from a variety of sources, including government (the New York City Social Service Department, Section of

214

Homemakers), voluntary agencies (the Visiting Nurse Association of New York), and occasionally from private organizations if the patient has money to pay for help. In many instances, however, there is no money available, and yet the patient is not eligible for outside assistance. Therefore, we have a homemaker on our own payroll, free to step in and provide assistance without delay, red tape, or limitations of any kind. Her job description (Fig. 13-1) is designed to encourage multiple functions in patient care. Her title, community health aide, is deliberately general in nature and indicates that she is free of limits in her service to patients.

GOALS AND PURPOSES

The ultimate purpose of the homemaker is to help patients meet home health and social needs. Specifically, homemakers work under the supervision of professional members of the health team to help make viable the plan of care.[9]

The homemaker is the eyes and ears of the team, able to report about patient status when others are not present, while at the same time performing domestic chores and personal and paraprofessional duties.

The homemaker performs a valuable function simply by monitoring the condition of the patient. She sees the patient more frequently than any

---

Job Summary: To provide household assistance and to meet the physical and emotional needs of aged and chronically ill individuals.

Responsibility: Under the direction of the Director of the Chelsea–Village Program

1. Provides the following functions to chronically ill and aged persons: personal care, general cleaning, nutrition planning, marketing, meal preparation, laundry, ironing, bathing, errands, and other sickroom chores.
2. Relates to the emotional needs of patients and provides reassurance.
3. Receives assignments and reports on tasks completed regularly.
4. Reports on unusual changes in patients' personal and environmental condition.
5. Performs related assigned duties and performs clearly unrelated assigned duties in times of emergency.

Skill: Must have ability to perform housekeeping, homemaking, and personal care tasks. Must have ability to empathize with the needs of patients and service these needs in a sensitive manner. Must have ability to climb stairs. Must be bilingual in English/Spanish or English/Italian.

Effort: Standing, sitting, walking, bending, climbing stairs, etc.

Working Conditions: Indoor and outdoors in all types of weather.

FIG. 13-1.   Job description for community health aide.

215

other member of the health care team, in more intimate circumstances, and is thus in the best position to note changes. Her ability to report alterations in the patient's condition to the professional health team can be of critical value.

One of the major difficulties which the chronically ill patient at home had to face was the fact that since he is in a sense invisible, he can easily be forgotten. Patients in a hospital bed must be looked after. The patient at home, whose need for a specific service has terminated and who may later need something else, does not automatically receive the necessary assistance, but usually comes to someone's attention in another crisis situation which might have been avoided. We found that sometimes when we closed a case to homemaker service because it really seemed that we were no longer needed a whole new set of needs developed over a period of weeks or several months, and by the time we were brought back into the picture (if we were), institutional care was the only solution. Often it was a solution that could have been averted.[2]

In the training process the goals of cleanliness, punctuality, responsibility, and team cooperation are stressed. A proper attitude toward the patient is vital, one in which the dignity and privacy of the older person are respected. The homemaker must recognize that she is not the ultimate authority or decision maker. This responsibility belongs to the patient and to the doctor, nurse, and social worker. She must avoid becoming emotionally entrapped in the patient's problems and yet be sensitive and responsive.[4] She should be flexible enough to plan her schedule of household duties to fit in most comfortably with her patient's daily routine and conform most closely with his or her wishes.[6] She should keep in mind that she is in the home of another person and avoid being domineering. She should try in every way to include the patient in her plans for the maintenance of the environment.[4]

Working hours can be defined to meet the goals of the employee, the patient, and the program. Women recruited and trained as homemakers want and need full-time employment. It is possible to provide this for them while at the same time responding appropriately to the needs of their patients, for it is a virtue of in-home services that hours can be gauged to the amount of time actually needed to complete the necessary tasks.[6] A full-time homemaker can have her schedule so arranged that she provides part-time service in several homes, the few hours of service required by the well aged in many homes during the week or portions of the round-the-clock care required by seriously ill people.[10]

216

TERMINOLOGY AT ITS CONFUSING WORST

Homemakers, Home Health Aides, Housekeepers, Home Attendants, and Homemaker–Home Health Aides

The functions of all the variously titled classifications of helpers-in-the-home revolve around the same set of duties: domestic chores, personal care, paraprofessional health care, and other related services. There is, however, variation in the way the function of each particular classification of home helper is defined, depending on the traditions and conventions of the providing agency. The different titles create confusion, and serve very little useful purpose.

Generally, the basic distinctions are between responsibility for personal care as opposed to strictly housekeeping chores. The titles homemaker and housekeeper denote a worker whose primary duty is the upkeep of the patient's environment, but a homemaker often has responsibility for some personal care tasks as well. The titles home health aide and home attendant are given to a worker whose duties center on the provision of personal and paraprofessional health care, but a home health aide is often responsible for routine housekeeping tasks as well insofar as those contribute to the safety and comfort of her patient.

Thus, in the spectrum of home helpers, the housekeeper is responsible almost solely for the upkeep of the environment, perhaps including meal preparation. The homemaker's function is essentially the performance of domestic chores, with some responsibility for personal care. The home health aide's role is basically personal and paraprofessional health care and performance of domestic duties necessary to the safety and comfort of the patient. The home attendant is responsible almost solely for daily personal and paraprofessional health care services, including escorting services and trying to keep the patient active and interested in events beyond the walls of the home.

People experienced in this field have suggested that patient needs would be better served by the integration of these services into a single job.[11]

The multiplication of titles [for subprofessional workers in the home] troubles me for several reasons. The least important, from my point of view, is that we are going to be wasting a good deal of time defining function, establishing criteria for selection, setting up specialized training programs, which differ slightly but in which those slight differences are going to become important to the people who set them up. The most crucial danger, from my point of view, is . . . further fragmentation in what is already a somewhat chopped up picture.[4]

217

Personal care has been recognized by reimbursement authorities as a valid health need, while housekeeping service has not. Therefore, the cumbersome term *homemaker–home health aide* has been created to cover all of the preceding functions.[3] Under this title, some of the rigidities of definition that create fragmentation are avoided, and there is the added advantage that the employee can be paid for under Medicare law.

SPECIFIC FUNCTIONS

While the duties of these employees fall naturally into the categories of domestic chores, personal care, and paraprofessional health services, every effort should be made to integrate these skills in daily work. Beyond these specific duties, it is important to recognize that the very presence of the homemaker is a benefit. For many older people, the homemaker is the only human being they see. She reduces the patient's isolation and often is more important than the professional staff in maintaining morale and averting depression.[12, 13]

Domestic Chores

Aged people are often unable to maintain a reasonable standard of upkeep in their homes. Occasionally the basis of the problem is confusion,[14-16] but more often the elderly simply lack the strength, energy, and agility necessary to clean the house, do the laundry, and prepare meals. Furthermore, as we have noted in Chapter 1, there are forces at work in contemporary society that tend to isolate older people at the same time that the chances of disability are rising. Often there is no family member or friend to step in and help. Two-thirds of the patients we have cared for in the Chelsea–Village Program, for instance, live alone. The homemaker, therefore, can be a critically important support for independence simply by taking over some of the household tasks or can relieve to some degree the pressure on a friend or relative, if there is one.[10]

A list of domestic chores commonly needed includes:

Preparing and serving meals
Making and changing beds
Dusting and vacuuming rooms
Dishwashing
Tidying kitchen, bathroom, and bedroom
Listing needed supplies

Shopping for supplies and doing errands
Doing personal laundry of patient
Ironing and mending
Sending linen to the laundry
Emptying trash and garbage
Cleaning and defrosting refrigerator
Reading and writing for the patient, paying bills
Escorting[17]

Personal Care

In the past, there has been a persistent line of demarcation in the homemaker service field between responsibility for the environment of the patient, the strictly housekeeping functions, and responsibility for the body of the patient, duties that involve touching the patient and are thus defined as supplemental to the nursing role. This distinction is arbitrary. Is meal preparation and assistance in eating a housekeeping or a nursing function, for instance?

Close professional supervision of the employee who performs personal care is a necessity, with careful attention supplied to the details of each individual patient's need. The supervising nurse or social worker must take responsibility for the proper training and conduct of employees.[18]

Personal care tasks generally include assistance with:

Care of teeth and mouth
Grooming: care of the hair, shaving, and care of the nails
Bathing, in the bed, tub, or shower
Getting on and off the bedpan, commode, or toilet
Moving from bed to chair or wheelchair
Walking, and in the use of crutches
Dressing and exercising
Preparing and serving meals on diets prescribed by the physician[17, 18]

Paraprofessional Health Care

Paraprofessional health care means routine health care tasks, or the specialized aspects of personal service, which require training and supervision of the homemaker by the physician or nurse responsible for the patient. Therefore, the home health aide is really a nurse's aide transferred to the home setting.

After the professional members of the home health team have worked

219

out the treatment regimen, the parts which can safely be carried out by the homemaker or home health aide are clarified.

Paraprofessional or routine health care tasks include:

Assistance with prescribed skin care and prevention of body deterioration due to bed confinement (back rubs, exercises, massages)

Help in use of support devices

Dressing changes

Observation and record making of important signs (temperature, pulse, and respiration) and general monitoring of the patient's condition

Irrigation of Foley catheter

Assistance with change of colostomy bag

Administration of medication

Application of heat or cold[17]

SUPERVISION

Competent professional supervision of the homemaker, both administrative and directly on-the-spot, is essential to the success of a homemaker program.[19-21]

The director of the home health care program should be responsible for:

Screening and selection of applicants

Coordination of training

Assignment of homemaker to patient

Decision on termination of services

Hours, wages, and benefits

Evaluation of the employee[20]

The coordinator should be available for discussion about job-related problems and grievances.

Day-to-day supervision of the homemaker in her work with individual patients is the responsibility of the nurses, doctors, and social workers who make up the health care team. The professional staff provides guidance in matters related to medical and psychological care of the patient, decides which services are necessary, and how they should be carried out.

Appropriate assignment of employee to patient depends upon the demonstrated skills of the worker and patient requirements. Intangible factors—the personalities and psychological makeup of both patient and aide—as well as clear-cut issues, such as particular health needs, enter into each of these decisions.

Unusual problems may arise, and it can take a high level of wisdom and judgment to resolve them. Aged people may develop paranoid thoughts and ideas of reference. The aide may be accused of theft or of physical abuse. The dependent situation of aged men may create unrealistic or unacceptable feelings toward the aide, often sexually oriented. We have experienced, for instance, a situation in which our aide was accused by a man in his 90s of prostitution, selling herself to him for $900. This matter reached the police before we managed to resolve it.

Be prepared, because these loaded issues will inevitably arise. Their resolution requires (1) knowing the employee thoroughly, (2) regular monitoring of each case, and (3) understanding the patient.

QUALIFICATIONS AND TRAINING

There is substantial agreement as to the qualities that make for a good homemaker. Age and educational background are less important than:

1. Experience in personal care and/or homemaking
2. Good physical and emotional health
3. Ability to read and write to at least an eighth grade level, to carry out directions and instructions, record messages, and keep simple records.[17]

We stress the importance of the proper attitude toward patients. The director of the program, whose responsibility it is to screen and select applicants for homemaker positions, should be aware of important personality traits in potential homemakers. The homemaker must be willing to learn and able to work under supervision as an employee of the agency, accepting criticism in a constructive spirit. She must be able to cope with the difficult situations she will encounter in her place of work[6] and be able to deal with crises. She must be mature, well adjusted, and contented, positive in outlook, interested and concerned about the welfare of others.[2,4] She should be able to treat her aged clients with tact, discretion, friendly politeness, and display a sensitivity to their desires, needs, and fears.

The homemaker must be trained in the maintenance of acceptable standards of home management and personal care. She should be taught how to deal with the behavioral problems that she is likely to encounter, and should be provided with general knowledge about the processes of

221

aging, diseases, and disabilities of her patients and techniques for dealing with the associated physical and psychological difficulties. Resource material for the development of training programs is available.[6-8, 11, 17, 18, 22-24]

In addition to the formal aspects of preparation for the job, the homemaker should be introduced to the concepts of the program and its relationship to the community, her place in the agency, and her responsibility for working cooperatively under the supervision of the coordinator and the professional staff.

FINANCING

Payment Mechanisms

Homemaker service agencies, public and voluntary, independent or sub-organizations within a larger agency, seek financial support from a variety of resources. No agency relies totally on fees.[2, 5] Among these sources, public tax monies figure as the largest and most important for most homemaker agencies, both public and private. The federal government supplies substantial funds to the states for homemaker services through grants from various governmental departments, including the Department of Health, Education, and Welfare, the Welfare Administration, The Bureau of Family Services, the Children's Bureau, the United States Public Health Service, and the Vocational Rehabilitation Administration.

Voluntary sources available for support of homemaker service include community welfare organization funds, endowments, foundation support, and gifts.

The fragmentation of funding is perhaps the greatest obstacle to be overcome in the whole of the homemaker service field.[25, 26] Each of the many sources is governed by its own regulations. The need to respond to the myriad of rules and contractual obligations tends to limit the service's sensitivity to the real needs of the community. "What is lacking is an assured public funding arrangement which will call into existence a personal care service network which can be assured of a stable basis for existence. Once in being, the basic service can grow as needed through private purchase of care."[27]

Federal and State Legislation

The Medicare and Medicaid legislation of 1965 (Titles XVIII and XIX of the Social Security Act) provided 80 percent of cost reimbursement rate to properly qualified "home-health agencies" for a wide range of home health services, including home health aides. In reality, however, this source of funds remains hedged with restrictions, especially with regard to the use of the service for the assistance of the chronically ill.[11] Medicare permits reimbursement for home health aide service only when it is provided in connection with an active program of *medical* treatment in the home. The potential beneficiary must require skilled nursing care, physical therapy, or speech therapy. The providing home health agency is reimbursed only for the personal care services its aide performs, not her housekeeping tasks, unless they are incidental and do not increase the amount of time she spends in the household.[3]

The provisions of Medicaid are not so restrictive. They provide broad coverage for home health aides to persons receiving or eligible for public assistance and more limited coverage to other groups. In reality, however, the implementation of the home health sections of Medicaid have been unreliable and inefficient. The Medicaid program suffers from a constant financial pinch. It has never made good on its promise to make home health care a reality.[11] In 1974 all home health programs represented less than 1 percent of Medicare expenditures and about 0.4 percent of federal-state expenditures under Medicaid. The percentage within that amount spent for home health aide service is so small as to be negligible.[6]

The federal government has made some progress in responding to the need

. . . by gradually increasing the scope of services which can be provided in-home to patients who qualify for Medical Assistance. Under the provisions of the 1973 amendments to the Social Security Act, a home health aide may perform simple procedures as an extension of therapy services, personal care, ambulation and exercise, household services essential to health care at home, assistance with medications that are ordinarily self-administered, reporting changes in the patient's condition and needs, and completing appropriate records.[17]

Yet restrictions in the Medicare legislation are still a major barrier to the expansion of home health care services and a force working for unnecessary institutionalization. Since funds from federal and state sources could offer the best assurance of continuous support of home health aide service programs, it is recommended that an all-out effort should be made to support legislation at the federal and state levels which will expand the provisions of the Medicare and Medicaid programs to meet the actual needs of the ill person and his family in the home. This will remove the limiting features of the program so home health aides can be used more flexibly and helpfully.[11]

COSTS

A study undertaken by the National Council for Homemaker–Home Health Aide Services, Inc., based on data from 43 home health agencies in 1971 and 1972, reported an average cost per hour of service of $3.98. The median cost was $3.79, from within a range of $2.09 to $7.50. The average cost per case, per year, was $467.79. These figures were compiled from data made available by programs approved by the National Council and include information from agencies under the three classifications of homemaker service: strictly housekeeping, mainly personal care, and agencies providing both services under professional supervision.[28]

A more recent study of homemaker–home health aide service as an alternative to nursing home care in Milwaukee found an average cost of $5.70 per hour for an average of four hours per week and an average cost of $100 per month per client.[12] This figure included the administrative costs of the providing agency. Unpublished data reported to the National Council for Homemaker–Home Health Aide Services by 74 approved programs from all sections of the country showed a 1974–1975 average cost per hour for homemaking services of $5.28.[3]

Evaluating the cost of the homemaker component of home health programs is more difficult than measuring the housekeeping costs of institutional care. The characteristics of home health care that make it desirable to the patient—its flexibility and responsiveness to personal needs—also make it less uniform and therefore more difficult to measure and to compare with other services. Advocates of home health care and advocates of institutional care present differing comparisons of cost-effectiveness because criteria used in their respective studies are not the same.[3] The fact is that home health care and institutional services are not alternatives to each other if utilized properly. Each type of care is cost-effective for appropriate patients.

REFERENCES

Starred publications are available from the National Council for Homemaker–Home Health Aide Services, Inc., 67 Irving Place, New York, NY 10003. Tel.: (212) 674-4990

1. Winston E: Homemaker service and social welfare. In Readings in Homemaker Service. New York, National Council for Homemaker Services, 1969, pp 18-19
2. Trager B: Homemaker services for the aged and chronically ill. In Readings in Homemaker Services. New York, National Council for Homemaker Services, 1969, p 61

3. Somers AR, Moore FM: Homemaker services—essential option for the elderly. Public Health Rep 91:354, 1976
4. Trager R: Recruitment and training of homemaker–home health aides. In Readings in Homemaker Services. New York, National Council for Homemaker Services, 1969, p 130
5. Soyka PW: Homemaker–home health aide services for handicapped children. Child Welfare 55:241, 1976
6. Shinn EB, Robinson ND: Trends in homemaker–home health aide services. Abstr Social Workers 10:3, 1974
7. Standards for Homemaker–Home Health Aide Services. New York, National Council for Homemaker–Home Health Aide Services, 1965*
8. Addenda to Standards for Homemaker–Home Health Aide Services. New York, National Council for Homemaker–Home Health Aide Services, 1969*
9. Rioux C: Health and social services under the same roof. Can Nurse 71:24, 1975
10. Nielsen M, Blenkner M, Downs T, Beggs H: Older persons after hospitalization: a controlled study of home-aide service. Am J Public Health 62:1094, 1972
11. Powers R, Weis SE: How Homemaker Services Meet Medical Needs. Hospital Homemaker/Home Health Aide Study. Department of Central Services and Institute of Welfare Research. Community Service Society of New York, 105 East 22 St, New York, February 1971
12. Berg WE, Atlas L, Zeiger J: Integrated homemaking services for the aged in urban neighborhoods. Gerontologist 14:388, 1974
13. Tunstall J: Old and Alone. London, Cox and Wyman, 1966
14. Stevens RS: Self-neglect in the elderly. Br J Geriatr Prac 2:88, 1963
15. MacMillan D, Shaw P: Senile breakdown in standards of personal and environmental cleanliness. Br Med J 2:1032, 1966
16. Clark ANG, Mankikar GD, Grey I: Diogenes syndrome—a clinical study of gross neglect in old age. Lancet 1:366, 1975
17. Health Occupations Education: Home Health Assisting, Program Development Guide No. 4 Albany, New York, The University of the State of New York, State Education Department and the Bureau of Home Economics Department, 1975
18. Guidelines regarding personal care in homemaker services. In Readings in Homemaker Service. New York, National Council for Homemaker Services, 1969, p 80
19. Supervision of homemakers. In Readings in Homemaker Services. New York, National Council for Homemaker Services, 1969, p 135
20. Essential ingredients of supervision. In Readings in Homemaker Services. New York, National Council for Homemaker Services, 1969, p 136
21. Williams C: Supervision and the homemaker–health aide. In Readings in Homemaker Services. New York, National Council for Homemaker Services, 1969, p 139
22. Training Manual—Homemaker–Home Health Aides. New York, National Council for Homemaker–Home Health Aide Services, 1967*
23. When Your Community Needs Homemaker–Home Health Aide Service, A Brief Guide to Starting One. New York, National Council for Homemaker–Home Health Aide Services, 1977*
24. Supplementary Services Guidelines, for Services Supplementary to Home Health and Homemaker–Home Health Aide Services. New York, National Council for Homemaker–Home Health Aide Services, 1977*

25. Homemaker–Home Health Aide Services in the United States, 1966 Survey Report. In Readings in Homemaker Services. New York, National Council for Homemaker Services, 1969, p 189
26. Moore FM: New issues for in-home services. Public Welfare 35:26, 1977
27. Morris R, Harris E: Home health services in Massachusetts, 1971: their role in care of the long-term sick. Am J Public Health 62:1088, 1972
28. Costs of Homemaker–Home Health Aide and Alternative Forms of Service: A Survey of the Literature. New York, National Council for Homemaker–Home Health Aide Services, 1974*

SECTION FOUR
The Financial Basis

CHAPTER 14

ANALYZING THE COST

with Linda Keen Scharer, M.U.P.

Health planners and legislators must have available accurate cost measures of home health care services in order to develop public policy. The questions of eligibility and utilization are related issues. This chapter reviews these points and analyzes costs in detail. In the next chapter, a similar study is performed of nursing home costs, and comparisons between the two are reviewed.

THE COMPONENTS OF COST ANALYSIS

Reliable measures of cost for the maintenance at home of disabled older people must include not only medical and health-related expenses but also all other living costs. These include housing (rent, mortgage, maintenance, utilities, telephone), food, clothing, transportation and entertainment (if any), supplies, and allowance for incidentals. Only by developing an all-inclusive total can proper comparison be made with institutional costs.[1]

A source of difficulty in developing believable financial information is lack of consistency in the available data. The problems include (1) confusion in the defining of terms, for example, what constitutes a visit, what is a homemaker, what is home health care?[2] (2) geographic differences in the nature of institutions, state laws and regulations, salary scale of staff, reimbursement rates, Medicaid eligibility levels, (3) variations in the quality of care, which are hard to define, and (4) the uncertain cost value of social factors, such as the psychologic benefit of being in one's own home instead of an institution.

More subtle variables which must be considered in comparing home health care costs with those of institutions are (1) the degree of functional impairment borne by the patient. To take an extreme example, if all nursing home patients are bedbound and all patients in a home-health care program are able to walk, cost comparisons would be meaningless. (2) The extent to which human contacts are available. If an individual is surviving at home instead of in a nursing home because friends and relatives are helping, the value of their services must be included in the total cost of maintenance. (3) The extent to which quality of services can be measured. For instance, can the value of housing be considered equal when the choice lies between occupancy of a four-bedded room in an institution and a private bedroom in one's own home, if each costs the same?

Once methods for developing uniform cost comparisons are established, the issue of anticipated utilization of services remains. Uncertainty about the number of people who would require care if it becomes available is a major deterrent to effective planning.

COST STUDIES

In recent years useful studies have appeared[1-9] which analyze costs of service for homebound, aged people, the subjects of this book. This work should not be confused with earlier material related to the financing of traditional home care[10-16] (Chap. 3).

None of the present analyses are entirely successful in meeting the difficult challenges of comparability and comprehensiveness, but they are nonetheless substantial attempts to provide data.

The most important information gap concerns the number of aged people in need of care. For this, the most accurate information available—a guess—is 1.7 million to 3 million aged individuals. These figures, cited in a report prepared by the Levinson Gerontological Policy Institute of Brandeis University,[17] include "people confined to home or institutionalized for some measurable physical illness, injury or handicap, or who are severely limited in movement or mobility." Excluded are those with mild restrictions, mental illness, or retardation, or disability so severe that institutional care is mandatory.

In general, cost studies tend to use sources of financial information most easily available. The more comprehensive analyses, obviously, include a greater number of cost components. The only valid comparisons are those which are all-inclusive. Furthermore, as Gavett points out, "one must really know how data are collected at the origin before valid interpretation is assured."[2] The following reports contain significant weaknesses but provide important data and are worth study.

Southern California Medical Center (Los Angeles) Home Care Program[7, 8]

For over 10 years, Dr. Robert Mims and staff have provided hospital-based services for people in their own homes. The program has grown to include over 300 active patients per year, most of whom are aged. Cost figures based on data from 1973 through 1976 show substantial savings. For instance, 40 patients with medical disorders saved $156,000 for anticipated in-hospital costs in 1976 because they were entered in the program. Between 1 and 3 percent of patients were hospitalized at any one time, but their length of stay is significantly (P < 0.001) less than during a control period.

Mims estimates that the daily program cost for patients is less than $3.00. This figure does not include standard living expenses. The available references on this program do not attempt to compare total costs with those of long-term facilities in the Los Angeles area. It is a characteristic problem of these cost analyses that they compare with acute care hospitals rather than with nursing homes.[18]

District of Columbia and Wicomico County, Maryland, Comparison[9]

William Pollak developed cost estimates for care of four aged patients with varying degrees of functional impairment, in four different physical settings: at home, in foster care, at an intermediate care facility, and in a nursing home. He then compared the costs in a rural setting—Wicomico County, Maryland, to those in an urban area—Washington, DC.

For those patients in the city, care at home was cheapest for one, care in an intermediate care facility was cheaper for three. In the rural area, home care was cheapest for two, foster care and intermediate care for one each.

The lessons of this carefully devised study are costs vary with patient needs, geographic location, and availability of services.

Minneapolis Age and Opportunity Center (MAO)[19]

MAO is a multipurpose program for aged people. Daphne Krause, the Executive Director, in describing the home care component, indicates that cost savings can be remarkable. To cite one of her extreme examples:

A patient had been under care at home for 59 months. Services provided, with cost estimates, are:

231

Home-delivered meals	$ 817.80
Home care and chore service	
provided by family	7.98
Transportation	343.40
Counseling	284.75
Volunteer service	1.00
TOTAL	$1,454.93

If the patient had been in a nursing home, paid for under Title XIX, the cost estimates are as follows:

Average basic cost of nursing	
home care at $540 per month for	
59 months	$31,860.00
Less client's income of $121	
a month, with allowance to	
patient of $25 a month	7,139.00
COST TO TITLE XIX	$24,721.00

Therefore if Title XIX could pay for all home care services in this case it would save the taxpayer $23,266.07 over a 59 month period.

This striking report requires fleshing out before it can be used properly for comparison. It lacks adequate information about costs at home, including value of housing, medical costs, and estimated value of family services.

. . . the savings may not be universally applicable, and . . . it cannot be absolutely ascertained that the individuals assisted by MAO would otherwise have been institutionalized on a full-time basis; the evidence indicates a great potential for cost savings under certain conditions.[19]

A COMPREHENSIVE ANALYSIS—
THE BOEHRINGER REPORT

In 1975 the Florence V. Burden Foundation provided funds for a comprehensive analysis of home health care costs, conducted by Boehringer Associates.[20] The Chelsea–Village Program (CVP) of St. Vincent's Hospital, New York, was used as the prototype.

The purpose of the study was to determine the actual costs of the Chelsea–Village Program and then to provide a basis for comparing the costs of care for similar patients in nursing homes in New York City with patients in this program (Chap. 15). To complete the analysis, the study included auxiliary household help and living costs required by the aged who wished to remain at home. Living costs were provided as guides rather than precise, individual measurements.

The cost of the CVP was determined through time studies of patient visits and the associated office work required to support the program. From these studies, standard times were developed and standard costs calculated.

The costs of anticipated auxiliary services, such as homemakers, home attendants, housekeepers, visiting nurses, as well as rent and food allowances, were obtained through publicly available sources.

Patients in the CVP are served by a team consisting of a physician, nurse, and social worker, who visit alone or in combination with one another. The focus of the program, in terms of time and reported achievements, is the patient visits. In 1975, there were 886 visits. A trend line analysis indicated that if the rate of growth continued, 1,140 visits could be expected in 1976. During this study, 47 home visits were observed to determine differences in time and resulting costs. On analysis, the time did not vary significantly with the patient's physical disability, the interval between visits, or the number of team members present. The time determinants most closely correlated to the observations were age of patient and type of visit. Three different types of visits were observed that related to time spent.

INITIAL VISIT   The patient is seen for the first time by a member of the Chelsea–Village Program team. The visit usually consisted of a complete social and medical evaluation. Six visits of this category were studied.

FOLLOW-UP VISIT   Here a nurse, social worker, and/or physician go to the patient for routine care. The visit usually consisted of the following components: greetings and good-byes, physical examination, medication check, and a note written in the patient's chart. Twenty-nine visits of this category were studied.

SPECIFIC PURPOSE VISIT   On these occasions any member of the team attends the patient for a limited reason, such as blood drawing, an influenza immunization, or check of a particular ailment. The visit usually consisted of the following components: greetings and good-byes, a procedure or examination, note writing, and instructions. Twelve visits of this category were studied.

Within the follow-up group, the length of the visit increased with the age of the patient (Table 14-1, element 8). The increase in examination time occurred at the end of the reported decade.

The actual time spent with the patient is, of course, only one compo-

TABLE 14-1
Time Data by Type of Visit

ELEMENTS OF VISIT	TIME (MIN)	FREQ.	FOLLOW-UP VISITS, BY AGE (YR)					SPEC. PURP.	INITIAL VISIT	
			< 60	61–70	71–80	81–90	> 90		Without MD	With MD
Go to OPD Office	4.50	0.4	1.80	1.80	1.80	1.80	1.80	1.80	1.80	1.80
Possible page for doctor	1.00	–	0.30	0.30	0.30	0.30	0.30	0.30	0.30	0.30
Possible wait for team member	10.00	–	2.80	2.80	2.80	2.80	2.80	2.80	2.80	2.80
Review of visit purpose	2.00	1.0	2.00	2.00	2.00	2.00	2.00	2.00	2.00	2.00
Travel from OPD to vehicle	1.00	0.4	0.40	0.40	0.40	0.40	0.40	0.40	0.40	0.40
Travel to home			See Table 14–2							
Travel from vehicle to patient's home	1.93	1.0	1.93	1.93	1.93	1.93	1.93	1.93	1.93	1.93
Examine patient; record findings	–	1.0	13.00	13.00	19.00	25.00	31.00	11.90	23.70	32.50
Travel from patient's home to vehicle	1.93	1.0	1.93	1.93	1.93	1.93	1.93	1.93	1.93	1.93
Travel to next patient or return to OPD			See Table 14–2							
Travel from vehicle to OPD	1.00	0.4	0.40	0.40	0.40	0.40	0.40	0.40	0.40	0.40
Return to CVP Office	4.50	0.4	1.80	1.80	1.80	1.80	1.80	1.80	1.80	1.80
Total time (min)			26.36	26.36	32.36	38.36	44.36	25.26	37.06	45.86
20% PFD			31.63	31.63	38.83	46.03	52.23	30.31	44.47	55.03
80% performance			39.54	39.54	48.54	57.53	66.54	37.89	55.59	68.79
Total time (hr)			0.659	0.659	0.809	0.959	1.109	0.632	0.927	1.147

234

nent of the total visit. Elements of preparation and travel are common to all (Tables 14-1, 14-2, 14-3). The times recorded were adjusted for PFD (personal, fatigue, and unavoidable delay) and set at an 80 percent performance rate, a common level for health systems. Social worker and nurse office time were also analyzed for each visit (Tables 14-4, 14-5).

Table 14-6 shows the number of visits anticipated in each of eight categories, using the age distribution of the patient population in the Chelsea–Village Program. The third column of the table shows the standard time per visit, calculated from the studies discussed above. When this is multiplied by the percent of patients in each category, a weighted visit time in hours is calculated. Summing these components results in an average of 1.27 hours per visit.

Figure 14-1 shows a projection for 1976 of types of visits by the categories already discussed. It provides a visual representation of the proportion of one category to another. Using this projection and the time

TABLE 14–2
Travel Time (per visit) Elements by Distance

	UP TO 1 MILE	UP TO 2 MILES	UP TO 3 MILES
Travel time per Visit (min)	6	12	18
× 1.43 (multiple visits per trip)	8.58	17.16	25.74
20% PFD	10.3	20.59	30.88
At 80% performance	12.87	25.74	38.61
Total time allowed (min)	12.87	25.74	38.61
Total time allowed (hr)	0.215	0.429	0.644

TABLE 14–3
Standard Time in Hours Away From Office for
Every Staff Participant

TYPE OF VISIT	UP TO 1 MILE	UP TO 2 MILES	UP TO 3 MILES
Follow-up visits (by age)			
Under 60 years	0.87	1.09	1.30
61–70 years	0.87	1.09	1.30
71–80 years	1.02	1.24	1.45
81–90 years	1.17	1.39	1.60
Over 91 years	1.32	1.54	1.75
Specific purpose	0.85	1.06	1.28
Initial visit (without MD)	1.14	1.36	1.57
Initial visit (with MD)	1.36	1.58	1.79

TABLE 14-4
Social Worker: Office Time per Patient Visit (Minutes)

	TIME	FOLLOW-UP		SPECIFIC PURPOSE		INITIAL VISIT	
		Freq.	Time	Freq.	Time	Freq.	Time
Telephone calls							
Patient-related	2.86	0.75	2.15	0.40	1.14	0.75	2.15
To or from patient	4.10	0.50	2.05	0.25	1.02	0.10	0.41
To specific agency	3.73	0.50	1.87	0.25	0.93	0.50	1.87
Weekly conference	2.00	1.00	2.00	1.00	2.00	1.00	2.00
Forms	3.30	0.50	1.65	0.50	1.65	0.25	0.83
Chart note	6.00	0.50	3.00	0.25	1.50		—
Chart note: initial evaluation	30.00	—	—	—	—	1.00	30.00
Conference with staff	1.50	0.50	0.75	0.50	0.75	0.09	1.35
Totals			13.47		8.99		38.61
PFD			16.16		10.79		46.33
80% performance			20.21		13.49		57.92
Standard hours			0.34		0.22		0.97

TABLE 14-5
Nurse: Office Time per Patient Visit (Minutes)

	TIME	FREQUENCY	TIME/VISIT
Bring specimens to lab	2.5	0.19	0.48
Read lab results, notify patient	4.0	0.19	0.76
Pick up medical bag, inspect contents	2.0	0.43	0.86
Report at weekly meeting	2.0	1.0	2.0
Confer with staff	2.47	0.85	1.85
Read hospital chart	4.0	0.33	1.32
Review CHP chart	2.0	0.85	1.70
Write in chart	2.0	0.19	0.38
Miscellaneous paper work	1.0	0.85	0.85
Totals			10.20
PFD			12.24
80% performance			15.30
Standard hours			0.26

TABLE 14-6
Weighted Average Visit Time

TYPE OF VISIT	NO.	% VISITS	STD TIME (HR/VISIT)	WEIGHTED VISIT TIME (HR)
Follow-up visits (by age)				
Under 60 years	85	7.5	1.09	0.082
61–70 years	151	13.2	1.09	0.144
71–80 years	357	31.4	1.24	0.389
81–90 years	292	25.6	1.39	0.356
Over 91 years	56	4.9	1.54	0.075
Specific purpose	105	9.2	1.06	0.098
Initial visit (without MD)	9	0.8	1.36	0.011
Initial visit (with MD)	85	7.5	1.58	0.119
		100.0		1.27*

Projected for 1976: 1140 patient visits.
*Weighted standard hours/visit.

studies discussed above, a standard cost table was constructed with fixed and variable cost analyses. Table 14-7, the standard cost per visit, shows the anticipated cost for each category and for an average visit.

The variable costs are composed of the salary of each team member attributable to the visit, the monetary value of related office work, and the costs of supplies and other visit-related expenses. Within the variable costs, the salary allocations for each profession are computed by multi-

237

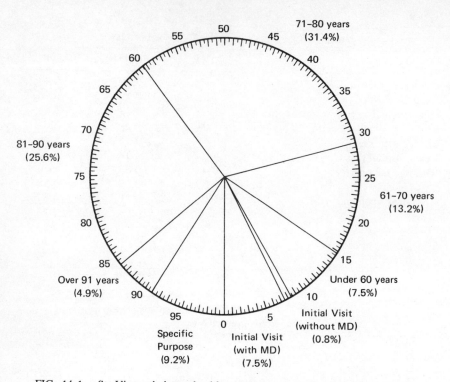

FIG. 14-1. St. Vincent's home health care program—type of visit by category.

plying the hourly rate by the anticipated frequency by the standard time of the visit. The frequency for staff visits is based on 1975 patient statistics of the CVP.

The fixed costs of the program consist of the salaries of administrative personnel, social worker and nurse time unrelated to the visits, the program's share in hospital overhead, and those expenses unrelated to particular visits.

Salary rates currently reported by the hospital were generally used for the budget calculations. Physician fees, however, are higher than those paid to the St. Vincent's Hospital house staff, who contribute their time to the program. Step-down information was based on the unaudited 1974 Uniform Financial Report of the hospital, adjusted for 1975 dollars.

The standard cost table (Table 14-7) incorporates certain staffing changes from current practices. In addition to the physician change noted above, the van driving has been distributed to members of the health care team. Table 14-7, furthermore, shows that an additional part-time nurse is needed to meet the required hours for 1,140 visits. No additional social worker staffing is necessary.

TABLE 14-7
Standard Cost per Visit

TYPE	INITIAL VISIT		FOLLOW-UP					SPEC. PURP.	TOTAL
	With MD	Without MD	0-60	61-70	71-80	81-90	> 90		
No. of visits	85	9	85	151	357	292	56	105	1140
Team hr/visit	1.58	1.36	1.09	1.09	1.24	1.39	1.54	1.06	1.27
Total team hr.	134.30	12.24	92.65	164.59	442.68	405.88	86.24	111.30	1450
Variable Costs per Visit									
Visit site									
Sal. & fringes									
Nurse ($9.72/hr)	14.59	13.22	8.05	7.95	9.16	10.27	11.38	8.76	9.72
Soc. Worker ($11.23/hr)	15.96	15.27	6.12	7.34	8.36	7.80	4.32	2.38	7.80
Physician ($26.69/hr)	42.17	0	22.11	21.82	24.82	28.57	31.65	23.20	26.49
Office-related									
Nurse (0.26 hr/visit)	2.53	2.53	2.53	2.53	2.53	2.53	2.53	2.53	2.53
Soc. Worker (0.38 hr/visit)	10.89	10.89	3.82	3.82	3.82	3.82	3.82	2.47	4.29
Physician (0.038 hr/visit)	0.77	0.77	0.77	0.77	0.77	0.77	0.77	0.77	0.77
Cons. Phys. ($26.69/hr)	0	0	2.61	2.61	2.97	3.33	3.69	2.54	2.74
Variable expenses									
Van costs ($0.20/mi)	0.40	0.40	0.40	0.40	0.40	0.40	0.40	0.40	0.40
Med Records ($0.80/call)	0.80	0.08	0.20	0.20	0.20	0.20	0.20	0.64	0.29
Lab Service ($6.05/occ)	1.01	1.01	1.01	1.01	1.01	1.01	1.01	1.01	1.01
Med Supplies ($0.34/visit)	0.34	0.34	0.34	0.34	0.34	0.34	0.34	0.34	0.34

(continued)

TABLE 14-7
Standard Cost per Visit (cont.)

TYPE	INITIAL VISIT		FOLLOW-UP					SPEC PURP.	TOTAL
	With MD	Without MD	0-60	61-70	71-80	81-90	> 90		
Variable Costs per Visit (cont.)									
Variable expenses (cont.)									
Telephone ($0.19/visit)	0.19	0.19	0.19	0.19	0.19	0.19	0.19	0.19	0.19
Forms and office supplies	0.20	0.20	0.10	0.10	0.10	0.10	0.10	0.10	0.11
Misc @ 5%	4.49	2.25	2.41	2.45	2.73	2.97	3.02	2.27	2.83
Variable cost/scheduled visit	94.34	47.15	50.66	51.53	57.40	62.30	63.42	47.60	59.51
Missed visit allowance	1.84	0.91	0.98	0.99	1.11	1.21	1.23	0.92	1.15
Variable cost/actual visit	96.18	48.06	51.64	52.52	58.51	63.51	64.65	48.52	60.66
Program Fixed Budget Costs									
Fixed salaries									
Project director									7550
Supervisor									6338
Codirector									2112
Coordinator									12368
Social worker—admin.									2361
Typist									500
Fixed portion of visits									
Nurse (317 hr @ $9.72)									3081
Social Worker (304 hr @ $11.23)									3413

Fixed expenses									
Laundry & linen	60								
Depreciation	370								
Deprec. equip.	82								
Op. and maint.	370								
Housekeeping	1500								
Share of cafe	100								
Nursing admin	420								
Gen and admin	2618								
Hsg allow	1500								
Soc service	1650								
Office supplies	800								
Meetings and publ	500								
Telephone	200								
Misc @ 5%	2070								
1974 $	12,240								
× 1.08 (1975 $)	13,219								
Total	50,942								
Team hours	1450								
Rate/team hour	35.13								
× Team hours/visit	1.58	1.36	1.09	1.09	1.24	1.39	1.54	1.06	1.27
Fixed cost/visit	55.51	47.78	38.29	38.29	43.56	48.83	54.10	37.24	44.62
Variable cost/visit	96.18	48.06	51.64	52.52	58.51	63.51	64.65	48.52	60.66
Fixed cost/visit	55.51	47.78	38.29	38.29	43.56	48.83	54.10	37.24	44.62
Total cost/visit	151.69	95.84	89.93	90.81	102.07	112.34	118.75	85.76	105.28

A missed visit allowance is included to cover occasions when the staff travels to a patient's home but is not admitted. This allowance omits the examination time, lab services, and medical supplies.

The fixed cost is based on 1,140 team visits per year and is adequate for volume swings of plus or minus 20 percent. Above that 20 percent volume increase, staff additions must be made, and costs must be recalculated. These costs are all based on optimum use of staff, including part-time employment, where whole person utilization is not indicated. If the forecast of 1,140 visits is met, the cost per visit is achieved. If the planned volume is less than this, attention will be given to reducing the fixed cost budgets accordingly, to maintain the cost per visit.

The frequency of visits to each patient is an important component of costs in the program. In this study, there was an average of 10 visits per year for ambulatory patients, 11.1 visits for semiambulatory patients, and 14.8 visits for bedbound patients. Each patient in the program is described by the staff in terms of general motor ability and need for assistance. The group of patients seen by the program are, in general, semiambulatory.

Conclusions and Recommendations

Conclusions and recommendations were divided into two main sections: those related to the CVP and those directed to the issue of providing alternatives to nursing home care.

CONCLUSIONS.

1. The per visit cost of the CVP during 1976, if the forecast is obtained, staffing recommendations followed, and past visit patterns continue, is $105.28. This cost will decrease as the patient base widens, up to the point that the fixed costs must be increased, based on the census forecast. Monitoring of patient visits, staff time, and cost keeping must be continuous, so that staffing requirements and expense levels can be adjusted to the census.
2. The average patient in the Chelsea–Village Program is visited by the staff approximately 11.1 times a year, producing an annual visit cost of $1,169.
3. This visit cost, along with the additional expenses of rent, food, auxiliary nursing, or household services, is below the amount of money needed to care for this type of patient in a nursing home (Chap. 15).
4. There is adequate evidence to warrant further study of home health

care in different environments to determine if the cost advantage measured here can be generalized.

RECOMMENDATIONS FOR FURTHER STUDY. Issues to be considered in providing alternatives to nursing home care are the applicability of the Chelsea–Village Program to other urban centers, housing patterns, financial incentives to families, utilization of services, appropriate rural and suburban alternatives to nursing home care, and development of pilot projects.

1. Applicability of the Chelsea–Village Program to other urban centers should be explored. Among the points to investigate are the availability of hospital-based programs, their geographic proximity to a patient population, the receptivity of the population to this type of care, the relative costs of nursing homes in the geographic area, and the availability of homemaking, housekeeping, and other ranges of support services. These factors should be looked at in terms of present use, methods of reimbursement, and anticipated demands.
2. Investigation of current housing patterns may show that a cost-effective program of health care can be provided on-site to patients living in apartments near one another. This study could also investigate how informal assistance for the elderly, provided by relatives and neighbors, can be used to supplement more costly support services.
3. A study should be undertaken to determine the feasibility of providing payments to families to provide care for patients at home. An appropriate screening mechanism would have to be developed for patient qualification, along with some financial commitment on the part of the family.
4. Evidence should be obtained to determine the extent that reimbursement to a hospital-based program would provide coverage to a new group of patients and whether it would create alternatives to care for the nursing home patient.
5. An assessment of appropriate alternatives to nursing home care for people in rural and suburban locations should also be investigated. The size of the population to be served should be defined, as well as the health center that would service the group, and the costs related to geographic dispersion.
6. A study should be made to determine the impact on people who would be covered in a home health care program, either urban or rural, but who have no medical facility to organize delivery of this care.
7. Development of pilot programs in housekeeping and homemaking

243

should be encouraged, to experiment with the use of more flexible units of time in the care of particular types of patients. Some semiambulatory patients might benefit by daily help for one- or two-hour periods. The use of a homemaker to supervise more than one patient per visit should also be evaluated. This approach would seem particularly applicable to single-room-occupancy hotels or to apartment complexes with large numbers of elderly patients. Here, homemaker productivity could be greatly improved as a result of geographic concentration of the patients.

REFERENCES

1. Opit LJ: Domiciliary care for the elderly sick; economy or neglect? Br Med J 6052:30, 1977
2. Gavett JW: Measuring the Community's Utilization of a Health Service. Department of Preventive Medicine and Community Health, University of Rochester, School of Medicine and Dentistry, Rochester, NY, July, 1974
3. Bell WG: Community care for the elderly: an alternative to institutionalization. Gerontologist 13:349, 1973
4. Williams TF, Hill JG, Fairbank ME, Knox KG: Appropriate placement of the chronically ill and aged. JAMA 226:1332, 1973
5. Adamovich GG: Testimony presented to the United States House of Representatives, Committee on Aging, Subcommittee on Long-term Care. July 8, 1975. Washington, DC: US Government Printing Office, 1975
6. Robinson N, Shinn E, Adam E, Moore F: Costs of Homemaker–Home Health Aide and Alternative Forms of Service. New York, National Council for Homemaker –Home Health Aide Services, 1974
7. Mims RB, Thomas LL, Conroy MV: Physician house calls: a complement to hospital-based medical care. J Am Geriatr Soc 25:28, 1977
8. Yeager R: Hospital treats patients at home. Mod Health Care 4:29, 1975
9. Pollak W: Costs of Alternative Care Settings for the Elderly. The Urban Institute, 2100 M Street NW, Washington DC 20037, March 12, 1973
10. Laverty R: Nonresident aid; community versus institutional care for older people. J Gerontol 5:370, 1950
11. Rossman I: Alternatives to institutional care. Bull NY Acad Med 49:1084, 1973
12. White DW: A community-based home care program. Hospitals 37:63, 1963
13. Cherkasky M, Rossman I, Rogatz P: Guide to Organized Home Care. Chicago, Hospital Research and Educational Trust, 1961, p 34
14. Rossman I: Environments of geriatric care. In Rossman (ed): Clinical Geriatrics. Philadelphia, Lippincott, 1971, p 491
15. Bryant NH, Candland L, Loewenstein R: Comparison of care and cost outcomes for stroke patients with and without home care. Stroke 5:54, 1974
16. Hurtado AV, Greenlick MR, Saward EW: Home Care and Extended Care in a Comprehensive Prepayment Plan. Chicago, Hospital Research and Educational Trust, 1972

244

17. Special Committee on Aging, United States Senate: Alternatives to Nursing Home Care, A Proposal. Prepared by Staff Specialists at the Levinson Gerontological Policy Institute, Brandeis University, Waltham, Massachusetts. Washington DC, US Government Printing Office, October, 1971

18. Weiler P: Cost-effective analysis: a quandary for geriatric health care systems. Gerontologist 14:414, 1974

19. Select Committee on Aging, United States House of Representatives, Subcommittee on Health and Long-term Care: New Perspectives in Health Care for Older Americans (Recommendations and Policy Directions). Washington DC, US Government Printing Office, 1976, pp 15-20

20. Scharer LK, Boehringer JR: Home Health Care for the Aged: The Program of St. Vincent's Hospital. New York, The Florence V. Burden Foundation, 1976

CHAPTER 15

ME HEALTH CARE VS. INSTITUTIONAL CARE: COST COMPARISON

with Linda Keen Scharer, M.U.P

The idea that institutions must inevitably be the setting for care of aged, disabled people has been taken for granted, and the real financial price of such care has not been questioned deeply. The cost must be measured and compared with that of home health care services (discussed in Chap 14) in order for valid legislative and planning decisions to be made.

THE PROBLEMS

The problems of developing reliable estimates of institutional costs are severe, similar to those for evaluating the costs of home health care.

1. We lack definition of terms which are useful countrywide. In New York State, for instance, there exist nursing homes, extended care facilities, day care services, foster homes, senior residential facilities, and proprietary homes for adults. Each has defined funding limits, none of which apply in other states.
2. We do not know the total number of institutions in the United States that provide long-term care. There exist approximately 23,000 nursing homes[1] in the country, but this total does not include other types of accommodation.

3. Documents which provide information about costs not only fail the test of comparability but are also outdated quickly by inflation.
4. These documents, further, are often incomplete and rarely say what was included or excluded in arriving at total figures of cost. In summarizing a number of reports, Robinson et al. note[2]:

. . . often it is not stated whether organizations include capital costs, or the costs of maintaining and replacing major equipment. Most cost reports reviewed omitted some of the professional costs involved, e.g., those services provided by a public welfare department or other placement and supervisory agency. . . . Physician's fees were also . . . omitted from reported analyses of bed costs.

None of the available cost analyses overcome all of these problems. Several are worth study, however, and provide useful information.

MASSACHUSETTS ANALYSIS

Ruchlin and Levey[3] gathered data from a sample of nursing homes in Massachusetts and subjected the cost factors to a rigorous analysis. The average per day cost rose from $8.95 to $14.56 in the five-year period studied (1965-1969). This growth was similar to nationwide trends, and the inflationary surge in these costs continues.[4] While the dollar figures in this 1971 report are by now hopelessly outdated, the conclusions remain valid. These are as follows:

1. Major cost increases occurred immediately after passage of the Title XVIII and XIX laws, which permitted payment by government for nursing home care.
2. For the study period, costs to Medicaid grew faster than the average of costs.
3. Expenditures for some elements of care directly involving quality, such as recreation and rehabilitation services, were insignificant, accounting for only 1.5 percent of costs.
4. Many patients in Massachusetts nursing homes have been placed inappropriately, with decisions based on expediency rather than proper health planning.

The authors' summary[3]:

State agencies responsible for licensing and regulation of nursing homes have been almost universally understaffed at the regulatory and rate setting levels. Data upon which rates are formulated are frequently unsatisfactory, and reim-

247

bursement for welfare patients is linked to the availability of Medicaid monies which generally have not been sufficient to provide for service of high quality. Unfortunately, development of a consistent and rational policy for long-term care patient services has been lacking at both the national and state levels.

MORE RECENT DATA FROM ACROSS THE COUNTRY

1. In Maine, during 1970, the cost of maintaining a patient in an intermediate care facility ranged from $240 to $810 a month.[5]
2. In Maryland, during 1972, nursing home costs averaged $39 for chronic care, $32 for skilled care, and $24 for intermediate care per patient day, or $1,170, $960, and $720 per month.[6] These figures include salaries, food, insurance, utilities, supplies, and equipment. Costs for physician's services, drugs, tests, administration, and capital expenditures were excluded.
3. In New York State, during 1974, the minimum figure for care in a health-related facility was $417 per month, the maximum $2,311. Public home infirmaries, part of the New York City Municipal Hospital System, charged $1,682.[7]
4. Similar information for Illinois, circa 1976, places the cost of skilled institutional care at $13 to $45 per day, with an average of $25, or $750 monthly.[8]
5. The average cost of nursing home care in 1973, across the country, was $600 per month.[9] This figure, a product of studies by the United States Senate Special Committee on Aging, is by now outdated, but it supports generally the validity of the before-mentioned analyses.

BOEHRINGER STUDY

In 1975 the Florence V. Burden Foundation provided funds for a cost analysis of a home health program, conducted by Boehringer Associates, using the Chelsea–Village Program of St. Vincent's Hospital as the prototype.[10] As part of this study, nursing home costs in New York State were assessed for the purposes of comparison. Other aspects of this report are discussed in Chapter 14.

In the analysis it was essential to determine whether the patients studied—all of whom were registered in the Chelsea–Village Program—were, in fact, candidates for nursing home care.

A panel of physicians with experience in ambulatory care reviewed the charts of 29 patients. They were asked to state on a questionnaire (Fig. 15-1) if they felt the patient was a candidate for a nursing home, the

248

```
┌─────────────────────────────────────────────────────────────────────┐
│                                          PATIENT I.D. _____ ___ │
│                                                                       │
│  1. Would this patient be a nursing home patient if there was no available home │
│     health care program?                                              │
│                                                                       │
│     _____      _____                                              │
│       Yes          No                                                 │
│                                                                       │
│  2. Would you classify this patient as (please check)                 │
│                                                                       │
│     _____   _____   _____                         │
│     Ambulatory    Semiambulatory     Bedbound                         │
│                                                                       │
│  3. How many hours per day, if any, of care provided by a Registered Nurse (RN), │
│     Licensed Practical Nurse (LPN), and/or a Nurse's Aide does this patient require? │
│                                                                       │
│     _____                                                  │
│     Total daily hours                                                 │
│                                                                       │
└─────────────────────────────────────────────────────────────────────┘
```

FIG. 15-1.   Home health care study.

person's physical classification, and the number of nursing care hours required. Six were rejected because the panel believed the patient's disability was minor enough for standard outpatient care, and/or there was enough strong family support at home to provide most of the necessary service, without significant additional help. The results of the review show that the remaining 23 patients would be candidates for nursing home care if the Chelsea–Village Program was unavailable. Of these, 20 patients were classified as semiambulatory and 3 as bedbound. General nursing care hours required, including bathing, dressing, grooming, feeding, were tabulated. The average number of hours for the 23 patients judged necessary by the panel was 2.75 hours per day.

Nursing home costs were established through a sample of 23 homes in the New York City area by a regression analysis, using 1974 HE-2 forms, the statistical and financial reports submitted to the Bureau of Reimbursement Rate Setting of the New York State Department of Health.

The New York State Hospital Code, Section 731, Subchapter 6, mandates a combined average of direct nursing care for each 24-hour period for specific patient categories.[11] The total number of patients in each category is reported on the HE-2 forms each year, to the New York State Health Department. For each nursing home in the sample (7 voluntary and 16 proprietary), the total nursing hours for all patients in the home were matched against the operating expenses of the same nursing home with a correlation coefficient of 0.913 (Fig. 15-2).

This analysis shows that the resulting cost of nursing care for one hour

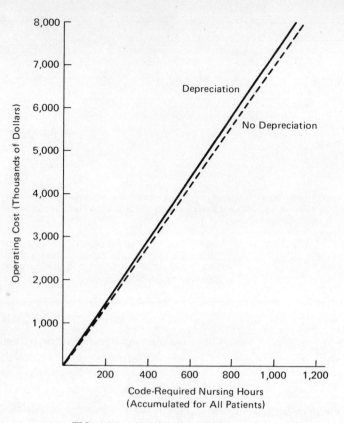

FIG. 15-2. Nursing home patient costs.

per day over a one year period, including all operating expenses, was $7,375.62. Costs were calculated with and without depreciation. A difference of only $232.96 per year occurred, so the curve with depreciation was used in the study.

In the sample studied, the average patient in the Chelsea–Village Program required 2.75 hours of nursing care per day, according to the findings of the panel. The average cost of this person would, therefore, be $20,283 per year in a nursing home. In reality, the reimbursement system used by Medicaid establishes a daily rate which includes all types of patients. The rate is calculated by dividing the approved yearly operating costs by the patient days. The average daily Medicaid reimbursement rate reported by the nursing homes in the sample was $41.65, or approximately $15,200 per year per patient, regardless of degree of care. This indicates that the ambulatory patients in a nursing home setting are subsidizing the bedbound patients.

250

The Boehringer report suggests that nursing home costs can be standardized by using a patient-rating scale and appropriate industrial engineering studies. The regression analysis performed for this report showed a strong correlation of cost per patient day to the mandated standard nursing hours of care. Further statistical studies and on-site observations may develop a system for reimbursement for this channel of care. Such a system would vary cost with the true requirement for care and more nearly reflect the true cost of providing this care.

COMPARING COSTS OF HOME HEALTH CARE
AND NURSING HOMES

General Accounting Office (GAO) Summary

In a 1975 report,[12] the GAO evaluated 20 publications and documents dealing with the costs of home care as compared to costs of alternative services. Of the 20, 19 presented data which supported the view that home health care can be less expensive under some circumstances.

The one study which takes the opposite view[13] critically reviewed four other cost analyses but did not cite original data.

The GAO report emphasizes the problems of comparing costs.

1. While it is true that home care is less expensive than institutional care at lower levels of impairment, the savings tend to disappear when severely disabled people are cared for at home.
2. Cost studies do not adequately address differing intensity, duration, and complexity of service.
3. Before comparative costs can be established for an individual patient, the level of institutional care in which he or she would be placed must be known. An attempt to make this judgment is lacking in most studies.

Boehringer Report Comparison of Costs

The Boehringer report developed a detailed comparison between the costs of home health care and those of New York State nursing homes. Table 15-1 compares these costs for three types of patients: the ambulatory, semiambulatory, and bedbound.

The nursing home costs are those required for one, two, or four hours of nursing home care, adjusted for 1975 dollars. The living costs attributed to home health care patients are composed of rent, food, general

251

TABLE 15-1
Comparative Costs per Year of Home Health Care and Nursing Home Care

| | REF | CVP HOME HEALTH CARE | | | | | | NURSING HOME CARE | | |
| | | Using CVP Comm. Health Aid | | | Using NYC House-keeper/Homemaker Svc | | | | | |
		Ambul	Semi-ambul	Bed-bound	Ambul	Semi-ambul	Bed-bound	Ambul	Semi-ambul	Bed-bound
Chelsea–Village Program	A									
Per visit		105.28	105.28	105.28	105.28	105.28	105.28	Costs included		
Freq visits per year		10	11.1	14.8	10	11.1	14.8			
Cost per year		1053	1169	1558	1053	1169	1558			
Program Comm Health Aid	B									
Per visit		19.58	19.58	19.58				Costs included		
Freq visits per year		52	104	260						
Cost per year		1018	2036	5090						
New York City Home Attend/Housekeeper/Homemaker	C									
Avg cost per visit					17.20	17.20	17.20	Costs included		

252

Item	Ref									
4 hr @ $4.30 freq. visits/year		52	104	260						
Avg cost per year		894	1789	4472						
Cost for 24 hr Home Attend, 365 days/year @ $33/day		12,045*								
Visiting Nurse Service	D									
Per visit		24.02	24.02	24.02	24.02	24.02	24.02	Costs included		
Freq visits per year		12	25	52	12	25	52			
Cost per year		288	601	1249	288	601	1249			
Food	E	1440	1440	1440	1440	1440	1440	Costs included		
Rent	E	2190	2190	2190	2190	2190	2190	Costs included		
Other costs	E	1170	1170	1170	1170	1170	1170	Costs included		
Mandated physician visits	F							300	300	300
Total nursing home costs	G	Included as part of program								
Per nursing hour/year 1974								7376	7376	7376
Freq. hours/day								1	2	4
Cost per year 1974								7376	14751	29502
Add 8% inflation								7966	15931	31862
Total		7159	8606	12697	7035	8359	12079	8266	16231	32162

*19,652 for 24 hr/day care (option).

items, such as telephone and utilities, and estimates of the amount of care required for housekeeping and homemaking services (Figs. 15-3, 15-4, 15-5).

Obtaining reliable estimates for food, shelter, and other personal items is difficult, and the results are to be considered approximate. Food and shelter costs were calculated from information provided by the Bureau of Labor Statistics, in their Retired Couple budget for autumn 1974 and then adjusted for a single person, with the appropriate consumer price index rise, to 1975 dollars. Guides for estimating other living items were obtained through use of the budget standard service of the Community Council of New York. Many of the Chelsea–Village Program patients receive only Social Security or Supplemental Security Income and probably have less money to spend than is actually shown in these graphs.

A major difficulty in estimating the cost of keeping patients at home is knowing the intensity of housekeeping, homemaking, or home attendant services required. The report estimates housekeeping services at 4 hours per day: once a week for the ambulatory patient, twice per week (total 8 hours) for the semiambulatory patient, and five times per week (total 20 hours) for the bedbound patient, with a 24-hour, seven-day-a-week option also included. The rate is a weighted average of home attendant, housekeeper, and homemaker fees. The Department of Social Services in New York City has not yet provided data on the average use of these support services per patient category.

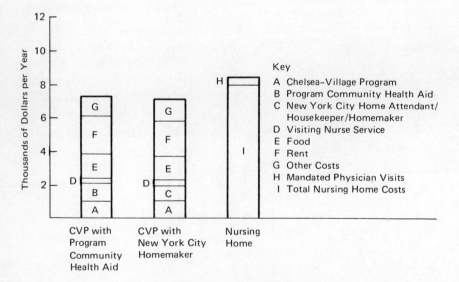

FIG. 15-3.   Costs for ambulatory patients.

254

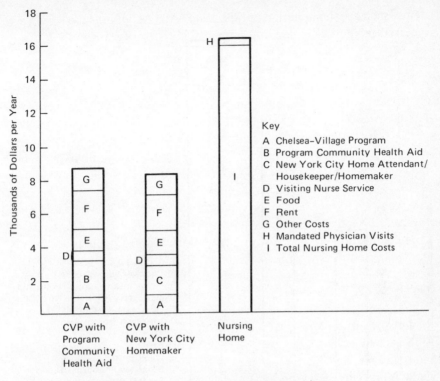

FIG. 15-4.   Costs for semiambulatory patients.

The Chelsea–Village Program also has its own community health aid. While the cost for New York City services appears to be lower, the greater flexibility of the Chelsea–Village Program health aide and the range of tasks she can perform make her a more versatile and efficient member of the support team. The costs shown in Table 15-1 assume that the health aide makes the same number of visits as the New York City worker. The Chelsea–Village Program health aide is supervised by the professional staff to help provide better continuity of care. Therefore, her performance is not subject to added costs (not shown here) of supervision provided by the Visiting Nurse Service (VNS) of New York to city aides. The intensity of VNS visits is also an estimate, since they do not currently record data about care provided to the categories of patients described above. The cost of drugs has been omitted from all comparisons.

The issue of providing appropriate support services is a key factor in preserving the differences in costs between the homebound patient and the patient in the nursing home. As more support is necessary at home, the cost distinction between these two alternatives diminishes.

255

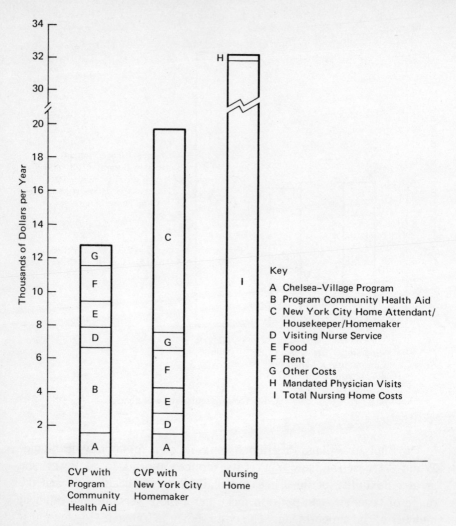

FIG. 15-5. Costs for bedbound patients.

In summary, the largest group of people under care at home in the Chelsea–Village Program—those who are semiambulatory—require about $8,500 per year each, all costs included. Comparable patients in a nursing home, based on the sample studied, require $16,200 yearly.

INAPPROPRIATE NURSING HOME PLACEMENT

If the information about comparative costs provided in this chapter is generally correct—and we believe that it is both correct and well supported—an obvious question arises. What is the proportion of people now living in nursing homes who have been placed inappropriately?

According to Robert Morris,[14] between 250,000 and 500,000 persons annually are assigned to long-term care institutions for reasons other than medical need. In elaboration, of 100 nursing home patients studied in Massachusetts in 1971, only 37 needed the full services of the institution. He concludes that unnecessary care costs more in public funds than it would cost to develop a system of home health services for the aged. This point is supported by other studies spanning the past two decades. Ruchlin and Levey, summarizing these reports,[15] note that from 48 to 62 percent of patients in skilled nursing homes could have received comparable care at home, did not require the level of care received, and/or were fully ambulatory.

What are the causes of misplacement? First, existing sources of money for care are directed toward institutions.[15-18] Second, alternatives are in short supply.[2,9,18] Third, nature abhors a vacuum,[19] and an empty nursing home bed functions as a vacuum. Overbuilding of nursing homes for profit in those parts of the country where regulation makes this possible has resulted in a concentrated effort to fill the institutions.

But the wisdom and authority of the legislator are seldom victorious in a contest with the vigilant dexterity of private interest.
—Edward Gibbon, *The Decline and Fall of the Roman Empire*[20]

As pointed out by the New York State Moreland Act Commission on Nursing Home and Residential Facilities[21]:

Although the elderly have been the fastest growing segment of the state's population, the expansion of long-term care beds over the decade has been far in excess of the growth of this population[;] . . . the rule that a new bed will eventually be occupied has apparently been borne out. Thus, despite the remarkable building program of recent years, occupancy rates at present average over 95 percent. . . .

The matter of misplacement has an additional practical aspect. People can—rarely—move out of nursing homes and return to an independent life in the community. In the Chelsea–Village Program, of our first 466 patients, 10 had previously been living in nursing homes.

As W.G. Bell puts the question[18]: "Should public resources for long-term care of [the] elderly continue to be allocated essentially to institutional programs or should alternate community based programs be supported to complement current nursing home sources?"

The financial data favoring home health care services in comparison to institutional care are solid when applied to appropriate patients. It is necessary to stress the point because another view emphasizes that no

257

form of service for aged people is cost-effective. They will never return to the work force, and therefore the money spent on their care is wasted.

A narrow economic cost-benefit analysis would . . . conclude that as society's investment in long-term care services cannot be financially recouped [these] services are not economically viable as long as other needs, such as pediatric and short-term care, exist whose servicing would yield a greater economic payoff. . . . The harsh realities of life dictate such an assertion. One must conclude that the rationale for providing long-term care services rests upon humane rather than financial considerations.[15]

REFERENCES

1. Directory of Nursing Home Facilities, Vol 1-4 (Northeast, South, North Central, West). DHEW Publication No (HRA) 76-20001. Health Resources Administration, National Center for Health Statistics, Rockville, Md 20852, December 1975
2. Robinson N, Shinn E, Adam E, Moore F: Costs of Homemaker–Home Health Aide and Alternative Forms of Service, A Survey of the Literature. New York, National Council for Homemaker–Home Health Aide Services, 1974, p 8
3. Ruchlin HS, Levey S: Nursing home cost analysis: a case study. Inquiry 9:3, 1972
4. Meiners MR: Selected operating and financial characteristics of nursing homes, United States: 1973-1974. Vital Health Stat 13:1-66, 1975
5. Governor's Committee on Aging: Steps for Maine's Elderly. Maine Committee on Aging, Augusta, Maine, 1970
6. Governor's Commission on Nursing Homes: Report of the Governor's Commission on Nursing Homes. Baltimore, Maryland, 1973
7. State of New York, Department of Health: Hospital Memorandum. Series 74-10, Jan 30, 1974
8. State of Illinois, Department of Public Aid: Notice. April 29, 1976
9. Eckman J, Furman W (eds): Handbook and Directory of Nursing Homes and Other Facilities for the Aged Within a Fifty Mile Radius of New York City. New York, Basic Books, 1975
10. Scharer L, Boehringer JR: Home Health Care for the Aged: The Program of St. Vincent's Hospital, New York City. The Florence V. Burden Foundation, February 17, 1976
11. New York State Hospital Code, Chap V, Subchap D, Nursing Home Operation, Part 731, Patient Services (Statutory Aathority: Public Health Law 2803, amended Sept 18, 1975)
12. General Accounting Office: Letter to Representative Edward I. Koch, Sept 17, 1975
13. Brooks CH: A Critical Review of Four Home Health Care Cost-Benefit Analyses. Cleveland, Ohio, Metropolitan Health Planning Corporation
14. Levinson Gerontological Policy Institute, Brandeis University: Alternatives to Nursing Home Care: A Proposal. The Special Committee on Aging, United States Senate, Washington DC. US Government Printing Office, October 1971, p III
15. Ruchlin HS, Levey S: An Economic Perspective of Long-term Care. Typescript, February 1974

16. General Accounting Office: Study of Health Facilities Construction Costs. Report to Congress, November 1972
17. Butler RN: Why Survive? Being Old in America. New York, Harper, 1975, p 272
18. Bell WG: Community care for the elderly; an alternative to institutionalization. Gerontologist 13:349, 1973
19. Spinoza B: Ethics. Part I, Prop. XV, Note, 1677
20. Gibbon E: The Decline and Fall of the Roman Empire. New York, Modern Library Edition, Vol. I, p 865
21. New York State Moreland Act Commission on Nursing Home and Residential Facilities: Nursing Home and Domiciliary Facility Planning, February 1976

CHAPTER 16

HOW TO FUND A PROGRAM

MONEY

If a community group or institution decides to start a home health care program for the aged, it will not thrive for very long without money. Organized efforts to obtain funds for the program should be part of the initial planning, and must continue until income is flowing at an adequate and reliable rate.

This chapter discusses methods of raising funds based upon our own experiences in the Chelsea–Village Program. We started with no background in the field and learned through our own efforts, with guidance from the development department of St. Vincent's Hospital. Whether we would have had greater success if we employed our own fundraiser is conjecture.

Goals

First, community financial resources must be assessed and joined with those of the planning body or organization. Once the program has started and begun to prove its value, larger sums of money may be obtained from philanthropic sources and businesses that have budgets for charitable contributions. Finally, application must be made for government funds, either in the form of grants or directly as a fee for services from Medicare or Medicaid. The difficulties in collecting funds from these two insurance programs are severe and require effort at the legislative level, both in state capitals and in Washington.

Local Financial Resources

In this discussion it is assumed that agreement in principle from a hospital administration has been obtained and that professional staff time is avail-

260

able to start the program (Chap. 3). Now money is needed to employ nonprofessional staff.

A reasonable financial goal should be identified, a budget drawn up, and a committee formed to solicit funds. A written preamble will be useful to give to potential donors. Typical examples follow:

Home Health Care for the Aged
A combined program of Blatherskate Hospital and the Rolling Dunes Community, its People and Agencies.

Budget
Fiscal Year 1978–1979

Coordinator (part-time)	$6,000
Telephone	600
Stationery, postage	150
Supplies for patients	250
TOTAL	$7,000

Preamble

Aged, isolated people in this community are regularly forced into institutions against their will because they cannot live safely at home alone any longer, or they are found too late and die unattended. We feel that the costs of this situation are too high in terms of common humanity. Furthermore, as we all know, paying for hospital or nursing home care is a burden on budgets at all levels. These institutions are expensive.

We are forming a program that will provide professional health care and other services at home for these older people and help to keep them there. We need your aid to get started.

Natural financial resources for this first stage of fundraising are:

The charitable arm of churches and synagogues
Fraternal orders
Employees' organizations of local businesses, who may collect funds at Christmas
Local individuals who have a known interest in charitable matters or in aged people
Specific fundraising events
The planning group itself

Members of the planning group must expect to provide personal funds, at a reasonable level, to the initial drive. Clearly, it is not fair to ask for the help of anyone else otherwise. A sense of conviction about the value

261

of the program, backed up by contributions from the founders, provides the spirit needed to ask for money from other people.

SEEKING MORE SUBSTANTIAL RESOURCES

Once the program has been in effect for six months or more, and proof is at hand about its value and viability, opportunities exist for obtaining more substantial contributions. The budget is larger because more staff members are now needed.

Each potential donor should receive a summary of the program's work to date, including number of patients seen, number of home visits, typical problems, supported by characteristic case histories. The portion of the budget requested from the donor is outlined separately, along with the total cost budget. For examples from the Chelsea–Village Program files see Tables 16-1 and 16-2.

At this stage of fundraising, donations from $1,000 to $25,000 or more should be sought. Potential sources include businesses, such as banks, insurance companies, the telephone company, utilities, large chains—all of which are likely to make charitable gifts, wealthy individuals, community agencies, such as the United Fund, and philanthropic foundations.

Foundations

Foundations exist in large numbers in the United States. *The Foundation Directory*[1] lists virtually all, with total assets, general purpose, and names of directors. In choosing which foundations to contact, concentrate on those with the following interests: health; older people or the process

TABLE 16-1
CVP Request for Support of Partial Program Cost from
The Grandmothers and Grandfathers Foundation,
July 1, 1977, to June 30, 1978

	POSITION	ANNUAL COST
Salaries and wages		
Physician	¼	$ 8,000
Staff nurse	1	14,300
Subtotal		$22,300
Fringe benefits		$ 2,700
Total		$25,000

These program costs represent a portion of the total Chelsea–Village Program budget. The detailed budget for the total program is attached for your review.

TABLE 16-2
CVP Cost Budget
July 1, 1977, to June 30, 1978

	POSITIONS	ANNUAL COST
Salaries and wages		
Coordinator	1	$13,000
Physician	¼	8,000
Staff nurse	1	14,300
Social worker MSW	1	16,500
Vehicle driver	1	11,500
Secretary	1	11,800
Community health aide	1	9,500
Total salaries and wages		$84,600
Other than salaries and wages		
Fringe benefits @ 15%		$12,700
Supplies and communications		1,400
Indirect costs		9,900
Total other than salaries and wages		$24,000
Total program cost		$108,600

The services of other professional staff (doctors, nurses and social workers) are donated by the hospital.

of aging; medical, nursing, or social work development as separate fields; local geographic focus.

It is wise to look up the names of foundation directors, trustees, and board members. *Standard and Poor's Register*[2] and the *Dun and Bradstreet Reference Book*[3] may be useful. Personal contact rarely hurts if applied with tact and judgment.

Barefaced honesty and a straightforward request for financial assistance are appropriate; begging is not. Assume that the potential donor is intelligent and perceptive. No stronger argument exists for funding than the merits of the home health care program as it is. No vivid elaboration is necessary. If the information is presented properly, with respect and conviction, and if the correct targets have been chosen, the chances for success are reasonable.

The keys to a successful grant request, in summary, are:

1. Select foundations that have appropriate objectives.
2. Request an amount of money that compares properly to other gifts made in the past by the foundation.
3. Prepare written budget material and documentation about the

program's work to date. Make certain that it is well organized and neat.

4. Request an interview with people on the foundation's staff to make a statement about the program and to hand over the documents personally. If staff members will make a site visit, even better. A grateful patient is a great advertisement.

5. Use relationships with trustees, but do so with judgment and dignity. Trustees can provide a favorable influence, but usually the staff of the foundation makes the decision, and usually the decision is based on merit.

GOVERNMENT FUNDS

The larger the organization supplying the money, the more cumbersome the application process, the more wearing the subsequent review of services rendered, and the more demanding the accounting of money spent. These dicta apply to government funding. It is tempting to ask whether the effort to obtain government money is worthwhile, considering the time spent on filling out forms and meeting paper work standards that are irrelevant. The cliché, "He who marries money earns it," applies neatly. And yet, these funds are essential to the long-term survival of home health care programs, so they must be sought.

City, state, and federal agencies differ in their submission requirements but are likely to insist upon complex financial accounting systems, devices for measuring results by numbers, and detailed methods of evaluation.[4-6]

The grant application may be so large that it requires a Table of Contents. An example follows:

Grant Request to Tendentious County Department of Health

Table of Contents

A. Summary of Purpose
B. Program Analysis
    1. Nature of problems faced by the homebound aged
    2. Number of potential patients
    3. Services needed
    4. Rate of program growth
    5. Relationship to community agencies
C. Budgets
    1. Overall program budget
    2. Funds requested from Tendentious County Department of Health
    3. Cost-sharing
D. Evaluation Methods
    1. Charts

2. Consumers
3. Providers
4. Conferences
   a. Didactic
   b. Patient care
E. Attached Documents
   1. Articles from professional journals
   2. Supporting letters from associated community agencies, hospital administration, board of trustees

Often a cost-sharing budget must be provided, requiring the program (or the institution which houses it) to find other funds or to contribute services of value (Table 16-3).

It is tempting to believe that government grant allocations are based on

TABLE 16-3
Cost Sharing

	% TIME	BASE SALARY + FRINGE BENEFITS	TOTAL
Overall Project Support			
Project director	80	$26,189	$ 20,951
Assistant director	20	22,036	4,407
Community organizer	50	20,013	10,007
Coordinator	100	16,042	16,042
Volunteer	20	8,934	1,787
Total project			53,194
Chelsea–Village Program			
Physician	100	25,000	25,000
Physician	50	25,000	12,500
Nurse	100	11,851	11,851
Social worker	100	13,918	13,918
Social worker	50	13,918	6,959
Subtotal			70,228
Total contributed personnel cost			123,422
Other than personnel cost			
Supplies			1,200
Printing and reproduction			1,000
Subtotal			2,200
Total contributed direct cost			123,442
Fringe benefits 15%			18,513
Indirect cost 5%			6,171
Total contributed cost by agency			$148,126

(1) the weight or mass of the application, (2) the prestige of the institution from which it stems, (3) the amount of jargon it contains, (4) the region of the country to be served, its rural or urban nature, and/or (5) political influence.

These may or may not be factors, but we have found that the merit of the application also carries weight. We have been most successful when we approach people in government straightforwardly, ask advice about how to submit applications and where the funds are to be found, enlist their sympathy and interest. We have failed when we attempted to swing money our way by exerting influence through our legislators.

LEGISLATION

As we have emphasized (Chap. 4), the original Medicare (Title XVIII) and Medicaid (Title XIX) laws simply omitted adequate provisions for home health care services. Amendments to these laws are necessary in order for home health care programs to flourish across the country because only through such change will money be available.

At present, there are bills before Congress and in state legislatures[7] which are drawn to serve the purpose. Those that are discussed here are among the most pertinent and are cited so they can serve as guides for the development of other legislation.

National Home Health Care Act of 1977 (H.R. 9829)

Chief Sponsor: *Representative Edward I. Koch*

1. *General Approach:* H.R. 9829 would amend Title XVIII of the Social Security Act to expand Medicare's home health benefit. The bill would increase the number of allowable home health visits, liberalize the requirements for receipt of services, and broaden the definition of reimbursable home health services.
2. *People Covered:* Individuals enrolled in Part A or Part B of Medicare.
3. *Scope of Benefits:* H.R. 9829 would increase the maximum number of allowable home health visits under the Hospital Insurance Program (Part A) from 100 to 200 and provide for unlimited visits under the Supplementary Medical Insurance Program (Part B). Home health services would be provided on the basis of need.
   a. For intermittent nursing care or other home health services as defined by Section 1861(m) of Title XVIII, or
   b. As an alternative to institutional care.
   The prior hospitalization requirement in present law would be retained under Part A, but the current requirement that the service be provided

266

for further treatment of the condition for which the patient was institutionalized is deleted. The requirement that the individual must be under the care of a physician while home health services are furnished is deleted.

4. *Definitions:* H.R. 9829 broadens Medicare's definition of home health services (Section 1861[m]) to include:

   a. Part-time or intermittent services of a homemaker,
   b. Services provided to certain blind or hearing-impaired beneficiaries to enable them to avoid institutionalization, and
   c. Any professional health services provided by hospitals or staff members of hospitals as alternatives to institutional care, if such services are not otherwise covered under Title XVIII.

   H.R. 9829 also

   a. Provides a statutory definition of "home health aide services," "homemaker services," and "medical supplies," and
   b. Clarifies the term "speech therapy services," when provided as a home health service, to mean speech pathology or audiology services.

5. *Administration:* No change to current Medicare procedures.

6. *Financing and/or Reimbursement:* H.R. 9829 would

   a. If necessary, finance the expenses incurred under amendments made by H.R. 9829 through general revenue appropriations to the Federal Hospital Insurance Trust Fund and the Federal Supplementary Medical Insurance Trust Fund, and
   b. Provide in certain circumstances payments for the purchase of goods and services from related organizations, on the basis of "actual costs" without allowance for profit or other considerations.

7. *Cost and/or Quality Controls:* H.R. 9829 would

   a. Prohibit payment for home health services, when provided as an alternative to institutionalization, if such services are more costly in the aggregate than corresponding care in a skilled nursing facility;
   b. For purposes of reimbursement, require the Secretary of Health, Education, and Welfare to assess a person's need for home health services and ensure that such person is referred to an appropriate level of care;
   c. Specify that need for Part B home health services must be recertified by a panel of three health care providers (at least one of whom must be a physician) within 30 days after initial physician certification. After initial certification and recertification, the panel is required to certify continued need for such care at least twice yearly as long as the individual is receiving or claiming entitlement to covered services;
   d. Amend Part C of Title XVIII to establish a home health patient program in the Department of Health, Education, and Welfare to be responsible for monitoring and maintaining oversight with respect to home health programs under Titles XVIII and XIX of the Social Security Act;
   e. Mandate a Department of Health, Education, and Welfare study of the desirability and feasibility of requiring Medicare to reimburse for home

health and nursing home services according to a prospective cost-based method utilizing the prudent buyer methods of purchase;

f. Require full disclosure of a Medicare home health agency's corporate interests, and the extent of its interests in businesses providing it with goods and services.

H.R. 12676 (No Short Title)

Chief Sponsor: *Representative Claude Pepper*

1. *General Approach:* H.R. 12676 would amend Title 18 of the Social Security Act to expand Medicare's home health benefit. The bill would remove limits on the number of allowable visits, liberalize the requirements for receipt of service, and broaden the definition of reimbursable home health services.
2. *People Covered:* Individuals enrolled in Parts A and B of Medicare.
3. *Scope of Benefit:* H.R. 12676 would provide for unlimited home health visits under Parts A and B and would remove the current prior hospitalization requirement under Part A. The Part A requirement that the service be provided for further treatment of the condition for which the patient was institutionalized is deleted. However, the requirement that the individual be in need of skilled nursing care or physical or speech therapy in order to receive services is retained.
4. *Definitions:* H.R. 12676 would broaden the current definition of "home health services" (Section 1861[m]) to:
    a. Include periodic chore services, hospital outreach services, nutritional counseling provided by or under the supervision of a registered dietitian, and professional guidance and personal counseling for aged and disabled individuals living at home alone. The present requirement that the individual be in need of skilled nursing care or therapy services and be under the care of a physician when services are furnished would not apply with respect to the provision of these new additional home health services;
    b. Delete the requirement that a physician must establish and periodically review an individual's home health care plan. Instead, the bill requires that the plan be established and reviewed by an appropriate health professional (as determined by regulation); and
    c. Delete the requirement that medical social services, when part of a home health service, be provided under the direction of a physician.
    In addition, H.R. 12676 would repeal the definition of posthospital home health services (Section 1861[h]), and provide a statutory definition of the terms "periodic chore services" and "hospital outreach services."
5. *Administration:* No change to current Medicare procedures.
6. *Financing and/or Reimbursement:* H.R. 12676 would amend Medicare's definition of "reasonable cost" (Section 1861 [v]) to permit the Secretary of

Health, Education, and Welfare to develop new or additional methods and standards for reimbursement, if such standards and methods, to the maximum extent feasible, are on a reasonable cost-related basis.

7. *Cost and/or Quality Controls:* H.R. 12676 would amend Section 1155 of the Social Security Act to make it a statutory function of Professional Standards Review Organizations to review health care services provided by home health agencies.

MODEL LAWS

Federal legislation can alter Medicare in favor of home health care services. For Medicaid to be revised will probably require efforts in every state capital, because Medicaid funds are controlled at the state level. We recommend that model laws support:

SPECIFIC INCLUSION OF HOSPITAL-BASED HOME HEALTH SERVICES IN THE MEDICAID REIMBURSEMENT PROCEDURE. At present, Medicaid does not provide coverage of medical services provided by hospitals on a home health basis but, by and large, reserves these payments for independent home health agencies and/or private practitioners. Yet hospitals are reservoirs of the expertise and training that are needed for quality home health care. Hospital-based home health services could be permitted the necessary reimbursement if this clause is incorporated:

Notwithstanding any other provisions of this title except those imposing limitations or requirements relating to cost, eligibility, or certification, the term ''home health services'' includes (without regard to any of the preceding provisions of this subsection) any professional health services provided in an individual's home by a hospital or by members of its staff acting as such (including its physicians, nurses, social workers, therapists, technicians, home health aides, dietitians, and other personnel) as an alternative to institutional care, if such services do not qualify for payment (as outpatient hospital services or otherwise) under the other provisions of this title.

EXPANSION OF HOME HEALTH SERVICES TO INCLUDE A VARIETY OF LONG-TERM HOME CARE NEEDS. Current restrictions on the types of services that can be reimbursed with Medicaid payments are unrealistic. The underlying assumption behind many of the service limitations is that the individual receiving the services will eventually become well and self-sufficient. The folly of this assumption is clear when one considers that the one group that could best benefit from a continuum of home health care is the chronically disabled, homebound aged. If hospitals

269

could be certified to provide long-term home health services in addition to standard home care services, they could prevent many elderly individuals from eventually needing costly institutionalization. The following clause should be incorporated:

For the purposes of providing long-term home health care services, a hospital may be certified to provide such services in addition to any certification it may now hold as a certified home health agency for the provision of standard home care services.

CONCLUSION

Only through programs which are comprehensive and hospital-based and supported at a reasonable level by a secure source of funds, can home health care grow across the country. Legislators are likely to respond well to suggestions in favor of this work. After all, ideas for programs which are both better and cheaper than the alternative do not come along very often.

REFERENCES

1. Lewis MO, Bowers P, Beck T: The Foundation Directory. New York, Columbia University Press, 1975
2. Standard and Poor's Register of Corporations, Directors, and Executives. New York, Standard and Poor's Corporation, Vol 2, 1977
3. Dun and Bradstreet Reference Book of Managements, 11th ed. New York, Dun and Bradstreet, 1977-1978
4. Guide for Non-profit Institutions. Superintendent of Documents, Washington DC, US Government Printing Office, 1975
5. Larson V: How to Write a Winning Proposal. Carmichael, Calif, Creative Book Co, 1976
6. Nowlan SE, Shayon DR, Smith DV, et al: How to Get Money for: Youth, the Elderly, the Handicapped, Women, and Civil Liberties. Radnor, Pa, Chilton Book Co, 1975
7. State of New York, 1977-1978 Regular Session in Senate, May 25, 1977, S6345; in Assembly, July 14, 1977, A8134

MAJOR FEDERAL PROGRAMS FOR OLDER PEOPLE

Program and Executive Agency   *Summary*

EMPLOYMENT

Program and Executive Agency	Summary
Age Discrimination in Employment—Department of Labor	Investigation of charges of discrimination by certain employers against persons between the ages of 40 and 65.
Employment Programs for Special Groups—Department of Labor	Secretary of Labor may establish and operate manpower programs for special groups, including older workers.
Foster Grandparent Program—Action	Federal grants to public and private nonprofit agencies for creating volunteer services opportunities for low-income persons aged 60 and over as companions to children and to older individuals. Volunteers receive at least the federal minimum wage.
Older Americans Community Service Employment Program—Department of Labor	Secretary of Labor may contract with public and private nonprofit agencies to develop and administer part-time work in public service activities for low-income, unemployed persons aged 55 or older, to be paid at least federal minimum wage.
Retired Senior Volunteer Program (RSVP)—Action	Federal grants to public or private nonprofit agencies to establish or expand volunteer activities for the elderly; providing compensation for out-of-pocket expenses incidental to their services.

Adapted from Federal Responsibility To The Elderly. Select Committee on Aging, the House of Representatives. Washington, DC, US Government Printing Office, 1976.

Program and Executive Agency	Summary
Service Corps of Retired Executives (SCORE)—Small Business Administration	Volunteer services organized through field offices of Small Business Administration; retired professional and business-related problems.
Volunteers in Service to America (VISTA)—Action	Provides volunteer service opportunities for persons aged 18 or older in urban and rural poverty areas, on Indian Reservations, with migrant families, and in federally assisted institutions for the mentally ill and retarded. Most older VISTA volunteers serve part-time.

HEALTH CARE

Health Resources Development—Health Services Administration	Federal formula grants and loans to public and private agencies, and to state governments for construction, expansion, or modernization of long-term care institutions and other outpatient and inpatient facilities. Federal share of project cost determined by designated state agency.
Construction of Nursing Homes and Intermediate Care Facilities—Housing and Urban Development (HUD)	Federal government insures loans to nonprofit agencies or individual sponsors to finance the construction, rehabilitation, or equipment supply of certified nursing homes or intermediate care facilities.
Grants to States for Medical Assistance Programs (Medicaid)—Social and Rehabilitation Service of Health, Education and Welfare (HEW)	Federal grants to states to cover 50 to 80 percent of costs of medical care for eligible low-income families and individuals. Within federal guidelines, states establish eligibility and scope of benefits.
Program of Health Insurance For the Aged and Disabled (Medicare)—Social Security Administration of HEW	Coverage of specified health care services for persons aged 65 or older and eligible disabled persons covered by Social Security. Part A (Hospital Insurance) covers hospital and posthospital skilled nursing home care and home health services. Part B (Supplementary Medical Insurance), subject to premiums, covers physicians and other specified outpatient services.
Veterans Domiciliary Care Program— Veterans Administration	Federal funds for federal facilities, and project grants to states to construct and

272

rehabilitate domiciliary care facilities for veterans, provides medical and personal care in residential type setting to aged and disabled veterans not requiring hospitalization, provides payments to facilities for provision of such services.

Veterans Nursing Home Care Program—
Veterans Administration

Federal funds for federal facilities, and grants to States for construction of homes providing nursing home care to veterans, and for covering medical care services for veterans receiving such care.

HOUSING

Housing for the Elderly—HUD

Federal loans for construction or rehabilitation of multifamily rental housing for elderly (age 62 and over). Tenants may qualify for rent supplements under the Section 8 program. Responsible for Management of Section 202 direct loan program.

Low and Moderate Income Housing—
HUD

Provides housing assistance payments for low-income persons and families who cannot afford ''decent and sanitary housing in the private sector.'' Rent supplements cover the difference between the community's fair market rent down to 15 to 25 percent of the tenants' adjusted income. Responsible for management of Section 8 rent subsidy program.

Mortgage Insurance on Rental Housing for the Elderly—HUD

Federal government insures against loss on mortgages for the construction and rehabilitation of multifamily rental housing for the elderly (aged 62 or over) or disabled whose income is higher than the low or moderate income level. Responsible for management of Section 231 mortgage insurance program.

Rural Rental Housing Loans—Agriculture

Federal government makes direct and guaranteed insured loans to construct, improve, or repair rental or cooperative housing in rural areas for low-income persons, including senior citizens aged 62 or over.

273

Program and Executive Agency	Summary
Community Development—HUD	Formula grants to urban communities, based on poverty population and other economic and population factors, for a variety of community development activities, including construction of senior citizens' centers.
Rental and Cooperative Housing for Lower and Moderate Income Families—HUD	The federal government subsidized down to 1 percent of the interest on mortgages for private developers of multifamily housing for low and moderate income families, persons 62 and over, and handicapped individuals. Responsible for management of Section 236 interest subsidy program.
Low Rent Public Housing—HUD	Local housing authorities receive federal loans to aid in the purchase, rehabilitation, leasing, or construction of multifamily housing for low income families, individuals aged 62 and over, and handicapped individuals. Housing designed for the elderly may have congregate dining rooms and other special features. Rents may not be more than 25 percent of the family's income. Responsible for management of public housing program.

SOCIAL SERVICE PROGRAMS

Education Program for Non-English Speaking Elderly—HEW	Federal grants to state and local educational institutions, or to other agencies for education programs designed to serve elderly persons with limited English-speaking abilities living in a culture different from their own; geared toward dealing with the practical problems of everyday life.
Food Stamp Program—Agriculture	Low-income families and individuals may buy food stamps worth more than the purchase amount, which varies with income. Persons over 60 who are homebound, handicapped, or otherwise unable to prepare meals may exchange food stamps for home-delivered meals.
Model Projects—HEW	Federal project grants to develop and operate model projects designed to

	demonstrate new or improved methods of providing needed services to older people, focusing especially on housing, transportation, education, preretirement counseling, and special services for older handicapped persons.
Multipurpose Senior Centers—HEW	The federal government may award grants or insure mortgages for purchasing, leasing, repairing, or altering a facility to serve as a multipurpose service center and may award grants for the initial staffing of these facilities. (Never funded.)
Legal Services Corporation—Legal Services Corporation	Project grants to private nonprofit organizations, universities, and bar-sponsored organizations to provide legal services to those who cannot afford them.
Nutrition Program for the Elderly—HEW	Formula grants through state agencies on aging to agencies to establish and operate low-cost group meals and home-delivered meals for elderly persons 60 years and older. The programs, located in community settings, include services introducing participants to other community resources and transportation to nutrition sites where feasible.
Older Reader Services—HEW	Formula grants through State Office of Education to public libraries to develop special library programs and services for the elderly, such as purchasing special materials for the elderly.
Revenue Sharing—Treasury	Direct payments to state and local governments based on factors including population, poverty incidence, and state-local tax effort. Local government may use these funds for eight categories of services, including social services for the poor and the elderly.
Senior Opportunities and Services—Community Services Administration	Funds to community action agencies which award grants to develop and operate projects providing economic, health, and employment services and activities for low-income elderly not adequately served by more general programs.

275

Program and Executive Agency	*Summary*
Social Services for Low-income Persons and Public Assistance Recipients— HEW	Formula grants to state welfare agencies to establish and operate social service programs for low-income individuals meeting state income limitations. Services for the elderly may include information and referral services, home health care services, and other support services.
State and Community Services—HEW	Formula grants to States to develop a comprehensive social service delivery system, establish area agencies on aging, and provide social services when otherwise inaccessible.

INCOME MAINTENANCE

Civil Service Retirement—US Civil Service Commission	Principal retirement system for federal civilian employees, financed by employee contributions matched by employing agency plus congressional appropriations. Provides monthly retirement benefits based on past earnings and length of service to eligible retirees and their survivors.
Old Age, Survivors Insurance Program— HEW	Financed through the payroll tax on employees, employers, and self-employed persons. Social Security pays monthly cash benefits to retired workers (their dependents or survivors). Entitlement and level of benefits is based on past covered earnings. Eligibility at age 65, or may opt for permanently reduced benefits at 62.
Railroad Retirement Program—Railroad Retirement Board	Financed through a payroll tax on employees and employers. Monthly benefits are paid to retired workers (their wives and survivors) after 10 years employment. Coverage for individuals with less than 10 years service is transferred to Social Security System.
Supplemental Security Income Program— HEW	Aged, blind, and disabled persons with no other income or with limited resources are guaranteed monthly income. States may, and in some cases must, supplement federal payments.

Program and Executive Agency	*Summary*
Veterans Pension Program—Veterans Administration	Provides monthly cash benefits to veterans aged 65 or older with at least 90 days military service and who meet income limitation requirements. Benefits are also paid to designated survivor. Benefits vary according to veteran's annual income.

TRAINING AND RESEARCH PROGRAMS

Multidisciplinary Centers of Gerontology —HEW	Grants to public and private nonprofit agencies and institutions to establish or support centers for such activities as training personnel, research and demonstration projects, and consultation services.
Nursing Home Care, Training, and Research Programs—HEW	Project grants and contracts to provide short-term training for employees of long-term care facilities and for supporting studies on long-term care. Office of Nursing Home Affairs responsible for training nursing home inspectors and certifying nursing homes participating in Medicare and Medicaid programs.
Personnel Training—HEW	Project grants for training persons employed or preparing for employment in the aging field and for publicizing available career opportunities in the field of aging.
Research and Demonstration Projects— HEW	Project grants for established research and demonstration projects involving the living patterns and living standards of the elderly and delivery of services to them, and to help identify and meet transportation problems of the elderly.
Research on Aging Process and Health Problems—HEW	Conducts and supports research relating to biologic, behavioral, and sociologic aspects of the aging process and the special health problems of the elderly.
Research on Problems of the Elderly— HEW	Federal grants to institutions of higher learning to plan, develop, and implement programs specifically designed to apply the resources of higher education to the problems of the elderly.

TRANSPORTATION

Capital Assistance Grants for Use by Public Agencies—Department of Transportation

Capital assistance grants to local public agencies for the acquisition of transit vehicles, equipment, and facilities. Grants may be used to meet special transportation needs of elderly and handicapped individuals.

Capital Assistance Grants for Use by Private Nonprofit Groups—Department of Transportation

Up to 2 percent of the annual allotment for capital assistance grants may be set aside for private nonprofit groups to provide mass transportation services for elderly and handicapped individuals.

Reduced Fares—Department of Transportation

Mass transportation companies who receive federal funds for either capital or operating expenses must charge elderly and handicapped individuals no more than half-fare during off-peak hours.

Rural Highway Public Transportation Demonstration Project—Department of Transportation

Project grants are awarded to public and private nonprofit agencies for projects designed to encourage the development, improvement, and use of public mass transportation in rural areas.

CHELSEA-VILLAGE PROGRAM DATA

QUALITY OF REFERRAL Our criteria for accepting people under care in the Chelsea–Village Program are:

1. Geographic accessibility—roughly speaking, the Chelsea and Greenwich Village areas of Manhattan
2. Homeboundedness
3. Lack of adequate presently existing health care
4. Willingness to receive us

Quality of Referral	Number of Cases
Satisfactory	416
Refused contact	12
Not homebound	24
Other source of medical care	14
Total	466

AGE AND SEX DISTRIBUTION Of the 466 patients, 299 are women and 167 men. The oldest patient is 107, the youngest 27. Age distribution by decade, upon entrance into the program is as follows:

Decade	Number of Patients
20–29	3
30–39	4
40–49	9
50–59	17
60–69	71
70–79	173
80–89	154
90–99	33
100+	2

From Brickner PW, Janeski JF: The Chelsea–Village Program, The Four-Year Report. Department of Community Medicine, St. Vincent's Hospital, 153 West 11th St., New York, NY 10011.

PRESENT STATUS OF PATIENTS: FOUR-YEAR SUMMARY

Under active care at home	125
Improved, receiving clinic care	72
In nursing home	73
Died in hospital	84
Died at home	33
In hospital now	12
Moved out of district	22
Improper referral	37
Inactive, refuses further contact	8

DEGREE OF ISOLATION

Alone	289
Living with others	177
Spouse	74
Child(ren)	57
Parent(s)	5
Other relatives	26
Same sex roommate	7
Opposite sex roommate	8

ETHNICITY AND COUNTRY OF ORIGIN   The diverse ethnic makeup of the Greenwich Village and Chelsea communities served by this program is reflected in the following tabulations of referred patients:

Ethnicity	Chelsea	Greenwich Village	Other Areas	Total
Austria	5	6	1	12
Brazil	1	0	0	1
Canada	1	4	0	5
Chile	0	1	0	1
Cuba	2	2	0	4
Czechoslovakia	0	2	0	2
Denmark	4	0	0	4
Ecuador	1	1	0	2
Finland	0	1	0	1
France	6	9	1	16
Germany	14	12	1	27
Greece	4	1	0	5
Great Britain	16	19	2	37
Hungary	1	0	0	1
Ireland	52	36	2	90
Italy	21	58	17	96

280

Ethnicity (Continued)	Chelsea	Greenwich Village	Other Areas	Total
Lithuania	0	1	0	1
Netherlands	1	1	0	2
Norway	0	2	0	2
Philippines	0	1	0	1
Portugal	1	0	0	1
Puerto Rico	20	1	6	27
Rumania	1	0	0	1
Russia	8	6	0	14
Spain	5	4	0	9
Sweden	1	0	0	1
Poland	10	0	0	10
Yugoslavia	3	1	0	4
Other Europe	11	3	0	14
Other Asia	1	0	0	1
Carribean	1	1	1	3
Unknown	15	15	1	31
American Indian	1	0	0	1
Black American	3	4	1	8
Black Caribbean	1	0	0	1
Jewish	20	10	0	30
Total	231	202	33	466

Country of Origin

	Chelsea	Greenwich Village	Other Areas	Total
Austria	6	4	0	10
Brazil	1	0	0	1
Canada	2	4	0	6
Chile	0	1	0	1
Cuba	2	2	0	4
Czechoslovakia	0	2	0	2
Denmark	1	0	0	1
Ecuador	1	1	0	2
France	4	3	1	8
Germany	1	3	0	4
Greece	3	1	0	4
Great Britain	7	2	0	9
Hungary	1	0	0	1
Ireland	12	6	1	19
Italy	6	31	11	48
Norway	0	1	0	1
Philippines	0	1	0	1
Portugal	1	0	0	1
Puerto Rico	19	1	5	25
Russia	11	7	0	18
Spain	5	3	0	8
Poland	12	0	0	12

Country of Origin	Chelsea	Greenwich Village	Other Areas	Total
United States	119	123	14	256
Yugoslavia	3	1	0	4
Other Europe	4	0	0	4
Other Asia	1	0	0	1
Caribbean	2	1	1	4
Unknown	7	4	0	11
Total	231	202	33	466

PROFESSIONAL VISITS: FOUR-YEAR TOTAL

Physician visits	2728
Nurse visits	2803
Social worker visits	1766
TOTAL (including visit of one or more professional staff members on same occasion)	3526

SOURCES OF REFERRAL Our 466 cases have been referred from the following sources:

Settlement house	52
Hudson Guild—Fulton Center	52
Community service agencies	103
Chelsea Action Center (OEO)	20
Catholic Charities	5
Village Visiting Neighbors	9
Visiting Nurse Service of NY	38
Neighborhood Council to Combat Poverty (OEO)	2
Village Independent Democrats	1
Other community service agencies	28
Government agencies	26
Mayor's Office for the Aging	2
Waverly Welfare Center	2
Department of Social Service, Division of Homemakers	14
Police department	5
Congressman's office	3
Church-related	14
Fur Center Synagogue	1
St. Bernard's Church	3
St. Joseph's Church	2
St. Francis Xavier Church	3
Legion of Mary of St. Anthony's	3
Other Church-related referrals	2

Community individuals	83
Superintendent	7
Friend	19
Neighbor	33
Relative	15
Self-referred	9

| Hotel managers | 5 |

| Other hospitals | 5 |

St. Vincent's Hospital referrals	178
Home Care Department	25
Social Service Department	83
Mental Health Clinic	4
Medical staff	42
Other St. Vincent's Hospital referrals	24

COMPLEMENTARY SERVICES Our goal of maintaining chronically ill persons in their homes cannot be accomplished solely by the provision of medical care. Other services are required to assist homebound people. Our program works closely with community agencies and individuals, as needed. The general range of these services for our active patients in the first four years of the program is as follows:

Visiting Nurse	96
Homemaker	89
Meals-on-Wheels	65
Community Workers	53
Friendly Visitor	39
Assistance by family	88
Assistance by a neighbor	76
Additional social service	93
Home health aide	40
Housekeeper	48
Telephone reassurance	10
Physical therapist	14
Respiratory therapist	5
SVH home care department	14

HOUSING We classify "inadequate housing" into two categories:

1. Housing not suitable for human habitation by anyone.
2. Housing inadequate because of the patient's particular limitation or handicap. This category includes, for instance, walk-up apartments for people disabled by arthritis.

283

Only those persons who are unable to survive at home in spite of all available assistance are candidates for transfer to a nursing home.

Fitness for human habitation	Adequate	Borderline	Inadequate
No move necessary	238	9	0
Move needed—patient refuses	18	18	10
Move needed—unable to find better housing	5	5	1
Move needed—other	7	11	1
Consideration of move in progress	10	20	6
Moved to chronic care institution	63	7	13
Moved out of district	20	3	1
Total	361	73	32

Fitness for patient	Adequate	Borderline	Inadequate
No move necessary	208	39	0
Move needed—patient refuses	3	20	23
Move needed—unable to find better housing	0	5	6
Move needed—other	4	13	2
Consideration of move in progress	1	23	12
Moved to chronic care institution	47	12	24
Moved out of district	15	2	7
Total	278	114	74

HOUSING INFORMATION REFERRAL SOURCES

Problem	*Department or Agency Responsible*
Air pollution: too much smoke, ashes, fumes from incinerators or other sources	Department of Air Resources; local police precinct if condition is acute
Basement: flooding, garbage, trash	Department of Water Resources
Bribes: asked by or given to city employees, general or anonymous complaints	Department of Investigation; District Attorney's Office
Disturbance: noise, harassment, nuisance	Local Police Department
Electricity: no electricity, wiring trouble, emergency service	Local Electric Utility
Elevator: not working properly	Department of Buildings
Environment: air, water, and sewer, and noise complaints	Environmental Protection Administration
Eviction: from rent-controlled apartments when tenant is receiving welfare assistance	Civil Court or District Rent Office; Department of Social Services
Faulty wiring	Department of Public Works; Bureau of Gas and Electricity
Fire: hazards, emergencies, complaints, and requests for fire inspection	Fire Department; Fire Prevention Division
Gas/gas leaks: emergency service	Local utility
Housing: emergency, no heat or hot water, complaints, repair and emergency, service for slum areas	Office of Code Enforcement of the local governing body

Problem	*Department or Agency Responsible*
Landlord registration/identification: to find out name and address of landlord and/or agent	Registration Division
Lead poisoning	Local Health Department
Light: no light in building, light fixtures not working, not enough light in hallway or stairway	District Rent Office
Locks: broken, not provided, tampered with	Office of Code Enforcement of the local governing body
Lot clean-up	Department of Sanitation
Mail: no mailbox provided, box broken, mail tampered with	Office of Code Enforcement of the local governing body; General Post Office
Noise and nuisance: noise, vibration and odors from boiler, central heating system, or incinerator, general noise and nuisance	Local Police Department
Occupancy, regulation of	Department of Buildings
Odors and fumes: inside building, outside building, sewage, smoke, or soot	Department of Water Resources; Office of Code Enforcement of the local governing body
Ownership, record of	Registration Division, local court
Paint: public areas, inside building, rent-controlled apartments	Office of Code Enforcement of the local governing body.
Pest and rodent control	Department of Health
Police: emergencies, information	Local Police Department
Public housing	Local Housing Authority
Rats: ratholes or rats	Department of Health
Refuse collection: garbage, bulk pickup	Department of Sanitation
Relocation: due to fire, government action	Department of Relocation and Management Services, Emergency Housing Bureau, Division of Site Relocation
Rent and rent control	Department of Rent and Housing Maintenance; District Rent Office
Rent stabilization	Rent Stabilization Association
Repairs	Office of Code Enforcement of the local governing body
Sewage: leakage or overflowing indoors; broken sewer lines indoors; standing sewage in vacant lots	Department of Water Resources; Department of Health

Problem	Department or Agency Responsible
Smoke: indoors from central heating or incinerators, from defective wiring, outside	Department of Air Resources
Sprinklers: tests, record of tests information	Fire Department; Office of Code Enforcement of the local governing body
Stairs: rickety, hazardous, or badly lighted	Office of Code Enforcement of the local governing body
Subletting, if rent-controlled	District Rent Office
Water: water supply, water pollution, catch basins, sewer backups, hydrants, indoor emergencies, outdoor emergencies	Department of Water Resources
Windows: broken windows, frames or sashes rotten, etc.	Office of Code Enforcement of the local governing body

Index

289

Basic data sheet, in CVP chart, 145, 147
Bay Area Rapid Transit System. *See*
    Transportation, public
Bereavement
  and health of elderly person, 14
  and reactions to spouse's death, 14
  and the solitary elderly person, 198
  and the threat of malnutrition, 162, 163
Biological assessment of elderly person,
    importance of, 10
Birthrate, and the number of aged in U.S.,
    10–11
Blue Cross, and physician participation in a
    home health care program, 40
Boehringer Associates, 232, 248
Boehringer Report
  CVP costs, 232–44, 248–56
  comparison of home health care and
    nursing home costs, 251–56
  on nursing home costs, 248–51
Brain, and effects of aging, 97–100
Budget, CVP
  example, showing portion of cost to be
    borne by donor to program, 262
  example, to be shown to potential
    donors, 261
  example of total cost budget to be
    submitted to foundations, 263
  need for, with growth of program, 61,
    63–64
Bureau of Labor Statistics, and estimation
    of cost of food, shelter, and
    personal items, 254

Case finding and evaluation, for a home
    health care program 45–46, 53,
    57
  evaluation as a nursing function, 76–77
  and food service programs, 162–63
Case history, inclusion of in grant requests
    to foundations, 262. *See also*
    Chart, CVP; Chelsea–Village
    Program, case conferences; case
    reports; staff conferences
Caterers, and a meals-on-wheels program,
    165

Chart, CVP, 141–53
  charting techniques, 144
  physical structure of, 144–52
  problem-oriented medical record style,
    148, 151–52
  problems in charting, 153
  purposes of, 141–44
  special requirements for home health
    care program chart, 144
Chelsea, New York City neighborhood, 56
Chelsea–Village Program (CVP), 52–70
  case conferences, 25, 66–68, 84,
    134–35, 136–38, 143–44
  development of concept, 52–53
  the dying patient, 68–70
  and emergencies, 207
  goals of, 23–31, 56–57, 133–35
  group conferences, 120–23
  growth of, 61–64, 77, 133, 134–35
  initial operation, 56–61
  and legal action, 142–43
  learning about the community, 56
  and number of patients estimated to have
    been maintained at home instead
    of in institutions, 30–31
  patients, 53, 64–68
    admission to and discharge from
      hospital of, 91–93
    attention soon after referral, 45–46,
      115
    complexity of problems of, 53, 55,
      82, 89, 91, 92, 93–94, 102,
      104–5
    the dying patient, 68–70
    education of, in health care, 79–81
    emotional support of, by physicians,
      102–4
    fear of institutions, 59–60
    income of, 254
    individuality of, 64, 104, 111–15
    isolation of, 29, 53, 89, 162–63
    management of, 93–94
    rejection of help, 59
    relationship to nurses, 79–83
    screening referrals, 59–61, 75–77
    winning the confidence of, 55–56,
      59–60, 82–83

291

292

294

296

Homemaking services *(cont.)*
New York City social service agency
homemakers, 61–63
organization and standards for, 214–15
Homes for adults, proprietary, 189. *See
also* Housing, semi-independent
Homes, foster, for adults, 190
Hospital administration. *See also* Hospitals
concerns of, 37
hospital–neighborhood relationship, 47
legislation on community influence on
hospitals, 39–40, 42, 47
and needs of the homebound aged,
37–41
reaction to requests for funding, 54–55
and time of hospital professional staff,
42, 53, 55
Hospital home care programs, 40–41
Hospital–neighborhood relationship,
39–40, 44–47, 53, 54
recent history of, 39
Hospitals
admission to and discharge from, for
CVP patients, 91–93, 134
as base of a home health care program,
35–42
community support of, 39–40
founding principles of, 40, 54–55
funding for a home health care program,
37–39
geographic proximity to patient
population, 243
patient perceptions of services provided,
37
and portable meals programs, 164–65
psychiatric sections of, 100
records of, 112, 142, 145, 153
staff of, 35–36, 41–42, 53–57, 58,
91
state mental, and the discharge of
patients, 100
types of patients served, 37, 92, 100
use of, due to lack of home health care
services, 8
Hotels, as housing for the aged, 191
Housekeepers. *See also* Homemaker;
Homemaking services
duties of, 213, 217–18

Housekeepers *(cont.)*
job descriptions, 213
Housing and the aged, 176–93
and the deterioration of urban housing,
192–93
and health, results of the 1960 Housing
Census, 184
the housing authority, 192
the housing court, 178, 192–93
limited profit housing, 188
moving, difficulty of, 185–86
problems of, 176–78, 180, 184, 192–93
Community Council of Greater New
York Report on, 176
CVP case report, 177
CVP patient data, housing study,
177
physical disability, 184
poverty, 176, 184
in rental housing, 176
Section 202 housing, 188
solutions to the problems of, 178–88
cash assistance, 178–84, 192
foster homes, 190
hotels, 191
housing emergencies, 191–92
semi-independent housing, 188–90
sources of housing information, 193
violations and legal assistance, 192–93
Housing Assistance Program of the United
States Department of Housing
and Urban Development, 182
Housing Authority, 181, 182, 186–88,
192–93
and aid to homeowners for repair of
building code violations, 192–93
CVP experience with, 186–87
and emergency housing, 186–88
in New York City, 181
responsibilities of, 186
Housing and Community Development Act
of 1974, 181
Housing codes, urban, 193
Housing, public, 186–88
delays in obtaining, 187
and emergency housing, 186
and relocation of CVP patients, 186–87
rents and maintenance problems in, 186

Housing public *(cont.)*
 shortage of, 188
 waiting list for, 186, 187
Housing, semi-independent, 188–90
 coverage of rent by Medicare and
  Medicaid, 189
 federal programs of financial support
  for, 189
 founder's fees and life-lease contracts,
  189–90
 services provided by, 188–89
 sponsorship of, 189
 supervision of, 188

Illness, chronic in the elderly. *See* Chronic
  illness, and the elderly
Immigration to U.S.
 changes in family organization as a result
  of, 11–12
 effects of neighborhood change, 12
 immigrant neighborhoods in Greenwich
  Village, 56
 immigrant population of Chelsea, 56
 isolation of elderly immigrants, 11–12
 and origins of public health nursing,
  79
Industrial revolution, 11
Industrialization
 and population movements, 11
 and position of the elderly in society, 11
Industries, attitudes of toward the aged, 10
Information and referral sources
 and housing, 193
 provision for funding of in Titles I and
  XVII of the Social Security Act,
  202
In-patient services, hospital, and the home
  health care program, 36–37
Institute for Health Team Development,
  130–31
Institutional costs, measuring, 246–47
Institutionalization of dependent elderly
 consequences of to family, 29
 due to family attitudes, 29
 fear of, by elderly people, 15–17, 23,
  24–25, 68
 inappropriate, 256–58

Institutionalization of dependent elderly
  (cont.)
 inappropriate *(cont.)*
  dangers of, 15–16, 24
  and label "senile," 97
 preference for home, 23–24
 reasons for, 17, 29, 30–31
 ways of reducing, 17
Institutions for care of the aged
 attitudes toward, 23–24, 246
 inappropriate placement in, 256–58
 lack of government policy for, 247–48
 regulation of, problems, 247–48
Intake
 card, for new CVP referrals, 60–62
 procedure for, in CVP, 60–61, 75–76
International Ladies Garment Workers
  Union, 56
Isolation, of the aged
 of CVP patients, 29, 162
 of elderly members of immigrant groups,
  12
 as price of uselessness in society, 11
 as a result of enforced
  institutionalization, 15–16

Job description
 for CVP homemaker, 215
 for homemakers, home health aides, and
  housekeepers, 213–14
 for nonprofessional CVP staff, 43

Language, and attitudes toward the
  elderly, 10
Leadership, in the CVP professional
  team, 133–35
Legislation
 changes in needed, 266
 and the health of the aged homebound, 17
 mandating community control over
  hospitals, 39–40, 47
 Medicare, expansion of benefits for home
  health care programs, 266–69
 National Home Health Care Act of 1977,
  266–69
Levinson Gerontological Policy Institute, of
  Brandeis University, 230

301

302

304

305

United States Department of Health,
    Education, and Welfare
  funds for friendly visiting programs,
    203
  funds for homemaker services, 222–24
  publication on sources of funds for
    transportation services, 208
United States Department of Housing and
    Urban Development
  housing improvement loan repayment
    program for Old Age Assistance
    beneficiaries, 182
  housing assistance program, 182
  regulations of on percentage of costs of
    public housing buildings to be
    covered by rents, 186
  and the Section 202 housing program,
    188
  subsidies of and the initiative of
    entrepreneurs, 179
United States Department of
    Transportation, 208
United States Senate Special Committee on
    Aging, 248
Urbanization, 10–11
  among European immigrants, 11, 12
  as part of industrialization process, 11
Urban Mass Transportation Act of 1964,
    208

Vehicles. *See also* Transportation
  necessity of in CVP, 59, 61, 206–8
  for a meals-on-wheels program, 167–68
  and safety of CVP staff, 207–8
  for a transportation program, 206–8
Village Visiting Neighbors Programs,
    199–203

Visiting Nurse Service Associations, 36,
    45, 52, 57, 80, 92, 142, 165, 199,
    214–15, 255
Visitor programs for the elderly, 43–44,
    44–45, 197
  benefits of, 196–97
  contributions of aged people to, 43–44
  example of budget for, 203
  financial resources for, 202–3
  Village Visiting Neighbor Program as
    prototype of, 199–203
  visits geared to patient's wishes, 197
Volunteers
  and food service programs, 165, 167–68
  in a friendly visitor program, 199
  as help to professional staff of a home
    health care program, 46–47
  and the medical profession, 105
  in a transportation program for the
    homebound, 206
  volunteerism, dangers of, 36

Waiting lists, for public housing, 186–88,
    192
Welfare, and income of the elderly for food
    purchases, 160–61
Welfare hotel (S.R.O.), 56
  clinic for residents of, 52–53
  numbers of in Chelsea and Greenwich
    Village, 56
  residents of as medically neglected
    group, 52–53
Welfare Island, 16–17
Widowhood, as factor leading to social
    isolation, 196
Withdrawal from society by the aged, 117,
    197

306